Patterns of WONDER

Inviting

Emergent Writers to Play

with the

CONVENTIONS OF LANGUAGE

PreK–1

WHITNEY LA ROCCA & JEFF ANDERSON

Foreword by Matt Glover

Stenhouse Publishers
Portsmouth, New Hampshire

Stenhouse
PUBLISHERS
www.stenhouse.com

Library of Congress Cataloging-in-Publication Data

Names: La Rocca, Whitney, author. | Anderson, Jeff, 1966- author.

Title: Patterns of wonder : inviting emergent writers to play with the conventions of language / Whitney La Rocca and Jeff Anderson.

Description: Portsmouth, New Hampshire : Stenhouse Publishers, 2021. |

Identifiers: LCCN 2021011345 (print) | LCCN 2021011346 (ebook) | ISBN 9781625314505 (paperback) | ISBN 9781625314512 (ebook)

Subjects: LCSH: English language—Grammar—Study and teaching (Primary) | English language—Grammar—Study and teaching (Kindergarten) | English language—Composition and exercises--Study and teaching (Primary) | English language—Composition and exercises—Study and teaching (Kindergarten)

Classification: LCC LB1528 .L37 2021 (print) | LCC LB1528 (ebook) | DDC 372.61—dc23

LC record available at https://lccn.loc.gov/2021011345

LC ebook record available at https://lccn.loc.gov/2021011346

Cover design by Martha Drury and adapted by Lynne Costa

Interior design by Martha Drury and Val Levy, Drawing Board Studios

Typesetting by Val Levy, Drawing Board Studios
Printed in the United States of America

This book is printed on paper certified by third-party standards for sustainably managed forestry.

27 26 25 24 23 22 21   4371   9 8 7 6 5 4 3

For my favorite kindergarten teacher, Amy Daley.
—W.L.

For my favorite kindergarten teacher, Rebecca Harrison.
—J.A.

Contents

Foreword
by Matt Glover

Deja is five years old and a unicorn expert. If you talk to her for a minute you will discover this, because Deja will tell you exactly how much she knows about unicorns (a horse with a horn), a Pegasus (a horse with wings), and an Alicorn (a horse with wings and horns). So, it isn't surprising that early in kindergarten Deja made her first of many books about unicorns.

When Deja excitedly read her book to her teacher, Lisa, in October, she composed beautiful language that supported her illustrations. On the page where she taught her readers about unicorn horns, Deja said, "Some horns are swirly and super long." On another page Deja exclaimed, "Unicorn horns are MAGIC!" Toward the end of her eight-page book, Deja said, "Unicorns can leap over trees."

Deja's book has illustrations on every page and for the most part you can tell which pictures are the unicorns. Deja also has a few words on each page, some with letters that correspond to some of the sounds in the word. But Deja's oral language composition conveys much more than is evidenced in her pictures and print. In order to truly appreciate her book, you have to hear Deja read it. And even more importantly, you would have to be comfortable with how approximated the actual book was. However, if you were comfortable with her approximations of illustrations and spelling and asked Deja to read her book, you would be rewarded with insights into Deja's compositional thinking, along with some new unicorn knowledge.

Whitney La Rocca and Jeff Anderson know how to notice and appreciate all that children like Deja understand about composing language and creating meaning through illustrations and words. For example, they would notice how Deja can compose informational text, long before her class studies informational writing later in the year (she divides her writing into sections, generalizes across a topic by saying unicorns rather than this unicorn, uses precise language, etc.). Whitney and Jeff also connect what they would notice in Deja's composition to important understandings about writing. For example, they would notice:

- The adjectives Deja uses when she describes the horn as "swirly and super long." (Lessons 1.5, 2.10, 3.13, and 4.12 in this book)
- When Deja says, "Unicorn horns are MAGIC!" she has the foundation for using a variety of techniques, including exclamation marks, to show voice and alter volume in print. (Lessons 2.8, 3.11, 4.11)
- Deja uses the precise, interesting verb "leap" when she says, "Unicorns can leap over trees." (Lessons 1.4, 2.6, 3.9, 4.10)

And, while keeping all of this in mind, Whitney and Jeff would also notice that Deja is using words to compose sentences and a combination of random letters and accurate letters to create words. By noticing all of the important, specific things Deja *can* do, rather than what she can't yet do, Whitney and Jeff value her approximations and can then nudge Deja and her classmates forward in precise, developmentally appropriate ways.

Whitney and Jeff's ability to notice, name, and support what children can do is crucial, especially in today's educational environment, which increasingly seems to promote isolated writing skills in rigid sequential steps. Too often I encounter administrators, parents, and teachers who view conventions as a prerequisite for teaching students to write well. They basically say, "First students need to learn letter-sound relationships, grammar, and punctuation, and *then* we can teach them to compose well." But if we take a prerequisite approach, we would have to wait several years to fully see and appreciate the brilliance of the language Deja is composing.

In *Patterns of Wonder*, Whitney and Jeff use a variety of strategies to avoid this prerequisite, limited view of children's writing development and show us how to think about composition and conventions as parallel, connected areas of development. They help the reader understand the individual developmental nature of writing and how children can compose powerful language regardless of how they are transcribing words on the page. For example, they show how children think about and use verbs, whether they are transcribing using Scribble Writing, Symbol and Letter Writing (like Deja), Transitional Writing, or Conventional Writing (all explained in-depth in Chapter 2). By structuring the lessons in this book around these four phases, Whitney and Jeff help the reader see how the intertwining of language and print develops right from the beginning, across phases.

Whitney and Jeff also make the important decision to not assign which phase children should be in at certain grades. They know that any kindergarten classroom, for example, might have children in all four of these transcription phases, and that children will grow and learn at different rates throughout the year. They understand that our responsibility as educators is to meet children where they are and help them move forward, one small nudge at a time. Whitney and Jeff push back on the idea that whole classrooms of young children need the exact same thing, on the same day, at the same time, and instead encourage responsive teaching and customized instruction for young writers.

Whitney and Jeff also know the importance of centering learning in authentic experiences. Each lesson in this book uses picture books as a springboard for understanding and using conventions, rather than isolated worksheets bought from a website. Alongside each lesson's recommended title, Whitney and Jeff also provide a list of alternative titles. Having a variety of titles is important because it provides teachers with the understanding of what to look for in a book, and how to use books they already know and love. They empower teachers by helping them see how language and illustrations are used to make meaning in a variety of books, rather than prescribing an exact title.

Whitney and Jeff use a predictable structure and process for each lesson, which helps both students and teachers. Once you are familiar with the process after a few lessons, it's easy to insert any new content, strategy, or idea into a lesson. This predictable structure also helps students by reinforcing that learning about language is rooted in noticing, play, oral rehearsal, and approximations across the year.

This predictable structure also makes it easier to focus on one small idea at a time. Children (and adults) learn best when they are working in the range just beyond what they can do on their own. By tackling one small, important idea in each lesson, Whitney and Jeff help us, and students, see how ideas are connected and built bit by bit over time. This allows teachers to avoid overscaffolding, the act of providing too much adult support in order to get a child to do much, much more than they can do on their own. Instead, Whitney and Jeff support teachers' ability to provide small scaffolds that nudge children forward over time.

Finally, and most importantly, Whitney and Jeff know that writing is about conveying meaning. As they state in the introduction, "conventions activate meaning." Conventions help a writer communicate a message clearly and effectively. But the focus in *Patterns of Wonder* is on composing meaning. The goal isn't to spell well or punctuate correctly. Students can spell and punctuate perfectly, and yet their writing can be boring to read and not well composed. Instead, Whitney and Jeff keep the goal of providing children with the tools and strategies they need to become powerful composers of language front and center.

Patterns of Wonder is a book that has aligned beliefs and actions. Whitney and Jeff start with a list of their beliefs about children and writing. These are beliefs that are easy to support, but more challenging to live into action each day. Whitney and Jeff show us how to live what they believe by ensuring that our interactions with children are built on the belief that children come to us full of knowledge, curiosity, language, and power—helping us see possibilities in children like Deja and create learning experiences they deserve.

Acknowledgments

From Whitney

I'm overwhelmed with the generosity and support provided during this project.

Teachers, coaches, principals, and district leaders stepped in to help by trying out lessons and collecting pictures for me to use in the lesson sets, even during the pandemic. Thank you to Sylvia Santos, Nancy Garcia, Hailey Volz, and Nancy Castillo in Lamar Consolidated Independent School District; Jacqueline Aguilar Martinez, Lesly Sanchez, Lisa Edwards, Bobbie Rodriguez, Tomi Dodson, and Rebecca Smith in Cleveland ISD; Evan Payne and Kami Anderson in Grapevine-Colleyville ISD; Tracey Bleakley in Leander ISD; Trish Gallery in Smithtown Central School District; and Cindy Baca, Elisabet Ney, Dana West, Tessa Rhyne, Quincie Bowling, and Mindy Peña in Brazosport ISD. The pictures and feedback you provided helped me tremendously to shape the lessons and provide even more support for teachers.

To Jessie Miller, Meghan Sweeney, Angel Bateman, Lisa Castecka, Erin Haack, Katharine Pie, Noé Robles Castañeda, Krystal Morales, and Cheree Hall, thank you for inviting me into your classrooms to work with your children. They gave me energy and inspiration each time I met with them.

To parents and educators who helped out when I put out the call for pictures to support my organization of the phases of writing: Chelsea Campbell, Kami Patik-Poledna, Erin Rocheleau, Kimberly Harrell, Cassandra Carlyle, Deborah Swallers, Leslie Zoehr, Lauren Calvert, Renee Houser, Shari Padron, Kallie Roman, Jayme Barron, Jessica Frank, Blair Miller, Amy Crawford, Jen Mallams, Jaime Shipley, Toby and Jamie Clouser, Morgan Ditchman, Janelle Coleman, Brittany Quedeza, Gulsah Weatherford, Amanda Thorin, Heather Fletes, Lindsey O'Neill, Angie Sadowski, and Yarrow Sledge. I loved seeing kids' play come to life in their writing and oral language.

Sarah Ramirez, you are incredible. Thank you for being a text away anytime I needed even the smallest things. Your excitement in our conversations inspired me even more. Keep sharing pictures with me!

To the parents of the four emergent writers I am lucky enough to work with remotely each week, thank you. Nawal and Jonathan Casiano, Kate Staff and Nick Movshon, Nilda and Sean, and Nada and Jordan Litwin, your children are the highlight of my week, and I have learned so much from them!

Thank you to everyone in our Facebook community who participated in surveys and shared your thinking with me along the way. And for our Twitter followers, I love seeing all that your writers do with this work. Thank you! And keep tweeting!

Thank you, Matt Glover, for being a brain to pick throughout this process. I've always turned to you and your work for early childhood expertise, but to be able to chat with you about language composition often has really helped me shape my thinking and dive deeper into the foundation of *Patterns of Wonder*. Thanks to my friends in Lamar Consolidated ISD for bringing us together!

Bill Varner, your talented editing skills and belief in *Patterns of Power* set the stage for *Patterns of Wonder*. You took a chance on me early on, trusted me to continue with this work, and have been with me from the beginning. I'm forever grateful. Thank you.

Shannon St. Peter, wow. You have been such a tremendous help behind the scenes from Day 1. I seriously cannot even express how much I appreciate you and the hours you put into this project, including answering my zillion questions. *Patterns of Wonder* would not be what it is if it weren't for you. Thank you, thank you, thank you!

To Lynne Costa, you know I love you! Your patience and talent with the pictures and requests I submit certainly doesn't go unnoticed. I'm so thankful for you and your positive energy! Thank you for producing such a beautiful book. Every time I look at it, my eyes fill with tears of joy.

To the rest of my Stenhouse family: Emily Hawkins, Dan Tobin, Nate Butler, Jill Backman, Faye LaCasse, Stephanie Turner, and Noele Faccidamo, as well as our sales team, thank you for the constant support and encouragement. You really are my family, and I love each and every one of you deeply. Thanks for being awesome!

Terry, our editor on this project, a simple thank-you is just not enough. I feel like I should make you some avocado toast and send over a Tiff's Trio every day. Your patience, conversations, feedback, and kindness grew my confidence and helped me to truly find the writer inside me.

Jeff, I love you. Thank you for encouraging me to take the lead on this one and supporting me every step of the way. You continue to be my mentor!

Finally, Keith and Emmeree, thank you for putting up with my writing process mess everywhere: books, papers, writing samples, anchor charts, and so much more strewn throughout our house. But among the mess, you cheered me on and took interest in what I was doing. I love you both. Emmeree, you got to see the true act of revising firsthand, and I hope it helped you grow as a writer as well.

Love,
Whitney

From Jeff

Of course, I say ditto to Whit's acknowledgments. This last year, the pandemic and my Parkinson's disease eked my life to a stop like I'd never before experienced. With this simpler life, I've written a simple acknowledgment. In the past year, I've allowed myself to rely on others more—like Whitney. I want to acknowledge her most of all as lead writer on *Patterns of Wonder*. Her name deserves to be first on this project. I participated a great deal in the writing and planning, but it is Whitney who guided the process—except a few times that I was Bossy the Cow. Next, I must acknowledge our brilliant editor, Terry Thompson, who kept us true to the task. His background in early literacy and his sense of what schools and teachers really need is matched by none in the industry. Sure, he's my husband, but I actually feel that way.

To the Stenhouse team from Bill Varner, Lynne Costa, Nate Butler, Emily Hawkins, Shannon St. Peter, Jill Backman, Faye LaCasse, Stephanie Turner, to Noele Faccidamo: Thanks for helping us produce magic. I am grateful for the readers and teachers and spreaders of the *Patterns of Power* family of products. It's a dream come true. I hope to meet you someday. Maybe it will be in person, an online staff development, our new podcast, POPCast, you can listen to.

But know most of all, I praise you teachers who make grammar about meaning and effect and not about right and wrong. I lift all educators up for making emergent writers curious about the wonders of patterns in language. Thank you for giving them a positive foundation with love and freedom and possibility.

Love,
Jeff

Introduction
A Space for Wonder Is a Space for Writing

Observe the wonders as they occur around you.

—Rumi

In a prekindergarten class, Yazen sits eagerly at the table with crayons in hand, making a book. Without talking to him, you might think he is simply scribbling something or adding a splash of color to a drawing. But when he shares his book, he explains each color represents someone in his family. And that big black scribble in the middle?

"That's a swimming pool." Yazan's eyes gleam, loving having an audience.

After a little more conversation, we discover Yazen is writing about a topic he cares deeply about and knows well: his family and what they do together.

If you think classrooms have lost their wonder, sit in a PreK or kindergarten class and listen to students talk about their pictures and writing. Wonder lives in these writer's eyes and pictures and words.

A note about how we define the word wonder . . .

The Oxford English Dictionary defines *wonder* in more than one way:

Wonder: (noun) a feeling of amazement and admiration, caused by something beautiful, remarkable, or unfamiliar.

Wonder: (verb) a desire to know something; feel curious.

For the purposes of this book, the word *wonder* can be either a noun or verb. It can be the wonder of reading and writing or what you wonder about. Our youngest students are full of wonder and wonder about most things they see—noticing, questioning, experimenting, playing, and learning. Our job is to keep their environment rich with things to wonder at and about, while giving them space to play with questions in the authentic world of literacy acquisition. What a wonder!

But behind the wonder is a carefully designed pattern of teaching that awakens curiosity and joy, while nurturing and maintaining it. We gladly create the space for it. This essential play and talk is foundational for emerging writing and reading skills to develop. Let's return to Yazen's classroom for a minute or two and explore some of those classroom patterns that create wonder and inspire the innovation of play. If you take a breath, lean back in the too-small chair, and look around Yazen's classroom, you can see it is print-rich: a reading center brims with a variety of picture books, both familiar and unfamiliar. Some of these books have already been enjoyed by the class through shared reading or read aloud, and others are yet to be explored. The reading center, a small library nook with some shelves and a well-worn rug, also includes concept books, big books, as well as class- and student-created books for previewing and reviewing.

Gaze to the left and follow the patterns of an alphabet word wall, hanging at the students' eye level, modeling words and pictures that represent initial letter sounds. On the wall to the right, a name chart displays student names with their pictures, a resource students often refer to for its rich treasury of classmates' names and the letters that make them. Opportunities for writing are everywhere: blank books are stacked in the writing center, dry erase boards with markers sit on each table, paper and small tablets are an integral part of the dramatic play center. All of these spaces invite students to pick up paper and pens and play on the page, discovering what they can do as writers.

Our Beliefs About Emergent Writers

Some educators and parents may believe that writing doesn't begin until children can write words conventionally or name all the parts of speech. Others warn we must wait until they can write a complete sentence, believing we can somehow avoid dreaded mistakes if we only front-load enough memorized terminology far above their current intellectual abilities:

- "They can't write unless they know sentences start with a capital letter and end with a period."
- "To write a sentence, you must understand the type of sentence you are writing and be able to define and categorize them: declarative, interrogative, and exclamatory."

We Believe Emergent Writers Are Already Writers

Like many researchers and thought leaders who came before us, we, like many of you, believe writing begins much earlier than this. It begins with an empty space and something the child can hold that leaves a mark behind. We believe when young children pick up a crayon and make marks on a page (or even a wall), they are writing. They are demonstrating humans' innate need to express themselves.

Children will write, if given space, inspiration, and healthy doses of acknowledgment, and when they are invited to question their big wonders that are always waiting to be discovered. They need time with pages, blank spaces. Yes, they will write, even if it's a scribble, a picture, or string of letters. Over time, as conventions or patterns are introduced, they become tools to help our youngest writers reach their audiences with more clarity and ease.

We acknowledge and invite and stay out of the way.

We Believe Emergent Writers Need Opportunities to Play and Wonder

Through the lens of our combined fifty-five years as literacy educators, we believe children flourish as writers when they spend their days in an environment that invites them to do things critical for emerging writers—every day. Teachers know about wonder and patterns. They create a space for writing, which creates a place for wonder, play, exploration, and experimentation. In a *Patterns of Wonder* classroom, every day, emergent writers do all of the following:

- Write.
- Listen to books read aloud.
- Talk about what they read and wonder.
- Explore books.
- Share their writing with others.

In learning environments that give these activities time and space, students like Yazen know that they can make meaning for their readers with what they put on the page. They can choose colors to represent the individuals in their family. They can draw, label, scribble, or innovate. Such meaning-based innovations blossom in intentional, safe classrooms. Here, meaning is explored and played with and nurtured rather than looked at as a pathway to be wrong, to miss the mark—or worse, an ever-growing scary list of things you *should* or *shouldn't* do. And let's be honest, no one likes to be *should* upon. Instead of *shoulds*, our youngest writers need to live in the *coulds*—things they might do, things they might try, things that might spark meaning or reach out from the page to amaze their audience.

To become literate citizens, emergent writers need to explore this menu of what is possible, to sample from the patterns of power language conventions provide, to lose themselves in the *Patterns of Wonder*. They come to know what writing moves make sense to them and others. What has meaning and what doesn't. They discover what writing moves help and what writing moves hinder.

A note about using worksheets to teach writing or conventions . . .

At the 2010 National Council of Teachers of English conference (Orlando, Florida), Jeff heard Arthur Appleby say, "Writing is not a fill-in-the-blank exercise." When writers are provided time to compose in ways that are meaningful to them, they compose more and take more risks. They become intentional with their decisions and how they write and illustrate, aiming to make meaning. Even our youngest writers benefit from a classroom environment that encourages decision making, choice, and intentionality, rather than a fill-in-the-blank cute template downloaded from the Internet.

We Believe Emergent Writers Need the Grace of Approximation

Approximation is the hallmark of emergent writing—getting nearer and nearer to their goals, moving toward things more conventional over time, not in a straight line but a wonderful wavy one. Emergent writers need space and grace

A note about whether unconventional is a thing . . .

Although we constantly expose emergent writers to the wonder and meaning of conventional print every day, we don't expect conventional perfection from students. We seek progress, not perfection. And by the way, unconventional is a thing; however, it means fresh and new, not riddled with error. As anyone tries anything new, mistakes are an expected part of learning. When we try to fix every mistake, we arrest students' growth, no matter our intention.

What good is sending the message that students must match conventions perfectly at all times to start writing? That stops writing. Of course, conventions continue to be learned for the rest of our lives—conventions, indeed, are not a one-time event. Patience and a generous allowance of approximation serve us well as teachers of emergent writers and readers.

to play. Through exploration and experimentation, emergent writers come to know conventions a bit at a time. Their words of wonder may not look anything like the actual words we conventionally know, but we remember they are the naturally developing words of three-, four-, five-, and six-year-olds. It takes time and then more time.

Of course, we believe in being there to nudge and support, but we also leave them be for their own growth and discovery, finding their own ways to spell or do whatever they're contemplating doing to create meaning. We believe it is important as teachers of emergent writers to back off, give space to play, and allow writers to blossom and stumble and recover.

They are writers, and we believe in them. We don't wait until they are ready to write. We don't have to. They *come* to us ready to write. Their writing just looks different than the writing we might find in other grade levels.

We acknowledge and invite and stay out of the way.

Approximation is the hallmark of emergent writing.

We Believe Emergent Writers Need Acknowledgment and Celebration

All along the way, we celebrate the writing students do, without ceasing.

It's not about what's right or wrong; it's about meaning and effect.

When we invite students to play with new concepts, they are encouraged by our acknowledgment and celebration. In fact, acknowledgment and celebration cause a flurry of more writing in the writer celebrated as well as others. It's nearly impossible for a young writer to get any level of competence without some level of confidence.

"I can see where that word ends and the other begins. That space that you put between them really helped me as a reader."

Jessica smiles.

"How'd you know to do that?"

"Because I *seen* it in a book."

"That's so smart," Whitney says, "I use books to help me know what writing can look like all of the time."

A large slice of working with emergent writers and readers is living in a state of acknowledgment, celebration, and invitation.

As the leader of our classroom, we acknowledge what students try and celebrate the work they are doing. Often, we share our excitement with statements like "Ooh, you're showing you're ready for another writer tool!" and other times, simply sitting quietly with them and relishing their accomplishments. Through these shared celebrations, we encourage young writers upward and onward.

Celebrate and acknowledge without ceasing, and you won't have to beg emergent writers to put a pencil to the page or share what they've written. In fact, you'll joyfully have more than you can respond to. And you don't have to respond to every piece, you just have to ensure they have an audience—teacher, whole class, center, small group, or peer pairing.

We Believe Emergent Writers Need Oral Rehearsal

Writing begins with oral language, or, as we think of it, oral rehearsal. These conversations, these rehearsals, both lend themselves to play and the evolution of discovery. Ideas bump up against one another through conversation, sharing, refining, and reshaping.

"What is that?" Elena asks Jordan as he works on his writing in the writing center.

"This is my mom's car." Jordan points and touches two pink circles. "See, it's got wheels."

"Oh yeah." Elena squints. "Are your Mom's wheels *really* pink?"

"Not really." Jordan's back straightens. "But it'd be cool if they were."

Elena nods. Anything is possible with paper and a crayon.

This test-driving of thought gives way to emerging organizational patterns of time, space, or relationship whether creating pictures, letters, or both. Given ample time, paper, and writing implements to play on the page, emergent writers often stumble upon familiar patterns or groupings to which they've been exposed, using attributes, time order, sameness, or differences. Organization often bubbles up from conversation and a need to make something clear to the listener.

Emergent writers build on illustrations and writing through oral language. We can invite children to put words on the page with their pictures. Or better yet, acknowledge scribbles and letters as they appear in open spaces and invite them into more open spaces where writing is waiting to happen.

> As teachers, we recognize this act and support the development of writing by building on what the child is already doing, and a primary way we do this is through the use of oral language.

A note about *Patterns of Power* . . .

In our grades 1–5 resource *Patterns of Power* (2017), we refer to grammar and conventions as the meaning-making activators that connect reading and writing. We believe this to be true at all the phases of writing, especially the emergent ones. However, when working with emergent writers, our development of grammar and conventions most authentically builds through conversations as we help students read their writing and tell their stories. This will lead well into the work writers and readers will do in future grade levels using *Patterns of Power*. To see how the *Patterns of Wonder* process is compared with the *Patterns of Power* process, see Appendix B.

Note, however, that the *Patterns of Wonder* process detailed in this book will benefit all emergent writers, even if their future doesn't include *Patterns of Power*.

Everything we do as we go through our busy days becomes an opportunity for language commentary—or talking about what we are doing, how we are doing it, or why we are doing it (functional language). This is a perfect way to invite children to think about and consider what writers and readers do and the reasons why (purpose). With all this tilling of the language and word soil, we trust that when writers are ready to try something out on their own, they will.

We Believe Emergent Writers Need Relevant and Diverse Text Models

We believe that emergent readers and writers need a wide range of diverse model texts from which to explore the conventions of reading and writing. Our students crave the opportunity to see themselves, to see others, and to step into the world of others, and books are one way we can facilitate this happening (Sims Bishop 1990). We took this to heart as we explored children's literature selected for the lessons in *Patterns of Wonder.* At a recent presentation, Dr. Sonja Cherry-Paul (2020) said, "The books we choose as teachers sends a clear message about what we value and the identities we are inspiring in our students. Book choice is either identity inspiring or identity silencing." We want our students to be inspired and informed and empathetic. We believe diverse texts are a beginning.

Above All, We Believe Conventions Activate Meaning

We believe writers are readers and readers are writers. "Grammar is reading and writing crashing together, making meaning" (Anderson and La Rocca 2017). The reciprocal and recursive processes of reading and writing are entwined and activated by the conventions of language. The conventions connect readers and writers through agreed meaning. It's important that we, over time, be explicit with our youngest learners about the connections between writing and reading, composition and comprehension.

We believe in the power of talking, playing, noticing, wondering, drawing, scribbling, inquiring, and tying all of these things to our young writers' beginning understanding of authors' purpose and craft. We believe in the power of literature. We believe in exploring how writers use conventions with real books that are already perched all around our classrooms. We believe that the driving purpose in all of this is to create a sense of curiosity and wonder about making meaning with the marks we leave on a page. When, as a class or group or pair, we take time to marvel in the beauty of language and notice or wonder about something an author or illustrator did, we support the process of writing with intention—making choices as writers with purpose and craft.

So find your kid heart, grab something to write with, and come play with us in the *Patterns of Wonder.*

XXOO,

Whit and Jeff

Part 1

GETTING STARTED

with the

Patterns

of

WONDER

PROCESS

1

The Patterns of Wonder Process

Play is our brain's favorite way of learning.

—Diane Ackerman

On a cool October morning, Whitney settles in to work with kindergarten students who, at the moment, mostly use symbols to represent letters in words. In the series of invitations she's about to introduce, we give you an overview of the *Patterns of Wonder* process. In these lessons, the intention is to support writers with the use of nouns—the stuff that writing is made of—in a playful, open exploration. These students' worlds are full of people, places, and things that they *love* to talk and draw and write about. Note how Whitney positions the grammar in this *Patterns of Wonder* lesson set as something emergent writers already use to express themselves, their thoughts, their feelings, their observations. She's not asking them to merely memorize a noun as a part of speech and be able to chant its definition.

The focus phrase, or learning target, she has preplanned is *I show and tell about people, places, and things*. (More on focus phrases in Chapter 3.) In this lesson set, students discover the purpose of nouns and learn about more possibilities to add to their pictures and words. With the foundational support of ample oral language, students explore how nouns help the reader navigate through the pictures and marks on the page.

Invitation to Wonder

What else do you wonder?

To kick off the several days of the *Patterns of Wonder* process, Whitney displays a page from Troy Cummings's *Can I Be Your Dog?* (2018). She selected a page with a picture full of people, places, and things. Of course, she could have used almost any text, but Whitney has found this book to be particularly strong for starting conversations about nouns with emergent writers. On the page they're studying, Whitney asks, "What do you wonder? Think about what Troy Cummings chose to do here as an author and illustrator. Is there anything you notice?"

Hands shoot into the air. Whitney pauses and then calls on Jasmine.
Jasmine squints. "I wonder what it says."

"Come up and point to the part that is making you wonder?" Whitney asks.

Jasmine strolls over to the chart and points to the letter in the postal worker's hand.

"Oh! I wonder about that, too!" Whitney looks at Jasmine, then the class. "It doesn't look like we really know what the letter says on this page. But Troy Cummings did add other details to his picture to help us know—"

"She's a lady," Thomas, excited, interrupts.

"Yes, the postal worker is a *lady* or *woman*," Whitney confirms.

The students stare intently at the displayed page.

"Hey, writers, *letter* is a noun. Let's write it on a sticky note." Whitney writes *letter*. "And another word Thomas added was who was in the story."

"A mail lady." Whitney writes *lady* and *woman* on a sticky note and adds both to a new piece of chart paper.

"What else do you wonder about?"

Curiosity cascades across the classroom as students all begin to wonder more about the mysterious mail and everything else in the picture.

"It's called a mailman," Joshua stands and starts swaying. "It's probably a bill."

"I've seen our mailwoman. She wears shorts!" Elisa adds.

"I'm hearing a lot of words that are people." Whitney adds *postal worker*, *mailman*. "And things." She adds *shorts* and *mail* on a sticky note, then turns back to the class, eyes wide, waiting.

Another student refers to the story itself and offers, "I wonder where the dog is. The book has a dog on the cover, and I don't see it."

"That's a good point, Deshawn." Whitney nods. "I don't see the dog, either. But we know a *dog* is on the cover picture and the word *dog* is in the title." Whitney holds up the cover and points to the words in the title as she reads them.

"Let me turn the page quickly to see if maybe the dog is on the next page." Cheering from the class erupts as Whitney turns the page and the dog is revealed. "There he is! *Dog* is another word we can add to our list here. Troy Cummings has added the dog to this page to show he's a character who reads this letter." Whitney points to the letter on that page to show how the perspective changes from page to page in the book. "Now let's go back to the page before this one. What else do you wonder about or notice or see?"

"There is a house and some kids playing." Jean Paul rocks back and forth.

> What else do you wonder about?

A note about determining places or things . . .

We all agree a house is a noun, but some may quibble over it being categorized as a *place* or a *thing*. Usually the quibble occurs when your answers don't match up. Take a quick survey. "A house is a noun, but is it a place or a thing?" The answers you will get will run the gambit of "Who cares?" to "It's definitely a place. I thought you were a teacher" to "It's a thing, of course. Everybody knows that."

Do they? Does it matter? Maybe to you, but we'd accept either answer with a reasoned explanation. Can there be more than one answer with grammar? Yes, there can.

Kindergarteners sharing their wonderings and noticings about the picture in the mentor text.

Whitney invites Jean Paul to come point to the noticing. She continues honoring, naming, and extending the wonderings and noticings from the students. "Oh, wow. Take a look at that! The author chose to put some important details in his picture here. We have a *house*, which is a place, and these *kids* playing, who are more people. We could add *house* and *kids* to our chart!" Whitney adds each noun to a new sticky note and places both on the chart paper.

"Hmm." Whitney taps on the display page. "What else do you see on this page?"

Several students call out other people, places, or things that they see.

Excited, the students point to everything they notice; Whitney helps add sticky notes to the list. "Oh, so much! So we are noticing that this writer included people, places, and things in his picture." At this point, Whitney reveals the focus phrase that she has previously written on a sentence strip. She reads it aloud, and the students repeat it with her a few times: *I show and tell about people, places, and things.*

Ongoing anchor chart created with the students' wonderings

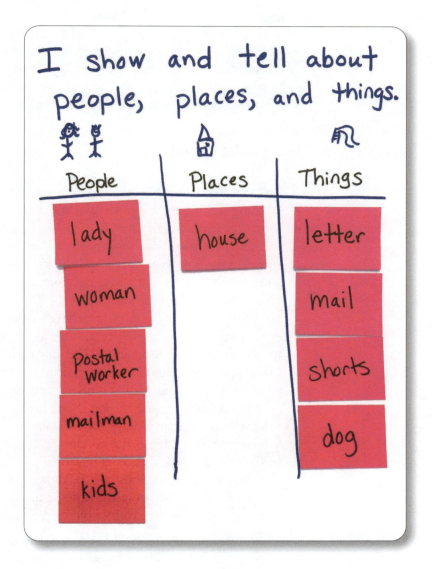

She adds the focus phrase to the top of her chart paper. "We need a quick sketch to help us remember *people*, *places*, and *things*. Hmm, we could draw a stick person here. Would that be good for a person?"

"Yes," the students agree.

"What could we draw to show a place?" Whitney asks.

Students share suggestions for the visuals that are added to the focus phrase. Then she quickly invites them to sort the sticky notes into people, places, and things. Even though Whitney is providing loads of support and scaffolds, she allows the young writers the time and space to do as much as they can.

Though this might seem like a friendly conversation, all of this noticing taps into the students' reticular activation system, more commonly referred to as the RAS (Jensen 2005). Basically, once something is brought to a person's attention, they start to see it everywhere. Nouns existed before this moment, but now that the idea of using people, places, and things to create meaning has been brought into their conscious level of awareness, the students notice the concept more the next time they see it. The brain sees far more things unconsciously than it consciously does (Eagleman 2011); therefore, once something like nouns become part of writers' conscious attention, they will engage with the concept each time they encounter it, which will deepen their awareness of nouns. That, in turn, will encourage them to use or experiment with these conventions in their daily writing.

Invitation to Compare and Contrast

The next day, the adventure continues with the power of the research-based teaching technique of comparison and contrast. Whitney shares another page from Troy Cummings's *Can I Be Your Dog?* on an interactive whiteboard, while she holds the page from yesterday's invitation open in her hand. Both pictures contain lots of people, places, and things, but the second page also has words within the picture, the name of the store, Chop Chop Butcher Shop, is written on the butcher shop picture.

This compare and contrast teaching structure gives students an opportunity to review, process, grow their thinking, and build curiosity around the choices writers make to create meaning. The moving from known to new, original page and a new page, helps consolidate learning as emergent writers actively process what is the same and what is different between the two pages.

"Yesterday, we talked a lot about this page from *Can I Be Your Dog?*" Whitney displays the page. "Now, let's take a look at another page in this book." Whitney makes sure all the children get a chance to look at the page they studied the day before and the new one.

She then asks questions one at a time and waits. *Patterns of Wonder* lessons are planned, but they are planned to be driven by student talk in reaction to a stimulus, like these two pages from the book Whitney is displaying,

- "What do you notice about the choices the writer made here?"
- "What did the writer do the same on both pages?"
- "What did the writer do differently?"

After a question, Whitney invites students to "turn and buzz with your partner about what you see." When using turn and talk, or buzz time, students talk excitedly about their comparisons, while we listen in and engage in some of the partner conversations. After a few minutes, direct the class's attention to the pages and ask someone to share what they talked about.

One boy notices both pages show the woman delivering the mail.

"Let's take a look. This page has this woman, and so does this page. Hmm. So interesting! We know that writers show and tell about people in their pictures and writing. Do you see any other people?"

"The lady in the shop! The kids!" Several kids yell. Whitney points to *lady* and *kids* on the nouns chart.

"What else do you see?" As students begin to note places and things that are different, she refers to the focus phrase as they repeat together: *I show and tell about people, places, and things.*

> When we write, we have choices, too.

Whitney continues the conversation by asking, "What else did you see is the same or different?" She invites her students to lead her on an adventure of curiosity and discovery. Whatever they compare and contrast, she supports.

"Both pictures have the color green in them," a student notes.

"Oh, I hadn't noticed that one. Hmm, I wonder why the illustrator decided to choose the color green? When we write, we have choices, too. You get to choose the colors that you think will show your thinking best. What else do you see that is the same or different?" Whitney honors the noticings and reminds her young writers that they always have choices to make, emphasizing that *they* get to decide.

"There are words on that page!" one student says as she points to the second example. Whitney invites the student up to point to the words. By asking students to come up and point, she makes sure she is not assuming she knows what they are referring to. "Oh wow! There are some words here. Let's see, these words say, 'Chop Chop Butcher Shop.' Hmm. That's interesting! This author chose to use the words to show what the store is called. You know, you could try that, too, when you write!" This step of the *Patterns of Wonder* process concludes by taking the students back to the focus phrase. "Writers, you have so many choices when you write! What's one way to help your reader understand your story?"

"Pictures!"

"And people."

"And things!"

"And places."

Whitney returns to the focus phrase, points to the words as she reads it, and has students repeat it with her: *I show and tell about people, places, and things*.

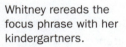

Whitney rereads the focus phrase with her kindergartners.

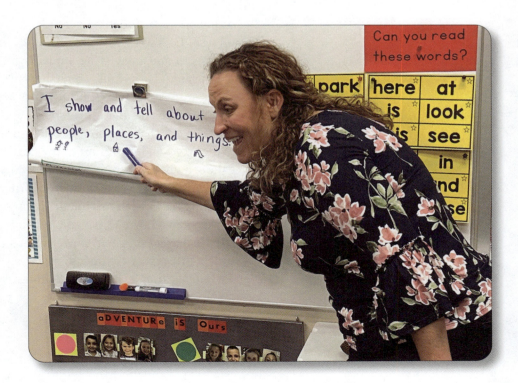

Invitation to Imitate Together

The following day, Whitney revisits the model and the compare and contrast example as well as the focus phrase: *I show and tell about people, places, and things*.

"Writers, we have been exploring how writers show and tell about people, places, and things in their writing." She points out some of the nouns in each picture to emphasize the focus phrase. "Now we are going to do this same work together. Let's think about something or someone we could draw or write about in our classroom. What would you tell someone about your classroom? What people are in our classroom? What places? What things?"

She provides wait time after each question.

"What happens with those people, places, and things? Turn and buzz with your partner." Whitney listens in on some of their conversations, encouraging students to share what people, places, or things the class might include in this piece of writing.

After a few minutes of buzzing, she brings the class back, and says, "Wow! I heard so many stories you were sharing and thinking about what people, places, and things are in those stories. Daniel mentioned that we have books in our classroom. Daniel, where are those books?"

Daniel shares that many of the books are in the classroom library, so Whitney draws a picture of the classroom library and invites Daniel to come add the books. While he is drawing, she invites students to share other people, places, or things they might add to the picture of the classroom and invites some of them to illustrate these on the chart paper as well. "Now we are going to write some words that tell about the people, places, or things in our picture. What might those words say?"

"It has tables!" one student suggests.

"That's true! Let's write **My classroom has tables**." Whitney says the words across her fingers and invites the students to say the sentence aloud across their fingers again. "Let's think about how we will write *my*." The students practice the m-m-m sound as Whitney writes *My*. "The next word is classroom. C-c-c-c," Whitney makes the initial sound and invites a student to write the letter that represents that sound. Once the student has finished the *c*, Whitney completes the word and moves on to the next word of the sentence.

Once the sentence is complete, Whitney invites writers to read the sentence with her while pointing to each word. "So writers, remember, we show and tell about people, places, and things in our writing. What are some people, places, and things we showed here? Turn and tell your partner."

Whitney listens in on their conversations to quickly check in. Next, she invites students to repeat the focus phrase again before ending the lesson: *I show and tell about people, places, and things*.

A kindergarten writer adds to the sentence during interactive writing.

Invitation to Play

Throughout the rest of the week or more, Whitney encourages students to play with this new learning about people, places, and things—or nouns—in a variety of settings and observes as they use the focus phrase at various places and times throughout the day. She shares as they become more intentional about adding to their pictures and words during writing workshop. "Look what Donelle did. He went back to his picture of a train and added pictures of things: windows, smoke, tracks."

Whitney discusses nouns
used in student writing
during a conference.

"And I added a person," Donelle says.

"That's right," Whitney replies. "Our pictures and writing are full of people, places, and things. Let's repeat our focus phrase a few times." Whitney points to the sentence strip: *I show and tell about people, places, and things*.

During centers, independent reading, social studies, and small-group reading instruction, emergent writers discover how the authors and illustrators show people, places, and things in the books they are reading. "Show me a page and tell me what you see and what you wonder."

She guides students through adding these noun details to the writing they do together. During recess and during choice time, she observes how they share with one another discussing people, places, and things as they play, draw, build, discover, wonder, and notice. She invites them to share and talk about their choices. Without prompting, students work together in a literacy station sorting pictures into people, places, and things. She makes note of how they are playing and decides what she will highlight during the Invitation to Share and Celebrate the next day.

Invitation to Share and Celebrate

At the end of the lesson set, Whitney gathers the class and begins by inviting Cole to share a story he created in the writing center this week. Cole tells about his pictures on each page of his three-page book. On the first page, he drew himself riding his bike with his brother. He points to the picture of himself and then of his brother. "This is me and my brother. We are riding bikes."

Whitney provides feedback, specifically naming what Cole has done as a writer. "Wow, Cole! You really show and tell about people, places, and things on this page! Look at this picture of you, a *person*, riding your *bike*, a *thing*, with your brother, another *person*! I'm noticing this part of your picture, too. Tell me more."

Cole, beaming, replies, "That's my house!"

"Wow! Your *house*, a place! Let's give Cole some snaps! Way to go, Cole!"

Cole asks, "Can I write house on one of those pink things?" (The sticky notes they'd been writing nouns on were pink.)

"Sure!" Whitney hands Cole a pink sticky note. She makes a choice not to guide him, not to help him unless he asks, and he doesn't. Students need space to approximate. Having laid the groundwork for now, Whitney trusts that her young writers will get to know the conventions as they play with them. We celebrate all the little attempts along the way.

The class snaps in celebratory excitement while Whitney invites another student to share.

Celebrating our writing gives students purpose, audience, and encouragement.

> We celebrate all the little attempts along the way.

Cole shares his writing with the class.

The *Patterns of Wonder* Process Is About Meaning, Not Correctness

> The ultimate goal of the *Patterns of Wonder* process is composing text with meaning.

This quick view into a *Patterns of Wonder* lesson is a glimpse into an instructional process that will have your emergent learners eager to share their worlds through writing as you invite them to wonder, compare and contrast, imitate, and play, while wrapping this all up with sharing and celebrating. As you continue to explore this pattern of engagement and play throughout this book and its lessons, the ease of this brain-based model will become second nature for you and your writers.

The ultimate goal of the *Patterns of Wonder* process is composing text with meaning. We want students to see themselves as writers, composing language and writing through storytelling and teaching. We introduce the conventions of language and grammar as tools to help them do this.

2

The Patterns of Wonder Phases of Emergent Writing

Darling, the moon is still the moon in all of its phases.

—Isra Al-Thebeh

No matter where writers are in their development—they are writers.

If you google "emergent writing stages," you'll instantly become overwhelmed with multiple versions of stages, frameworks, or continuums from various state and national curriculum documents, professional organizations, and professional literacy resources—all created with the intent to help us understand and guide the development of our youngest writers. In our own attempts to analyze such a wide range of approaches, we noticed that some depictions were so painstakingly long and detailed that things got more confusing the more we tried to disentangle them. And, though the less cumbersome alternatives appealed to us, many were comparably insubstantial, leaving far too much unsaid. In the end, as we considered where these lists originated, what their common threads were, and which of their tenets would actually be helpful to those of us who work with emergent writers, we found ourselves pulling threads from several resources, primarily leaning on the following:

> **"**
>
> No matter where writers are in their development—they are writers.

- The National Association for the Education of Young Children (NAEYC) and their 2017 *Young Children* article "Promoting Preschoolers' Emergent Writing" (Byington and Kim)
- *Already Ready* (2008) by Katie Wood Ray and Matt Glover
- Common ground covered in most current national and state curriculum and guidelines
- Interviews and surveys of prekindergarten and kindergarten teachers (2017–2020)

Over time, and through careful study, we consolidated common characteristics found across multiple resources and condensed them down to four phases of writing as a way to help us think about the development of emergent writers that is both accessible and useful to practitioners. The following chart gives an overview of the outcome of that process—the *Patterns of Wonder* Phases of Emergent Writing.

Patterns of Wonder Phases of Emergent Writing

PHASE	HALLMARK WRITING BEHAVIORS
Scribble Writing	▶ Drawing to represent writing ▶ Relying heavily on oral language ▶ Using a variety of lines and dots to record language
Symbol and Letter Writing	▶ Using mock letters or symbols ▶ Including representational drawing ▶ Using letter strings intended to represent writing ▶ Exploring letter and sound correspondence ▶ Experimenting with labeling
Transitional Writing	▶ Labeling pictures using letter sounds ▶ Using letter sounds to write words with invented spelling ▶ Copying words from the room ▶ Beginning to use spaces as word boundaries in sentences ▶ Trying out capitalization and ending punctuation
Conventional Writing	▶ Conventionally spelling common words ▶ Approximating spelling of less common words using letter sounds ▶ Using spaces between words in sentences ▶ Using ending punctuation, may be approximated ▶ Using both uppercase and lowercase letters intentionally

These developmental phases may not always be linear, and students will move in and out of phases depending on complexity and familiarity with writing purpose. This recursiveness—think of it as two steps forward and one step back—is a hallmark of all writing development.

Taking a Closer Look at Phases

As you've observed emergent writers, you know they may fluctuate back and forth among phases, depending on the complexity or familiarity with the writing they are doing. We may even see characteristics of multiple phases within one piece of writing.

Likely, you've noticed that we choose the term *phases* rather than *stages*, *framework*, or *continuum*. This was intentional. First and foremost, we call these writing behaviors *phases* because no strict boundaries exist between them. In fact, in these four phases of development, we expect some degree of overlap. The *Oxford English Dictionary* traces the origin of *phases* to "appearance" or "to show." *Phase* is also defined as part of "a series of change or development." As emergent writers move in and out of these four phases—through their play and risk taking—the lines between them often blur as students tentatively show their developing skills and new understandings appear in the approximations found in their writing. For these same reasons, these phases are not considered levels of writing, but rather characteristics or writing behaviors that help us understand our emergent writers better.

In addition to offering us a structure to think about the development of our youngest writers, these four phases also help us analyze our students' work and plan intentional instruction that meets them where their strengths and needs show they need the most support. For our purposes, the *Patterns of Wonder* Phases of Emergent Writing also establish a blueprint upon which we organize the sample lessons you'll find later on in Part 2 of this book. With that in mind, let's take a closer look at the characteristics of each phase and explore some clarifying examples.

These phases are not considered levels of writing, but rather characteristics or writing behaviors that help us understand our emergent writers better.

Scribble Writing

During the first phase, Scribble Writing, children are making the connection that they can put something on paper to represent something from their mind. They may draw their story or use dots, lines, and random shapes to represent meaning. And, because they rely heavily on oral rehearsal, writers in this phase will change their stories often from one telling to another, so don't be surprised if this happens—it's a normal emergent writer behavior. When we see writing behaviors from this early Scribble Writing phase with children, we sit with them and encourage them to talk to us about what their story or picture says. We may prompt them:

- "Tell me about your picture."
- "Read your story to me."
- "What are you writing today?"
- "Tell me what you're doing as a writer today."

66

> We honor them as writers and what they can do, leaning heavily on oral language.

These interactions help emergent writers in this phase see that what they are doing is indeed writing, if only its first shoots. We honor them as writers and what they can do, leaning heavily on oral language. These conversations continue to be fertile ground. Over time, as we share more writing from picture books and use the language of those books, emergent writers absorb these language patterns and begin to incorporate them in their conversations about their own drawings or scribbles or both.

Scribble Writing Phase Behaviors

- ▶ Drawing to represent writing
- ▶ Relying heavily on oral language
- ▶ Using a variety of lines and dots to record language

Drawing to Represent Writing

Keep in mind that during this scribble phase of writing, young children will begin toying and experimenting with written language. Their writing often includes drawn images that could represent a picture or words in their minds. Students may also choose colors to represent certain things or parts of their story. For example, in Figure 2.1, Yazen uses yellow to represent "Mom," red to represent "Dad," and blue to represent himself. When first asked to share his picture with Whitney, he simply pointed to each color and orally labeled them as *Mom, Dad, me*. To address Yazen's oral language growth at this phase,

Figure 2.1
Yazen moves through a conversation about his writing from labels to simple sentences about his family and what they like to do together.

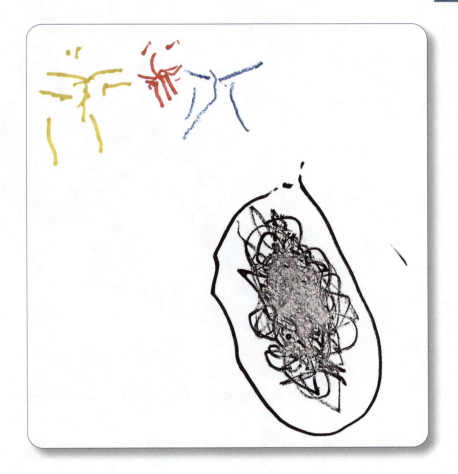

> During this earliest phase, our main work centers on honoring anything writers put on the page. We support their construction of conventional language through modeled texts and talk, not correction.

Whitney encouraged some revision by asking questions like, "Who was this one again? What was this black part again? What were you doing?"; together, they worked toward creating sentences around these drawings. Through this conversation, he refined his story saying, "This is Mom. This is Dad. This is me. We are going to swim in the pool," and he pointed to the big black scribble in the middle of the page that represented the pool.

During this earliest phase, our main work centers on honoring anything writers put on the page. We support their construction of conventional language through modeled texts and talk, not correction. We don't want to unintentionally squash their approximations.

Relying Heavily on Oral Language

Students working within the Scribble Writing phase are refining their oral language, which will act as a foundation for their progression through future phases. Importantly, these developing scribblers revise and build stronger language as they talk about their writing. For example, Ewyn explained his picture (Figure 2.2) with "This is a hygodo. It swims on the ocean floor near coral reefs. It's like a cuddle fish or a frog, but it's not. It's a hygodo!" Since this phase of writing relies heavily on oral language, we use our conversations with these writers to determine how best to support them in their language growth.

Figure 2.2
Ewyn shares what he learned about a sea creature called a hygodo in his writing. He talks about where it swims and compares and contrasts it with other living things.

Using a Variety of Lines and Dots to Record Language

In the scribble phase, we often see linear sequences of waves or lines that represent words (Figures 2.3 and 2.4). Children working in this phase attempt to replicate what they see others do in their writing by making lines that go across the page. With this type of writing, children often run their fingers along the waves or lines as they read their writing to you. This behavior is encouraging, because writers are playfully practicing the work that has been modeled for them by other readers and writers in their lives.

Figure 2.3
Braeley reads her wavy writing orally, "There was a horse named Rainbow. A princess girl came to ride her and then a mean girl came to steal her and cut her hair so she wouldn't have magical powers. The horse ran away with the nice girl to the forest."

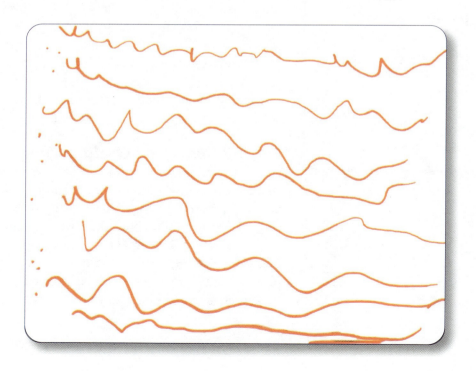

Figure 2.4
Leo orally shares his story while pointing to the linear lines, "One day I went to the slide with Tomi. We climb up and up and up and up. It was fun."

It's important to note that, though the lines or dots in this phase may seem random, they are often quite intentional. Jeff sat down with Leo to learn more about his intentions as a writer (Figure 2.4). "Hi, Leo. You're doing quite a bit of writing today. Will you read your story to me?" Leo pointed to some of the lines on his paper, while stopping to act out along the way, and shared, "One day I went to the slide with Tomi. We climb up and up and up and up. It was fun." Leo used storytelling language to share his intent behind his lines and scribbles. Through this work, he is discovering that marks are used to record thoughts and to share a message or story.

A note about names . . .

As you know, the first word most children learn to write is their name. Their names are valuable and hold strong meaning. During the Scribble Writing phase, students may begin to write their names, even though they are most likely still learning letter formation or they are grasping the fine motor skills it takes to form those letters. These early approximations of writing their names helps emergent writers find comfort in the written word and wonder in its patterns of meaning.

Symbol and Letter Writing

Students writing within the symbol and letter phase are discovering how letters and sounds can help them convey meaning through their writing. They may not yet know how to form letters, so they will often invent symbols to represent them. Still other writers developing through this phase may know how to write letters but are still gaining an understanding of the sounds that go with them. You'll find lots of connections to your work with phonological and phonemic awareness, segmenting and blending, concepts about print, and letter-sound correspondence during this phase, as children begin to make connections between the symbols and what they create in writing.

Within this phase, emergent writers use a wide variety of letters and symbols, and often the child's name is written somewhere within the piece of writing. Students tend to produce more detailed representational illustrations during the symbol and letter phase as well, and we can continue to build their oral language as we invite them to revise their oral tellings and add more to their illustrations.

Symbol and Letter Writing Phase Behaviors	▶ Using mock letters or symbols ▶ Including representational drawing ▶ Using letter strings intended to represent writing ▶ Exploring letter and sound correspondence ▶ Experimenting with labeling

Using Mock Letters or Symbols

Although students working early within this phase may use letters mixed with symbols that represent letters, we still ask them to share their stories with us orally and point to their pictures and words as they share them. When Whitney invites Nayra to share her story, she explains that she is writing about her family and using "lots of words." When Whitney asks her to read her words, Nayra says, "I love my family." As you can see from her symbols in Figure 2.5, Nayra is using the letters she knows from her name as well as other symbols, including an approximated formation of the letter *B*. Nayra may not yet understand that the letters have corresponding sounds, but she does understand that we use letters to make writing that has meaning. Again, our conversations are critical. We must talk with our writers to discover how they are playing with written language to support their growth.

Figure 2.5
Nayra reads her symbols and letters as "I love my family."

Including Representational Drawing

Illustrations in the symbol and letter phase become more developed and representational as children expand on their idea development and play with meaning and effect. We still heavily support writers in this phase through conversation, while also inviting students to add many of the details they share through oral language to their pictures—teaching them to revise by looking again and adding more to their writing. Rayne composed a story (Figure 2.6)

A note about letting students be the writers . . .

You'll notice that the student writing samples throughout this book don't include teacher writing or transcriptions. When we write for the child, we may unintentionally communicate to them that they can't write. We believe it is better to take notes about their intentions for instructional purposes, like remembering later what they said their writing says. These notes are not permanently written on the student's piece. Some teachers write on sticky notes and temporarily attach them for audiences to know what they say when they are displayed. Other teachers prefer to snap a picture of the writing with a device and keep digital notes. Whatever method you choose, it's important writers feel their work is valued for what they are currently doing, so we avoid sending the opposite message by doing it for them.

about a dinosaur using representational pictures and eagerly shared what it said with his classmates. His story is focused and follows a simple plot, something he is bringing in from his knowledge of how stories tend to go.

Figure 2.6

Figure 2.6

Rayne writes his story across pages, "The dinosaur was trying to eat me."

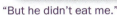

"But he didn't eat me."

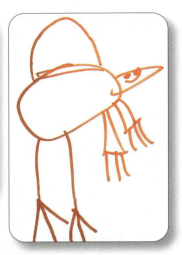

"I drove away."

Using Letter Strings to Represent Writing

When emergent writers scratch a variety of letters across a line, we call these letter strings. As students begin to understand how letters are formed and that they are written across a page to create meaning, young writers in the symbol and letter phase will give it a try with confidence, writing as many letters as they can. We often find their names or letters from their names within the strings of letters, too.

If writers are only using pictures with no letters as Rayne did in his dinosaur story earlier (Figure 2.6), we invite them to write their stories with both pictures and words. Madison wrote her name and then drew a picture of a unicorn on the first page of her book (Figure 2.7). To encourage her to include words, her teacher asked, "What will your words say?"

Figure 2.7
Madison adds letters to tell about her unicorn.

Madison replied, "I don't know any words yet."

"Well, let's see. You know your name. That's a word, and that means you also know some letters. You're five and five-year-olds write the letters they think will work best to tell their stories. What letters do you think would be best to tell about your unicorn?"

Madison, excited that she does what five-year-olds do, eagerly writes some letters she knows. This approach with Madison shows her that we value her learning process and we also value that she is the one that makes the choices in her writing. Notice Madison's name and then letters that make sense to her.

Exploring Letter and Sound Correspondence

In the symbol and letter phase, students learn more letters and the sounds they represent and begin to use those sounds to record their language. Although they are still using letter strings, the letters within the strings become more intentional, matching more and more with the sounds they represent. In Figure 2.8, Mia Bella wrote, "Once upon a time, there was a queen and king." She thought through each word as she wrote the letters she knew to represent the sounds she heard. Notice there are many additional letters included in her writing, too. We love this playfulness we find inside of the words students write during this phase. Their writing still may include spots that are difficult to read on our own, so it's important to still make note of the language the students use orally when reading their stories.

Figure 2.8

Mia Bella writes, "Once upon a time, there was a queen and king."

Experimenting with Labeling

In the symbol and letter phase, emergent writers may also begin tentatively playing around with labeling their pictures with symbols as well as some of the letters they have learned. Notice how Emmy has so much to say in her writing sample shown in Figure 2.9! We know this because of the details in her picture. When asked about her story, she explained each part of her picture in detail. In addition to reading her letter strings at the bottom, she beamed with pride as she pointed out the labeling she was trying out for the first time: "I like the beach. I build sand castles with lots of toys. We wear swimsuits. Sometimes I have to go to the bathroom. My mom likes to sit in this chair. This is me, and these are my cousins. We are yelling because we are outside and we can yell as loud as we want."

Figure 2.9
Using letter strings and approximated labels as an anchor, Emmy writes her story about going to the beach.

Transitional Writing

The transitional phase of writing encompasses a larger variety of writing moves as students begin to grasp concepts about print and letter-sound correspondence and develop a stronger understanding of the written language. It's also a phase that easily overlaps some of what we see in conventional writing. It's a phase that is constantly transforming, shifting from symbols and letters to conventional writing and all of the magic that happens between.

Writers in the transitional phase move into labeling pictures with letters or words that match the sounds they hear. Though often not spelled conventionally, their words are more easily read by others as many letters represent sounds in the words. In this phase, writers tend to use multiple words, though the words may run together. The transitional phase is also where you'll notice writers playing with punctuation and capitalization. We still may need to invite students to include words in their writing, but in the transitional phase you see far more conventionality seeping into their words, labels, and sentences.

Transitional Writing Phase Behaviors	▶ Labeling pictures using letter sounds ▶ Using letter sounds to write words with invented spelling ▶ Copying words from the room ▶ Beginning to use spaces as word boundaries in sentences ▶ Trying out capitalization and ending punctuation

Labeling Pictures Using Letter Sounds

In the transitional phase, labeling pictures continues to be a prominent way students share their thoughts with words that tie directly to their illustrations. When writers in this phase are first beginning to label their pictures, they may just write a letter representing the initial sound of the word. However, as they gain a better understanding of letter-sound correspondence, writers in the transitional phase become more intentional with the letters they choose to write. Over time, their approximations become increasingly successful as they learn to apply sounds across words in their labels. Wherever writers are in this process, we value this heavy work of putting letters to sounds and celebrate this step toward conventional writing. Pearly made a book about Peppa Pig and wrote one letter as a label on each page. Figure 2.10 is a page from her book showing Peppa's house. Notice how her choices were intentional as she thought about using initial sounds in her labels.

Wherever writers are in this process, we value this heavy work of putting letters to sounds and celebrate this step toward conventional writing.

Figure 2.10
Pearly uses the letter *H* to label the house in her book about Peppa Pig.

Evan labeled the swing and merry-go-round on the playground in Figure 2.11. When talking with Evan, he shared his writing by reading each of his labels, pointing to each corresponding word. He also shared the action that was happening on the playground by pointing to the red lines. You can see that Evan is comfortable with listening for the sounds he hears across words to craft his labels. As a next instructional step, we might invite him to use his labels in sentences below the picture to tell even more, but oral rehearsal will be the key here as he begins to play around with the words he has and what else he wants his readers to know.

Figure 2.11
Evan uses letter sounds to label the swing and merry-go-round on his playground.

Using Letter Sounds to Write Words With Invented Spelling

In addition to labeling pictures, writers progressing through the transitional phase begin to write sentences with words that we can read, even if they aren't conventionally spelled. William labeled his pictures on the page of his book in Figure 2.12 and wrote the sentence "I am walking my puppy." Though his spelling is approximated, William is clearly thinking through the sounds he hears as he writes his sentence.

Figure 2.12
William uses approximated spelling to write "I am walking my puppy."

Copying Words from the Room

Students begin to make more connections to written language as they discover that words are everywhere, and they can use these words in their own writing. We often see writers in the transitional phase use the words around the room including those from the word wall, shared reading poems or songs resting on the easel, and anchor charts. A print-rich environment invites students to read the room and use these words as anchors for spelling in their own writing.

Notice how Homero writes about his friends in Figure 2.13, spelling words from the word wall correctly and writing the letters of the sounds he hears for the other words.

Figure 2.13
Homero uses words from around the room to help him write "I love my friends. We do not fight!"

Beginning to Use Spaces as Word Boundaries

Concepts about print are still a focus as children in the transitional phase of writing learn that letters make words and words make sentences, and we separate those words with spaces. When talking to Jeremiah about his book on superheroes, he proudly showed us each page, pointing to his labels as he read. When he shared the page shown in Figure 2.14 with us, he said, "A superhero." Notice how Jeremiah recorded the initial sound, medial sounds, final sound, including vowels, and he added a space between the two words! In addition to what he wrote, he also shared more information through his oral language, adding conversationally, "He is strong and flies high." Jeremiah is transitioning toward conventional writing as he thinks about spelling and recognizing that words have boundaries by putting a space between them.

Figure 2.14
Jeremiah adds a sentence to his picture with a space between the words *A Superhero.*

Trying Out Capitalization and Ending Punctuation

> When we provide support for writers in written conventions, we always want to look at what they are doing and build on it.

We also see writers begin to play with using both uppercase and lowercase letters and even some punctuation as they shift away from the transitional phase and into conventional writing. As you can see in the two samples in Figures 2.15 and 2.16, these writers are dipping their writing toes into some conventional writing as they approximate capitalization and punctuation. In Figure 2.15, Charlotte is playing around with capitalization as she transitions to the conventional usage of using lowercase letters more often than capital letters, while Lauren plays with ending punctuation in Figure 2.16. When we provide support for writers in written conventions, we always want to look at what they are doing and build on it. So, as children begin taking risks like this in the transitional phase, we take those attempts as a sign of growth and teach into them.

Figure 2.15
Charlotte writes about a tea party with her mom and plays with the use of uppercase and lowercase letters.

Won. my. famlamay witoowto Coobech. ifoocuz. alontim. tim. teit. thir. the. brathde. witinto. The. wotre. thiur winon. lot. wwaper it wuz very. hot. at. coobech. Thire wunne shesh on

Figure 2.16
Lauren experiments with periods throughout her page about going to Coco Beach.

Conventional Writing

Writers in the conventional phase have an understanding of what makes a sentence on paper, and they continue to play with what they learn. They are intentional with their thoughts, placing ending punctuation in places they feel their readers should stop, ending that idea. Their spelling is accurate for sight words, most likely taken from the word wall, and the sounds across other words are intentionally thought out. Spacing between words is present, and spelling is more accurate. They continue to approximate with capitalization, but we see more consistency with beginnings of sentences and names with capital letters while leaving all other letters lowercase. We see more intentional use of punctuation, with writers in this phase often getting creative in their efforts to bring out meaning and effect. As conventional writers become accustomed to doing all of this with automaticity, their volume of writing expands as they include more words and use conventions more precisely in an effort to share everything they want their readers to know.

Conventional Writing Phase Behaviors	▸ Conventionally spelling common words ▸ Approximating spelling of less common words using letter sounds ▸ Using spaces between words in sentences ▸ Using ending punctuation, may be approximated ▸ Using both uppercase and lowercase letters intentionally

Conventionally Spelling Common Words

As in the transitional phase, writers in the conventional phase are spelling more and more words correctly. These words are often high-frequency words, words copied from the room, or words that can easily be spelled through segmenting, such as *c-a-t*. In the conventional phase, this spelling accuracy becomes more prominent and frequent, allowing us to easily read even more of what the child has written. Emily made a book about people she likes, concluding with someone she loves, her brother (Figure 2.17). Her spelling of the common words *I*, *love*, and *my* is accurate and, because she wrote the sounds she heard across the word, her readers can clearly tell her last word is *brother*—even though she heard the *d* sound for *th*.

Figure 2.17
Emily writes, "I love my brother!"

Approximating Spelling of Less Common Words Using Letter Sounds

Even in the Conventional Writing phase, writers will still make approximations for spelling. Children continue to learn about how letter sounds work together to make words for several years after first grade, and we value the thinking they do as they play with the words they are writing to make meaning for their readers. Zander wrote a book about being in a ninja warrior competeition and ended the story with this page in Figure 2.18. Zander took the time to really think through each word he wrote and considered everything he was learning about words and sounds as he played with this new knowledge to write *going*, with the *o* sound represented with *owe* and a silent *e* at the end of the word.

Figure 2.18
Zander approximates spelling as he concludes his ninja warrior competition story: "I am going to Vegas!"

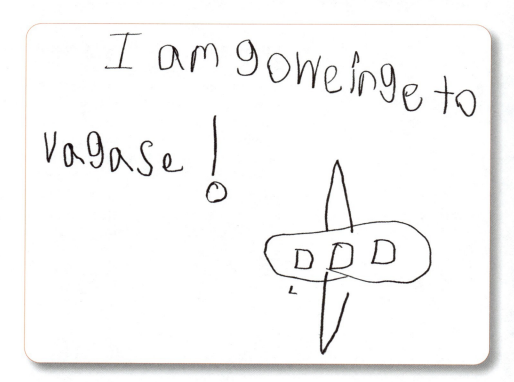

> Children continue to learn about how letter sounds work together to make words for several years after first grade, and we value the thinking they do as they play with the words they are writing to make meaning for their readers.

He has also added that silent *e* to the end of *Vegas*. Can you guess what he might be learning about during word study at the moment? We honor this play throughout the learning process, knowing that our emergent writers' spelling will become less approximated as they learn more about phonics and spelling, and as they read and write a variety of texts across their instructional years.

Using Spaces Between Words in Sentences

Though they may have only tentatively played around with spacing during their transitional phase, conventional writers begin to use clear spaces between their words more consistently. To support this, some teachers use popsicles sticks or the child's finger as a scaffold to help students self-monitor how much space they're using between each word. Spacing scaffolds are removed as writers begin to show their understanding of word boundaries. In Figure 2.19, Chandler, a *Titanic* expert, decided to share his knowledge with others. Notice the spacing between his words, showing his understanding that letters create words and words create sentences. He is still playing with punctuation, capitalization, and spelling, but his volume of writing is tremendous, showing excitement and confidence in his choice of topic.

Figure 2.19
Chandler uses spaces between his words to teach his readers: "Titanic: The Titanic was a big ship. It was built 107 years ago. It crashed when it was going somewhere with an iceberg. The Titanic was huge."

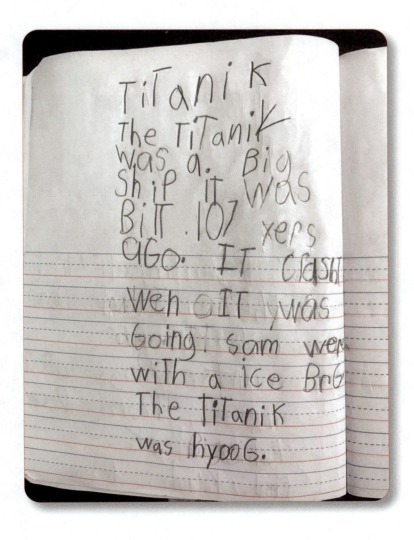

Using Ending Punctuation, May Be Approximated

As children learn why writers use ending punctuation and how they decide where it goes in the conventional phase, we often see periods at the end of each word or even at the end of each line. We're always encouraged by the risk and play involved in these approximations, because we trust that writers will become more and more accurate with ending punctuation as they grow in their conventional writing. In the second step of her book on how to brush your teeth (Figure 2.20), Julia demonstrates an emerging understanding that we use end marks, knowing they go at the end somewhere—and takes risks as she plays around with punctuation.

Figure 2.20
Julia teaches her readers how to brush their teeth while also taking risks with transition words and punctuation: "Next, you brush your teeth in a circle."

Using Both Uppercase and Lowercase Letters Intentionally

Writers in the conventional phase continue to grow in their knowledge of using capital letters, and—although we still may continue to see some approximation with this, even beyond kindergarten—they're increasingly consistent with using capitals accurately. Lydia wrote an informational book about turtles. She knows that her information can be shared through both pictures and words, and she has written more than one sentence to share her information on the page in Figure 2.21. She begins each sentence with a capital letter and, overall, uses lowercase letters appropriately. With more exploration through reading texts and continued practice during interactive writing, she will continue to play with and refine the way she uses capitalization for purpose and craft.

Figure 2.21
Lydia begins to use capitalization conventionally in her book about turtles: "Turtles lay eggs. The turtle's babies hatch out of the eggs."

We Don't Arrive: We Move Toward Conventionality

Though the fourth phase of writing is titled Conventional Writing, this does not mean students will need to be consistently following the conventions to be in this phase. Rather, conventional writing is the phase in which writers are ready to explore, at a deeper level, language's established patterns or conventions and what they mean to writers and readers. In fact, emergent writers who reach this phase will continue to evolve for the rest of their lives, as they hone their craft and take on greater understanding of the writing process. The next thing becomes the next convention they need to express or comprehend.

Since we know writers transfer what they have seen in books they have been exposed to through shared experiences as well as exploratory experiences, we continue these processes in any phase. They crave opportunities in their day to be immersed in fresh or familiar written language through read-alouds, shared reading, interactive writing, and shared writing. As these experiences change, so will what emergent writers learn. Through repeated play with standard patterns, they naturally begin to pick those conventions up.

> When we're intentional about providing writers with this time for exploration and immersion, they bring these experiences back to their own writing.

As emergent writers develop across the four phases, conventionally or otherwise, they continue to need time to talk with one another about what they see and notice, as well as choice time to read and browse self-selected books, play, build, and act out scenarios. This is how writers explore their world. Writing becomes a natural extension of these activities. Of course, they also need small-group time with the teacher to read and write at every phase as well. When we're intentional about providing writers with this time for exploration and immersion, they bring these experiences back to their own writing. As we look at what our students are creating in any phase, we ask ourselves:

- What is this writer doing to make meaning already?
- What can I teach this writer about what other writers do that will build on the meaning they are already making?

This is the power of considering patterns in writing instruction. No matter which of the four phases emergent writers find themselves in, they are moving to their next right place, then the next. Not in straight lines or steps, but in zigzag, forward, back, and across motions, becoming. We find our best teaching happens when we join them for the ride, following our writers as they lead the way. They invariably show us what they need next.

Scribble Writing

DeAndre uses a variety of color to show people, places, and things in his picture. He labels them orally as he points to each one: "This is the helicopter. This is the pool. This is a trampoline. A red table. The ladder. This is the color red. This is my mom. This is a turkey. A car. The stairs. I like the trampoline. It is at my new house." Through conversation with his teacher about how writers tell what's happening in the story, he revised his oral telling of the story and said, "The rolling pin is rolling here. This big dragon is blowing fire." Changing the telling of the story is common in this phase.

Sierra makes a book about what she likes. On one page, she shares, "I like Mrs. La Rocca. She's holding a flower, and this is her curly hair. She's wearing a black shirt."

Ben eagerly shares his story about ice cream. Notice his pictures of ice cream cones are representational and he writes his words using scribbles. As Ben learns more about letter formation and their sounds, his written language will become more representational as well.

Symbol and Letter Writing

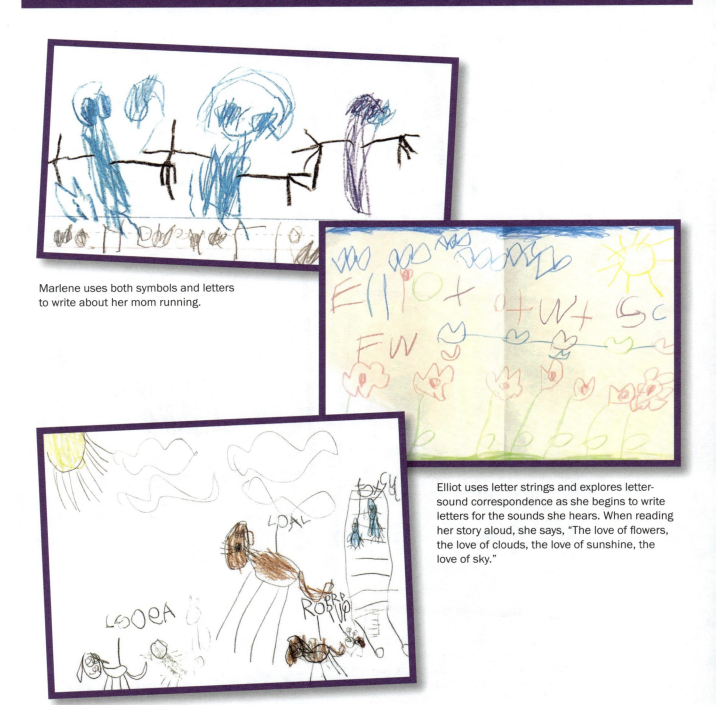

Marlene uses both symbols and letters to write about her mom running.

Elliot uses letter strings and explores letter-sound correspondence as she begins to write letters for the sounds she hears. When reading her story aloud, she says, "The love of flowers, the love of clouds, the love of sunshine, the love of sky."

Amilia labels her pictures to share her story about a visit to the pet store: "One day I went to a pet shop and they had pretty dogs. I had to pick one to take home with me."

Transitional Writing

Cash uses letter sounds to write words with approximation. Notice he also plays with ending punctuation.

Homero labels his picture with initial letter sounds and shares his story about his family orally by saying, "A visit to my grandma's house in Mexico."

Finn shares his story using letter sounds to write words with inventive spelling. He is beginning to play around with capitalization. When reading it aloud, he says, "We went to the pool."

Conventional Writing

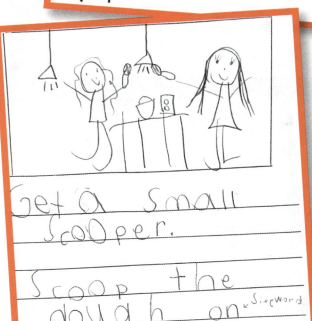

Peyton fills an entire page with writing as she tells her story about a dinosaur in danger. Notice how she plays with both uppercase and lowercase letters, inventive spelling, and spacing between words.

Keraya wrote a book about sharks. On this page, notice the approximated spelling, spaces between words, ending punctuation, and intentional capitalization at the beginning of her sentences.

Olivia wrote a book about how to make cookies. She uses conventions intentionally to make meaning for her readers. She even labeled where she used a sight word, celebrating what she knows about what writers do.

3
The Planning Behind the Patterns of Wonder Process

Where attention goes, neural firing flows, and neural connection grows.

—Siegel and Bryson, *The Yes Brain*

The wonder of inquiry is the driving force behind the *Patterns of Wonder* process. The conversations around conventions cause the brain to fire, connect, and grow, which etches a beginning understanding of the moves writers make to activate meaning. This inquiry creates a path of meaning-making that feeds reading, writing, and grammar as it unfolds naturally.

Writers come to us already full of this inquisitiveness, and it's a wonder to watch them follow a thread of thought while exploring their thinking out loud. To capitalize on this instructionally, we find a bit of intentional preplanning sets the stage to harness the curiosity they bring to our classrooms.

How to Plan for the *Patterns of Wonder* Process

In Chapter 1, we stepped into a kindergarten classroom and walked through a series of lessons in the *Patterns of Wonder* process. You got your first peek at how the process invites emergent writers to observe, explore, and experiment with conventions. In that series of lessons, we focused on nouns orally and in pictures, as well as words, letters, or symbols. How do we plan for this kind of engagement and growth over time?

	Planning to **Wonder** *Steps*
1	Select a standard and drill down to what your writers need to know.
2	Connect the convention to author's purpose and craft.
3	Choose a pathway of writing support.
4	Create a focus phrase.
5	Choose a text that demonstrates the standard.
6	Prepare a compare and contrast invitation.
7	Plan for how students will imitate the model with you.
8	Plan for play.
9	Plan a celebration.

Select a Standard

We use various standards—national, state, and local—to guide us as we teach our students. These standards cover a wide range of developmental writing levels within our classrooms. We also consider the different instructional needs students demonstrate as they write for different purposes and interests. Some students may come to us having never held a writing utensil, while others in the same class come writing letters and some words.

For our youngest writers, concepts about print are an essential component of learning to read and write, so we make sure to both connect and fold this into our work around conventions. Since we're working with emergent writers, we use two primary domains when thinking about standards in *Patterns of Wonder*:

- Concepts about print
- Grammar

> We encourage you to roll with the flow of student responses as much as you can.

Emergent writers are still learning how print works, so sometimes it may make more sense to focus our instruction on concepts about print. At other times, a grammar focus like using nouns, verbs, or prepositions to expand detail and clarify our sentences would be more useful to our blossoming writers. Our focus may adjust as a lesson unfolds, since the direction our curiosities lead us and the conversation they stir can create a fascinating playground in which to explore multiple reading and writing connections. We encourage you to roll with the flow of student responses as much as you can. Even though we plan our lessons, we want our students' curiosity to be center stage—alive, evolving, and open-ended.

Selecting the standard is our starting point. But this can seem deceptively simple. Consider these questions as you look at any standard:

- What is the standard really asking learners to do?
- Does the standard ask writers to use *or* identify a skill craft?
- What do your students need to know first?
- How can we deconstruct the standard into a teachable, bite-sized chunk(s)?

A note about concepts about print . . .

According to early literacy researcher and Reading Recovery founder, Marie Clay (2017), an understanding of concepts about how print works opens doors to literacy for our youngest readers and writers. This learning includes

▶ book orientation and layout (front and back of the book, where the story begins, when to turn the page, etc.);
▶ the difference between pictures and words;
▶ directionality (moving from left to right in both reading and writing);
▶ the understanding that letters make words and words make sentences;
▶ one-to-one correspondence;
▶ and the understanding of simple punctuation and capitalization.

Some children enter kindergarten with these understandings, and others do not. As we read and write together, we look for opportunities throughout our day to notice and share our thinking around these crucial concepts about print.

For example, common kindergarten standards tend to use wording like "use frequently occurring nouns." What does this really mean for students? (See "A note about 'frequently occurring' . . ." for more information.) How do we figure out what they need to actually know?

Drill Down to What Your Writers Need to Know

Here, we make an effort to drill down to what our learners need to know about any concept or standard. For example, with the concept of nouns, our students don't really need to know much before they can use them. That's right. They *already* use them—constantly.

"When's snack *time*?"
"Tell *Brian* to stop touching my *picture*."
"Yay! *Patricia* made me a *card*."

And they'll go on using nouns as they talk, read, and write for the rest of their lives. But what do our beginners actually need to *know* about nouns? How can the concept of nouns or verbs, or whatever convention we are introducing, help them as writers, readers, and learners? We can show students they *already* use the skill or craft in some way. They can't escape them. Nouns, nouns everywhere. And verbs. And adjectives. You get the point.

So we begin there, inviting beginning writers to use what they already know to tell us about their lives and inviting them to choose different kinds of nouns to describe people, places, and things in their writing. Using nouns is more than labeling people, places, and things in our pictures and writing—although we might begin there in some phases. What emergent writers really need to know is that using nouns allows us to fill our writing with the people, places, and things that make up the worlds we live in and construct, in real life and in the pretend world with blocks. The more writers know about nouns—or any concept—the more precisely they'll use them to compose and the more they'll use them to comprehend. With intention. With knowledge.

A note about frequently occurring . . .

Some standards call for students to use *frequently occurring* nouns, verbs, adjectives, prepositions, conjunctions, and so on. Students will use words that are part of the language they hear from others and see in books, so don't worry so much about including the words *frequently occurring* when talking with children. The words they use are already frequently occurring.

Resist making conventions complicated or overly important.

> Author's purpose informs why writers do what they do, and author's craft is how they do it.

Connect the Convention to Author's Purpose and Craft

Author's purpose informs *why* writers do what they do, and author's craft is *how* they do it. When considering nouns as people, places, and things, writers show their readers what the world is made of. They create a picture in their reader's mind that shows more than just stuff. They use words like *brother*, *bike*, and *park* to craft sentences for the reader to understand what's going on: "My brother rode his bike to the park." Without these details of *who* and *what* (*nouns*), the reader would be lost.

Choose a Pathway of Writing Support

Once you've chosen the standard for the lesson set; narrowed it down to a meaningful, sensible, digestible goal; and connected it to purpose and craft, you'll want to think about what type of focused support will be most effective, depending on the hallmarks of the phase your writers are developing within. In the *Patterns of Wonder* process, we consider three specific pathways of support for writers:

- Oral language
- Illustrations
- Written language

These three pathways allow for intentional flexibility in meeting emergent writers at their growing edge. For example, as we work through the standard on using nouns, we can plan a variety of supports for our emergent writers in multiple scaffolds across all four *Patterns of Wonder* phases. Some examples of these pathways follow.

Support in Oral Language: Scribble Phase

We can best support writers in the scribble phase through oral language, encouraging them to use nouns to tell about people, places, and things in their writing and pictures. As they speak about their lives and their writing, we invite them to tell us more by asking questions that probe for details about *who* or *what* in all our conversations across the day and in all subject areas.

This type of support builds on the language students are using orally to share their writing. Are they talking in simple labels or sentences? Do their sentences include various parts of speech such verbs that show action, adjectives that tell what kind or how many, or even prepositions that tell when or where? Are they expanding their sentences with conjunctions like *and*, *so*, or *because*?

While conferring, Whitney kneels alongside Andrew. He points to parts of his picture and labels them orally, "Car. Me. Road."

Whitney nudges him to compose sentences orally: "OK, now let's read your pictures as if they are sentences in a book. You might say, 'This is a car.' Or 'The car goes zoom.' What do you think it should say on this page?"

Andrew senses from his experiences of being read to how books and writing tend to go. He points to his picture again and says, "This is my car, and I am driving it really fast."

Whitney will continue to invite this oral rehearsal of his story every time they talk about his writing. She might nudge him further by asking, "What else could you write?" When students repeat what the page "says" several times, it builds their oral language and develops their writing muscles through oral rehearsal. For some students, this oral rehearsal might need to be modeled by the teacher at first, while asking for the writer's input: "Does that sound right to you? Is that what you're trying to say here?" Most young writers will correct you if it doesn't match their intended meaning. The teacher is really a writing coach, always putting the ball back in the writer's court.

Our focus as writing teachers is to help students compose written language—eventually. Composing or pulling together of words begins with oral language. We won't truly know what support we can offer the student in later compositions if

Composing or pulling together of words begins with oral language.

we don't talk with them about their writing and pictures early on. As we take note of what our emergent writers are showing us through their oral language, we can build on this, inviting them to tell more.

Support in Illustrations: Symbol and Letter Phase

Since writers in the symbol and letter phase are still learning how to talk through their writing, approximating mock letter attempts, and playing around with including more intentional images, we'll support them best by helping them enhance their illustrations while continuing to tap into their developing proficiency with oral language.

"Tell me about your picture, Emma," Jeff says.

"It's a wagon," she answers.

"What other things or people or places could you add to your picture?"

"Me! It's my wagon!" Her face brightens and she eagerly draws herself in the picture.

"So you show others about the people, places, and things in your picture by adding them, and you can tell about each one, too. Anyone want to see what Emma's doing in the writing center?" A few kids rush over, excited to celebrate Emma's writing with her.

And now they want to try.

When our instructional support focuses on the writer's illustrations, we continue to search for what they are already doing and build from there. We can still ask ourselves the same types of questions as we did with oral language, but search more and more for the answers in their illustrations or by asking, "How could you show what you're saying?" We can also look to see if writers are using color and if their illustrations are representational drawings. Are we able to recognize what they are? With this level of support we'll still likely need to engage writers in conversation around their pictures to help us discover the intent behind them. As we fine-tune our support to expand or refine what writers mean to say, we invite them to add more to their illustrations through drawing or experimental writing to show what they mean.

Support in Written Language: Transitional and Conventional Phases

As writers are ready, we'll turn our attention toward labeling pictures and writing words in the transitional phase, while the focus becomes including sentences later in the conventional phase. When students begin to write more on the page in these later phases of emergent writing, it's time to support this exciting development toward written language. Because these writers are still approaching conventionality, we continue to ask ourselves that same questions we considered when supporting them with their oral language and illustrations. But now we look at what they are showing in their words and sentences.

- Are they using spaces?
- How are they sharing their thoughts and ideas through words?
- Are they writing the letters of the sounds they hear?
- Are they playing with capitalization and punctuation?

Whitney sits down to confer with Chandler about his writing. She notices he wrote an entire page about playing Legos with his family. She celebrates that his language had not decreased when he began writing more conventionally. Chandler writes in a way that mirrors how he might talk about his picture. She notes how he's playing around with capitalization and punctuation. Most of his punctuation is being used accurately, but his capital letters are randomly mixed with lowercase letters throughout the words and sentences. She decides to build on what he's doing with his capitalization.

"Chandler, you have so much to say! Look at all of this writing. Wow. I noticed you are using capital letters at the beginning of your sentences." Whitney and Chandler celebrate this use of capitalization as she points to the beginning of each sentence.

"You also used capital letters at the beginning of names like Phoebe and Star Wars. That's what writers do. Let's take a minute to look at how other authors use upper- and lowercase letters." Whitney pulls a book from nearby and the two of them explore what the author has done with capital letters and lowercase letters on one page.

Through conversation, Chandler discovers words that are not names or the beginning of sentences don't usually begin with capital letters. Whitney moves him back into his writing to look for places where he might become more intentional about using capital and lowercase letters. She doesn't ask for perfection. She trusts he will use capitals more effectively as he gets to know more about what authors do.

It's important to note that, although we generally focus our support in the area of written language in the transitional and conventional phases, we can still choose to provide support through oral language or illustrations as we see fit. If Whitney had noticed that Chandler's picture had a great amount of detail but his writing did not, she may have chosen to focus on oral language for their conference to encourage Chandler to write more. Every time we sit down with children to confer about their writing, we try to choose one effective pathway of support. Avoid addressing all three pathways in one conference because you run the risk of overwhelming emergent writers.

> " Every time we sit down with children to confer about their writing, we try to choose one effective pathway of support.

Create a Focus Phrase

In Terry Thompson's book, *The Construction Zone* (2015), we learned about focus phrases, and our minds were blown. They became an essential part of the *Patterns of Wonder* process. We use focus phrases to help teachers and children commit to a concise and manageable learning target, using kid-friendly language. This frequently repeated focus phrase becomes a source of students' self-talk when they work independently. Eventually they internalize the focus phrase to become part of their independent thought. Crafting an effective focus phrase takes practice, so it may be helpful to remember these key points:

- Use language children are able to repeat and remember.
- Narrow a broad concept down to one thing writers can do with the convention.
- Explain why and how writers use the convention.
- For some examples of focus phrases and what makes them more or less effective, see the following chart:

How to Make Focus Phrases Stronger

Weaker	Stronger
Standard: Use frequently occurring nouns.	
I use frequently occurring nouns.	I use nouns to show people, places, and things in my writing.
What makes this focus phrase weaker? *It uses the direct language from the standards rather than kid-friendly language, and it doesn't explain why and how writers use nouns as readers and writers. The words* frequently occurring *hold no meaning for emergent writers. The nouns they read, see, and write about by their very nature are frequently occurring.*	**What makes this focus phrase stronger?** *It is something that children can repeat and understand while also explaining in an exact way why and how writers use nouns. Abstract vocabulary doesn't belong in a focus phrase.*
Standard: Capitalize names of people, places, and holidays.	
I use capital letters. I capitalize proper nouns.	I start names with a capital letter. I start holidays with an uppercase letter.
What makes these focus phrases weaker? *This is too broad. Why do writers use capital letters? There are many ways (how) writers use capital letters. Since this focus phrase needs to be more specific, the idea of capitalization will need to be broken down into several different focus phrases.* *Proper nouns are just names.* *Why make it more complicated?*	**What makes these focus phrases stronger?** *These are specific and something the writer can repeat and do every time they write their name or the names of anything—even a holiday.*
Standard: Produce complete sentences.	
I write sentences. I write complete sentences. My sentences have a subject and a predicate.	My sentences answer the question *who?* or *what?* My sentences have a somebody or something. My sentences have a noun. My sentences have a verb.
What makes these focus phrases weaker? *These focus phrases are weaker because they don't really say anything a four-, five-, or six-year-old could understand.*	**What makes these focus phrases stronger?** *These focus phrases take on a bit at a time, not the whole. These gradual steps toward a crucial foundational skill work better with our youngest writers.*

Progression of Emergent Writer Focus Phrases

When shaping your focus phrases, consider the standard you're teaching alongside the needs of your students. Where are they working in the *Patterns of Wonder* Phases of Emergent Writing? As students progress through the windy road of development, we want to meet them where they are, acknowledge that, and then invite them upward and onward. The specific language we use can support that. Since our focus phrases progress toward a long-term goal across all four phases, we offer some suggested stems that correlate generally with the common avenues of instructional support we introduced earlier in this chapter. We say generally because, like always, our work with emergent writers needs to stay flexible. It's important to leave room for this. Still, we offer these stems as a scaffold, a starting place, from which to evolve your instructional language based on the needs of your writers.

Scribble Writing: "I tell . . ."
- Support is generally provided through oral language.
- Writers point to their marks and illustrations as they tell about them.
- Teachers build oracy by modeling how it would sound if it were written in words.

Symbol and Letter Writing: "I show and tell . . ."
- Support is generally focused on developing oral language and building meaning in illustrations.
- Writers add to their pictures and words to show more detail.
- As students learn letter formation and sounds, they begin to write the letters they know or symbols that they consider to be letters.
- Writers point to their marks and illustrations as they tell about them.
- Teachers build oracy by modeling how it would sound if it were written in words.

Transitional Writing: "I write words that show . . ."
- Support is generally provided in written language and illustrations.
- Students label their pictures with letters or words.
- Students write words to represent a sentence (words may be missing letters and parts; the focus is on writing the letters of the sounds they hear).
- Writers point to their letters and words as they read their writing.

Conventional Writing "I use . . ."
- Support is generally provided in written language.
- Students write words in sentences with spaces, capitalization, and punctuation.
- The capitalization and punctuation may be approximated.
- Writers point to their words as they read their writing.

You'll notice that these stems are a recurring feature in the demonstration lessons throughout Part 2 of this book. Again, this language commonly coordinates with the typical needs of emergent writers working on that lesson's particular standard in that phase. But you know your learners best. If a more concise wording would be more appropriate for the emergent writers in your classroom, by all means, make this adjustment and shift your language as

> The *Patterns of Wonder* process is about introducing and playing with concepts, not rigidity without regard for students' needs.

needed. Alternatively, if a broader focus phrase would better meet their needs, go with that. For instance, when emergent writers learn about sentences, there are multiple principles they'll need to understand in first and second grade. Therefore, we break the standard down and adjust our instructional language accordingly. We might plant the conceptual seed during shared writing stating, "Every sentence has to have a *somebody* or *something*." And then, later, move on to a focus phrase such as, *My sentences are about somebody or something*. The *Patterns of Wonder* process is about introducing and playing with concepts, not rigidity without regard for students' needs. Consider the language that would be most helpful and clear for your writers when making decisions on how to word your focus phrase.

Focus Phrases with Visuals

Emergent writers and readers need many visuals to help them connect the written word to its meaning, so we invite our writers to help decide what visuals would best help everyone read, remember, and access our focus phrase. Because we think making these decisions together is a valuable experience for the class, we generally don't plan these ahead of time. However, we do try to keep a few possibilities in our heads in case we need to nudge things along during this part of the lesson. Kids are incredibly creative with these visuals. We'd love to see what your writers come up with and, since we learn best from one another, we invite you to share some of them in the *Patterns of Wonder* unit or subthread in the *Patterns of Power* Facebook community. In the following chart, you can see examples of this type of visual support along with the progression language stems across several focus phrases. It is up to you and your students what type of visuals are needed. We show a variety of possibilities here.

Example of Focus Phrase Progression for Nouns by Phase

Scribble Writing	*I tell about people, places, and things in my writing.* I tell about people, places, and things in my writing.
Symbol and Letter Writing	*I show and tell about people, places, and things in my writing.* I show and tell about people, places, and things in my writing. IWMD
Transitional Writing	*I write words that show people, places, and things in my writing.* I write words that show people, places, and things in my writing. I WALK MY dog in the Park
Conventional Writing	*I use nouns to show people, places, and things.* I use nouns to show people, places, and things.

Choose a Text That Demonstrates the Standard

After we've defined our focus phrase, the next piece of planning is finding a model text that shows the convention in action. Depending on the phase of writing, the model may be a picture, a picture with text, or a sentence from a book. Consider what your students are already doing in their writing and how you can build on that with the text you've selected. When choosing a text, consider these qualities:

- **Is the book engaging?**
  Consider books that invite children in and make them want to keep reading or exploring the text further.

- **Is the book inclusive?**
  Select texts that represent a variety of audiences, allowing children to see themselves and others. Here, consider race, ethnicity, culture, and gender as well as diversity, equity, and inclusion.

- **Do the illustrations invite close study and conversation?**
  If pictures will be part of the conversation, look for illustrations that are clearly visible, support the concept of the lesson, and stir community conversations.

- **Is the text easily read and visible?**
  If the text will be a part of the conversation, find works that have larger print or think about how you will display the texts for clearer visibility, so students can read them easily.

- **Do the text or illustrations lend themselves to imitating?**
  Pick works with illustrations that include characteristics similar to the ones you want students to emulate in their own pictures. For instance, if labeling is part of the imitation, look for books with labeled pictures. When working with text, select books with sentence structures that demonstrate the focus phrase, yet are also easily imitated by your students.

Prepare a Compare and Contrast Invitation

The next step is to decide what type of piece will be used to compare and contrast alongside the model text you'll have explored in the Invitation to Wonder. This might be another page from the same book, a page from another book, or something you create. This second example provides another model for students to use when imitating.

If you decide to create your own example for this step, keep the phase of writing in mind as you draw a picture or add words. This will help you showcase the types of things students can do in their own writing. Because your writers will use this model as another mentor, conventions, including spelling, should be correctly written. We find that more effective compare and contrast invitations include the following qualities:

- Legible writing
- Accessible text
- Simple pictures

Plan for How Students Will Imitate the Model with You

The next step of the planning process is to decide how you will invite students to compose an imitation of the model with you. This shared experience of composing together could happen through *shared writing* or through *interactive writing*.

Shared Writing

During shared writing, the students and teacher share the work of thinking and composing orally, and the written composition is modeled by the teacher. For example, if the imitation is about including additional details in an illustration, students are invited to share what should be added to the picture, and the teacher draws it. The teacher then invites the students to come up with a sentence that goes with the picture, and the teacher writes the sentence, modeling the act of writing for the students.

Interactive Writing

On the other hand, during interactive writing, children are invited to share the pen with the teacher, taking part in the work of composing the written text. Here, the thinking and composing are still done together orally, but when it's time to create, the teacher chooses which parts they will write and which parts the students will be invited to write. Sometimes, students are invited to write a letter representing the sound they hear, like the initial sound or the ending sound of a word. Other times, the invited student might write a sight word or another word using sounds they hear. This engaging practice of encoding together has a high payoff as students become more comfortable composing with written words and transfer what they learn from these experiences to their independent writing throughout the day. We've seen even more growth and engagement during interactive writing when students mimic the class composition on individual dry erase boards, simultaneously writing what they can throughout the invitation.

Whichever method you choose, make a plan for how the students will take part in the imitation. Think about what levels of support and modeling they need. Will they tell you what pictures to draw, or will they take part in drawing some of the pictures? Will you write the words they come up with, or will they write some of them? You may also choose to imitate together in small groups, differentiating the support as needed.

Plan for Play

This step in the *Patterns of Wonder* process invites students to see writing as a form of play. It provides opportunities in alternate settings across a few days to try out the focus phrase, lingering in it a little longer, approximating the use of it in the speaking and writing students do everywhere. Think about how you will invite students to play with the focus phrase in a variety of settings. For instance, we might choose from several options to invite play around nouns.

Play During *Patterns of Wonder* Time

If you have a time in your day reserved for *Patterns of Wonder*, you can build some playful imitation into it. Most teachers schedule this extra time as an optional extension of the conversation just after their Invitation to Imitate Together. Students can work with a partner or independently to imitate the model or create another piece of writing to try out the skill.

Play During Writing Workshop or Independent Writing Time

Since the focus phrase and the imitation you created together as a class is on display, students might play around with convention, such as nouns, in their writing whether they add them to their pictures or words. To invite the play, nudge writers to use the convention during a writing conference or highlight the way some writers tried using the convention during a share session.

Play During Centers or Literacy Stations

With a writing station full of inviting writing tools, like different kinds of paper, writers play around with their own imitations by drawing a picture or composing a story that shows people, places, and things. In the reading station, they may look for examples in books they are reading or start a collection on a shared anchor chart. You might even set up a sorting station where teams sort picture cards into categories of people, places, and things so writers visually see what nouns are.

Play During Choice Time

Children can call back to the convention and the focus phrase during dramatic play by discussing the people, places, and things in their play. When building with blocks or Legos, children could be encouraged to share with each other some of the people, places, or things they have built. When creating paintings or drawings in the art center, students might try adding people, places, or things to their work. When reading the room, children point out people, places, or things they find. They can even label them with sticky notes!

Play During Small-Group Instruction

During guided reading or guided writing, students share the people, places, or things they see in the pictures or words of the books they are reading, or they write together about people, places, and things. The small group is a nice place to revisit some concepts that may be confusing or to practice using the convention through interactive writing in a more intimate setting. It may also be a time to confer with individual group members about taking risks around the convention, inviting them to play with it in different ways.

Plan a Celebration

"Celebrate often and watch what happens with your young writers" (Anderson 2007). We take time to celebrate our writers and their efforts because they deserve it and they need lots of feedback that says "Yes! You *are* a writer!" Use this part of the planning process to decide how writers' efforts will be celebrated. As students share their work during the celebration, find some way to display it or in some way continue the celebration beyond the conversation. This celebration invites your students to continue their play and grow as writers. Some favorite ways to celebrate include the following:

- Sit in a circle and share in turn.
- Play music as students move through the room and, when the music stops, they share with someone nearby.
- Place a piece of butcher paper out on the floor to act as a pretend stage. Encourage students to share their writing with a prop microphone.
- Invite other teachers, principals, or classes in for a sharing session.

Sharing by reading writers' work aloud is only one way to celebrate. You'll also want to think about creative ways they can display their work to be read by multiple audiences such as posting their writing on the wall, placing class created books in the classroom library, or uploading writing samples for online display. The possibilities are endless.

At this point in planning, you will have done the bulk of your preparation. The rest will come to you in the moment, developing organically as you put the process into action. As you do, pay attention to your students and be responsive, knowing your plan is flexible and following them intuitively. Trust your writers to show you what they need.

In time, planning for *Patterns of Wonder* lessons will become second nature to you. But for now, you may find the following chart as well as the planning template in Appendix C to be useful resources as you get started.

> As students share their work during the celebration, find some way to display it or in some way continue the celebration beyond the conversation.

> Trust your writers to show you what they need.

Patterns of Wonder Planning Process	
Standard/Concept	Review your students' writing samples or refer to your curriculum standards. Choose a standard or concept and break it down. Uncover what it asks writers to do. Decide if you need to have a grammar focus or focus on concepts about print.
Author's Purpose and Craft	Connect the convention to the author's purpose (*why* writers do that they do) and craft (*how* they do it).
Pathways of Writing Support	Determine where your heavy support will be for your writers: oral language, illustrations, written language.
Focus Phrase	Create a focus phrase grounded in the *Patterns of Wonder* Phases of Emergent Writing: kid-friendly language that states a clearly defined learning goal.
Invitation to Wonder	Choose a text that demonstrates the focus phrase, and decide if you will explore a picture, a picture with words, or a sentence from the text.
Invitation to Compare and Contrast	Select or create an imitation of the model that the students can use for a compare and contrast conversation.
Invitation to Imitate Together	Decide if you and your students will imitate the model through shared writing or interactive writing.
Invitation to Play	Incorporate opportunities throughout the day or week for your writers to play (explore, try, talk, act) with the standard in their reading, writing, and speaking.
Invitation to Share and Celebrate	Determine how you will celebrate writers' application of the standard and how you might display and honor their efforts.

As you prepare for each step of the process, remember to consider where your writers are in the *Patterns of Wonder* Phases of Emergent Writing and plan accordingly to meet their needs. See Appendix C for a blank template for this planning process.

4
The Patterns of Wonder Process in Action

Most of what we know about the world was not given to us by our genes: we had to learn it from our environment or from those around us.

—Stanislas Dehaene, *How We Learn*

> Each step of the process takes ten minutes or less, and stretching them out across several days allows for a deeper understanding of what writers do and how they do it.

Once a provisional plan is in place for the *Patterns of Wonder* process, it's time to put it into action. We recommend creating a ten-minute time slot in your day for the *Patterns of Wonder* inquiry process. This is a valuable time where students are able to playfully connect reading and writing with the bridge of meaning. Each step of the process takes ten minutes or less, and stretching them out across several days allows for a deeper understanding of what writers do and how they do it. Once your students have an understanding of the invitational process, you might find it more feasible to move the steps to other parts of your day, such as during your read-aloud time or your interactive writing time. (See Appendix A for some examples of how this could look.)

At this point, you have everything you need to move forward teaching with the *Patterns of Wonder* invitational process (Figure 4.1). However, before we move on to the lessons in Part 2, let's take a look at how everything we've discussed up to this point coordinates to play out in classrooms on a daily basis.

Invitation to Wonder

To begin the inquiry process in *Patterns of Wonder*, share a sentence or page from a published text and ask open-ended questions:

- "What do you wonder?"
- "What do you see?"
- "What do you notice?"

Figure 4.1
Initially, you may find it easiest to spread the five lesson steps across five days or more, but don't feel like you have to. In time, you'll find a schedule that works best for you and your writers.

As Jeff gathers a group of first graders to think about adjectives, he shows them a page from Maya Tatsukawa's *The Bear in My Family* (2020) and asks, "What do you Wonder?" He pauses and looks at their faces. "Let's look at the page, writers. What do you see?"

Students study the pictures, speech bubbles, labels, and sentences; on the page spread. He's not expecting them to notice adjectives or define them; he just wants them to observe the text and pictures.

"I see lots of words around the bear." Shondra says, even though she doesn't have the word for *label* yet. "I wonder if he's mean."

"I don't think he is," Jonathan says.

Jeff jumps in, saying, "Well, let's take a look at these words or labels that Shondra is curious about. Who wants to help me find the words or labels around the bear?"

"His arms are crossed," Darius says.

"What does it mean when we cross our arms? I tell you what—let's all cross our arms." Notice how Jeff didn't stop the inquiry with, "I said let's look at the words, not the picture."

"You look scary," Pricilla says, sitting up on her knees.

"Yeah, my grandma is mad when she crosses her arms," Dylan adds. We have to leave a little room in our conversations to honor all that is said.

Arms crossed, Emma says, "I thought we were going to talk about the labels around the bear."

"That's right, Emma. I'll start. Right here, this label says strong arms and the arrow points to his arms. We noticed the bear's arms were crossed. But this says he has what kind of arms?"

"Strong arms!" A few overly excited memory experts keep the momentum going.

"Who wants to come point to another one of the labels?"

Brian, who's often reticent to share, likes a sure thing so he raises his hand and points to the label with the arrow to the bear's eyes.

"It says mean eyes," Jaquiline says.

"What kind of eyes?" Jeff raised his eyebrows.

"Mean!"

"I was right," Shondra stands and bows.

In a similar way, the writers continue reading the labels and Jeff keeps emphasizing the kind: *big* ears, *sharp* teeth, *short* but *quick* legs.

"Why do you think Maya chose to use these labels? Turn and buzz with your partner about why you think she did that," Jeff listens in on some of the conversations.

"Maya wants us to know the parts of the bear," Joel explains.

"Yeah and he seems mean to me. It even says mean eyes and sharp teeth." Shondra sticks to her original thinking about the bear.

"I think the boy is just trying to make us think he's mean by telling us he's scary in that speech thing," Joel counters.

"Oh, maybe it is a trick!" Shondra's eyes grow wide.

As students' curiosity builds around the choices that Maya Tatsukawa made as a writer and illustrator, Jeff makes sure to honor their responses, then invites them back to the whole-class conversation. "Writers, I heard some of you wondering about how Maya may have used the labels to show us the parts of the bear, and some of you even talked about how these words told us more about the bear, like instead of just ears, Maya said, 'Big ears.' Big shows *what kind* of ears. What about sharp teeth? What word did Maya use to help us know what kind of teeth?"

"Sharp!"

"So those very helpful words are magic for writers. Do you want to know what they are called?"

"Yes!"

"Writers use adjectives to tell what kind. Say it with me, 'Ad-jec-tives.' And they tell what kind. What do adjectives do for writers?"

"Tell what kind."

Sometimes, when kids are ready to—or need to know—a term or a bit more information about the meaning-making move connected to what they note or wonder about, we stretch out the conversation. We always connect these discussions about why the author might have chosen to do it that way and emphasize the idea that writers make choices.

Once the conversation touches on to the focus phrase concept, or something related, reveal it. Say it as you write it, and invite students to read it with you a few times. Display it in some way—like on a sentence strip, butcher paper, or chart—so students can return to the focus phrase often.

"What kind of teeth?" Jeff asks, pointing to the labeled picture.

"*Sharp teeth!*" shouts the excited class in unison.

"You're right," Jeff says as he seizes this opportunity to connect the conversation to the focus phrase. "*Sharp* is a word that tells what kind. And that's what you can do as writers, too." Jeff writes out the focus phrase and points to it as he invites the group to reread it together a few times. *I write words that tell what kind.* Note that, depending on the readiness of the group, Jeff might have just as easily gone with, *I use adjectives to tell what kind.*

Sometimes students will come to the focus phrase early in the conversations, and, at other times, this may require more conversation. Regardless, once the focus phrase is discovered and introduced, keep going. The curiosity doesn't end there. Continue the adventure, asking students, "What else do you wonder or notice?"

Our youngest children have brains full of wonderings, so take the time to listen and pay attention to the curiosity they are building around the choices authors make and often how their pictures and words connect. Enjoy this part of the inquiry process. So much can be uncovered and built through these conversations.

On the other hand, you might worry about finding your way organically to the focus phrase. But remember, this is a conversation. During the invitation to wonder, honor and name student wonderings, no matter what they are. After asking, "What else?" you might try "What are the words telling us?" If the focus phrase remains undiscovered, don't fret. The conversation during the Invitation to Compare and Contrast that follows will surely lead to it.

> Once the conversation touches on to the focus phrase concept, or something related, reveal it.

A note about wondering across the day and curriculum . . .

In *Already Ready*, Katie Wood Ray and Matt Glover (2008) state, "Noticing and naming what writers and illustrators do in their books helps children build a repertoire of possibilities for things they might try in their writing and illustrating—a repertoire of *crafting techniques*." We can model this noticing and wondering during read-alouds. This will guide children to naturally notice and wonder and play. As you share texts with children throughout the day, pepper some *Patterns of Wonder* language into the experience, giving the process of wondering about the writing time to take root with your writers. Through these interactions, students will begin to read like writers, building curiosity and wonder around an author's purpose and craft.

Invitation to Compare and Contrast

As the conversation begins, take the time to listen to what the students have to say, honoring their wonderings and guiding their attention to the choices writers make.

Keep in mind, though the selected standard is the prime focus of the lesson, this compare and contrast process allows for extensions and new discoveries.

Next, display the original sentence or page that was used in the Invitation to Wonder alongside another example that closely follows the original pattern. Invite students to think about how the two samples are similar or different. Recall that this second text might be from the same book, an additional book, or something you create on your own. As you display both texts, ask students, "What do you see is the same? What is different?" or "What did the writer do that is alike on both pages? What did the writer do differently?" As the conversation begins, take the time to listen to what the students have to say, honoring their wonderings and guiding their attention to the choices writers make.

With the students gathered on the rug, Jeff shares a page of another labeled picture, this time of a monster in Jory John's *Quit Calling Me a Monster!* (2016). He invites his students to compare and contrast this page with the labeled bear page from the Invitation to Wonder.

"Writers, yesterday we wondered about and noticed some things in this book *The Bear in My Family*." Jeff holds this page spread in his hands. "Now, let's take a look at this page in one of our favorite books, *Quit Calling Me a Monster!*" He turns on the document camera to display the second page. "What do you see is the same in both pages? What is different?" Jeff points to each picture a few times. "Turn and buzz with your partner."

Students point out that both pictures have labels and both of the characters have sharp teeth. Jeff invites them to share their thoughts with the whole class and lets their observations lead the way.

Keep in mind, though the selected standard is the prime focus of the lesson, this compare and contrast process allows for extensions and new discoveries. This develops students' ability to build the observational cognitive structure. And all other cognitive structures rest upon observation (Garner 2007).

"The bear is standing still and the monster is moving," Zoey shares.

"Aah, how do you know the monster is moving, Zoey?" Jeff invites Zoey to share her thinking.

"There are those white lines to show him moving," Zoey continues.

"Action marks!" Zach shouts.

Jeff takes this moment to invite students to think about what they, too, can do as a writer in their pictures. "Oh yes! We can call these white lines action marks and they show us the monster is moving. Show me what he's doing." The students drop onto their backs, mimicking the monster in the picture, squirming and giggling. Conventions are fun.

After a minute Jeff returns the class to their nonmonster positions. "What else do you see is the same or different?" Jeff brings the conversation back to focus.

Students who are ready to share out new extensions and discoveries will, while others will stick with the safety of the focus phrase.

"They both have labels."

"Yes, they sure do. Let's read these labels in the monster book." Jeff and his first graders read the labels together. "Why did the author, Jory, use these labels?"

"To tell what kind of horns and eyes just like our focus phrase, Mr. Anderson!" Joel shares excitedly, sprinting over to the focus phrase.

Jeff invites Joel to point to the words in the focus phrase as the class rereads it together. "What else tells what kind?" he asks as the conversation continues.

Allow space for your writers to share everything they notice and wonder. That's the driving force of the *Patterns of Wonder* process!

Invitation to Imitate Together

Now that students have explored a model sentence or page, discovered a pattern or craft move writers use, and compared and contrasted it with another example, it's time to invite them to compose an imitation together as a class or small group. This is the practical application that grammar research supports (Graham and Perin 2007).

In our ongoing example from the classroom, Jeff invites young writers into an interactive writing experience. He revisits the model and the compare and contrast example as well as the focus phrase.

"Writers, we have been exploring how writers write words that tell what kind." Jeff points out some of the adjectives in the labeled pictures from *The Bear in My Family* and *Quit Calling Me a Monster!* to emphasize the focus phrase. "Now we are going to do this same work together. Let's think about some pictures we could draw and label. Turn to your partner and share something you would draw. It could be a person or a place or a thing or even an animal."

This brainstorming session helps writers think about what they could also write about in the future. As Jeff listens in on some of their ideas, he encourages students to share what labels they might add to tell what kind. After a few minutes of buzzing, Jeff brings the class back, and says, "Wow! I heard so many ideas that you were sharing and thinking about what labels you could add. Some of you even thought about what words you would use to tell what kind in your labels. One idea I heard that I thought we could do together is our playground. What might we label on our playground?" As students get excited about the possibilities, Jeff quickly sketches a picture of the playground based on ideas shared by the class. The students have dry erase boards in their laps and also draw quick pictures that represent what will be labeled. Jeff then invites them to help label the picture using words that tell what kind. "What kind of slide do we have on our playground?"

"A tall swirly slide!" one student shares.

"Oh yes! Let's label the slide with the words: *tall swirly slide*," Jeff says the words across his fingers and adds three lines to the chart paper to hold a place for each word next to the slide. "OK, writers, let's think about how we will write *tall*. T-t-t and then *all* as in *ball* or *wall*." While Jeff writes *tall* on the chart paper, the students write the word on their dry erase boards.

"The next word is swirly. S-s-s-s-w-w-w-w," Jeff makes the initial blend sound and invites a student to write the blend on the chart paper. While the class continues to work through the word *swirly*, the student at the board writes how he thinks it would be spelled. Jeff continues to invite children to the board to label the rest of the picture, choosing which words he will write and which words the students will write. Staying with his writers' strengths and needs, Jeff chooses which parts of the words and the sentence he wants to focus their attention to while moving the other parts along quickly. Once the labeling is complete, Jeff invites his writers to read the labels with him while pointing to each word.

Invitation to Play

Play invites inquiry. Play provides opportunities for kids "to linger, to examine, to wonder, to notice, to look closely, to ask why things are the way they are, and to share their thinking." (Mraz, Porcelli, and Tyler 2016).

Now that students have composed something together, they can bring the focus phrase to life even more. We want emergent writers to play with it in different ways. This invitation may offer another shared imitation with the whole group, another experience with guided groups, a chance to use the pattern independently during their writing workshop, or time to experiment with the standard in centers.

Jeff begins the play by inviting students to draw their own pictures with labels during the *Patterns of Wonder* time. He then releases them to continue this work in the writing center, which he has stocked with fun paper, colorful markers, and a variety of different pens. Here, students work on pages for a class book that will be added to the book shelf for future reading.

"Writers, you have paper at your table. You've been thinking about pictures you could draw and label using words that tell what kind, and now you get to do that! Let's say our focus phrase together."

"*I write words that tell what kind!*" The class reads excitedly.

"And there is always paper in our writing center, so if you want to draw more pictures or write more labels using words that tell what kind, you can do that during your writing center rotation! We will use all of the pages you make to make an *Adjective (What Kind?)* book for our classroom library."

Then, during writing workshop, the class repeats the focus phrase, and Jeff invites the students to continue to use words that tell what kind in their writing. "Remember writers, as you work on your stories today, you could write words that tell what kind. You can add these words to your labels and your sentences."

Later that week, when working with a small group, students compose a sentence about a picture using words that tell what kind. "Writers, let's take a look at this picture. What do you see? Let's think about words we can use that tell what kind."

"There is a big tree right there with green leaves," Andrew chimes in.

"There sure is! Let's write a sentence about that big tree with the green leaves."

In our busyness of teaching and learning, this play-driven step may seem dispensable, but it's important to note that having fun with language is a critical piece of the *Patterns of Wonder* progression. Continue this play in multiple areas, across as many days as needed, and then add in some more for good measure.

> In our busyness of teaching and learning, this play-driven step may seem dispensable, but it's important to note that having fun with language is a critical piece of the *Patterns of Wonder* progression.

Invitation to Share and Celebrate

Young children love to share their writing. We provide multiple opportunities to celebrate them as writers, composers, risk-takers, and meaning-makers. Through their noticings, conversations, interactive or shared writing experiences, and play, they've been immersed in the focus phrase, adopting it as their own. These experiences are anchored in what writers do rather than mistakes they could make. To continue this work, Jeff plans for time to display what his writers have tried and celebrate their efforts.

"Writers, you have been working so hard to write words that tell what kind. I've asked you to bring the story you wrote in writing workshop to the rug today, so you can share a part where you wrote words that tell what kind. When it's your turn, you get to put your writing under the document camera and hold our special microphone. Zayden, would you like to get this party started?"

Essentially, the Invitation to Share and Celebrate is a time for our emergent authors to share how they have incorporated the focus phrase into their writing and any other concepts taking form with them as a writer. Celebrating their approximations—their progress, not their perfection—encourages young writers to continue to play with their new learning as they grow safer and more confident to make future writing choices.

> Celebrating their approximations—their progress, not their perfection—encourages young writers to continue to play with their new learning as they grow safer and more confident to make future writing choices.

An Invitation to Explore and Experiment

As you dive into the lessons in Part 2 of this book, we'll be right there by your side—if only on the page—connecting you to standards, focus phrases, literature, and tips, as well as suggestions for every invitation. Scaffolds, background information, and alternative texts are all included to support you when you need it. And remember, you can always return to the foundational conversation of the first four chapters as often as you like.

We hope a friend will join you as you step into teaching the *Patterns of Wonder* process, but if not, you'll find lots of ways to connect with others who are doing the same work you are on social media. Ask questions. Celebrate successes. But don't feel that you have to wait until you're sure you have it all under your belt to begin. Approximation and inquiry are important to leading rich teaching lives as well. The worst thing that can happen is that your students will be exposed to some great literature, which will lead to richer conversations about writing and the work writers do. And, with that, the wisdom that comes out of their little genius minds will teach you just as much as you (and the texts you share) will teach them.

The time is now. Let's get started!

INTO THE

Patterns

of

WONDER

LESSONS

Using the Patterns of Wonder Process in Your Classroom

Carry the map as a guide, but explore those trails not drawn on paper.

—Rebecca Kai Dotlich, *The Knowing Book*

Now that we've laid out the planning and process of *Patterns of Wonder*, the lessons that follow in Part 2 are designed to help you to start right away while further refining your understanding with some concrete examples. You will see that each lesson set is organized in a way that follows the process, making it a ready-to-go resource to flexibly meet the needs of all of your writers, regardless of the phases of writing they are working through. We invite you to think of Part 2 as a guide that launches your adventure into the world of language and its wonders. But as Rebecca Kai Dotlich reminds us, let's not forget to explore those meaning trails not drawn on paper—yet.

Each group of lessons in Part 2 is color-coded, representing which of the four *Patterns of Wonder* Phases of Emergent Writing they support:

- **Scribble Writing**
- **Symbol and Letter Writing**
- **Transitional Writing**
- **Conventional Writing**

The lesson standards are presented cumulatively across the four phases, so you can differentiate your instruction based on your emergent writers' needs. For example, we teach writers how to use nouns in each phase of writing, so there is a noun lesson in each phase's section. These lessons help you consider where your writers are in their developmental path and provide the appropriate levels of instruction and support. For instance, if you set out to teach nouns, and a large part of your class is working within the symbol and letter phase, you can use a lesson on nouns from the purple section in a whole-group setting. To supplement this, you can refer to the companion lessons in the other phase sections to revisit or extend the concept of nouns in small groups or conferences, fine-tuning your instruction to meet your writers where they are developmentally. To further help you find the right instructional fit, we've included a list of all the lessons along with their correlated standards and focus phrases at the end of this introduction.

How Are the Lessons Formatted?

Each lesson is built around a favorite picture book that invites engagement and wonder while showcasing the selected standard in action. Let's take a closer look at how the lessons that follow in Part 2 are structured.

Standard: Standards are selected from state and national documents, worded in their most universal form for clarity and ease of use.

Teacher Considerations: Here, you'll find helpful background discussions that offer more details about how the lesson supports the particular developmental needs of writers in the correlating phase.

Mentor Text: Each lesson is grounded in a discussion based on a favorite picture book introduced during the Invitation to Wonder.

Alternative Titles: This title list offers additional picture book options that can be explored to support the standard and focus phrase, introduced during the Invitation to Compare and Contrast, or written into additional lessons for reteaching or extension.

Companion Lessons: Since most standards are covered cumulatively across the *Patterns of Wonder* Phases of Emergent Writing, corresponding lessons for the selected standard are listed here, color-coded by phase for quick access.

Helpful Icons: Look for icons to pinpoint the focus of the lesson as well as avenues of support. These icons are explained in detail on page 84.

Focus Phrase: The focus phrase is unveiled in the Invitation to Wonder as children share their thinking about what they see authors and illustrators doing. It is written to match the goal of the lesson and the phase of writing it supports.

Take Note Boxes: These notes, indicated with a paper clip icon, have additional information for the teacher, often extending concepts from the lesson, adding interesting commentary, or clarifying the standard.

Lesson Set 3: Tr... 239

3.9   Verbs Gotta MOVE: Verbs Show Action

Standards and Connections	Teacher Considerations	Texts
Standard Use frequently occurring verbs. *Companion Lessons* • Lesson 1.4 • Lesson 2.6 • Lesson 4.10 	In this lesson, we move from adding action to our pictures to writing words to show action. *Move!* by Steve Jenkins and Robin Page labels each page with a verb and uses it in a sentence to show that animals move in different ways. When sharing the text with your students multiple times, invite them to read and act out the verbs with you. You might even collect these verbs on an ongoing "I write words to show action" anchor chart to be used in writing workshop.	*Move!* Written by Steve Jenkins and Robin Page and illustrated by Steve Jenkins **Alternative Titles** *Some Pets* Written by Angela DiTerlizzi and illustrated by Brendan Wenzel *An Island Grows* Written by Lola M. Schaefer and illustrated by Cathie Felstead *It's Hard to Be a Verb!* Written by Julia Cook and illustrated by Carrie Hartman

Focus Phrase   I write words to show action.

A note about verbs . . .

Sentences wouldn't *do* or *be* much without verbs. Verbs activate sentences, bringing them to life, identifying actions, setting a mood, or telling time. Quite simply, verbs help us *do* and *be*. That's right. In addition to action, verbs also signal a state of existence, linking nouns or pronouns to a description: you *are* a magnificent writer. They even help out other verbs from time to time. When working with young writers, we needn't worry whether they know the difference between a *be* verb or an action verb or a helping verb, or even if they are using past, present, or future tense. Instead, we want them thinking about how the actions in their writing help to create meaning for their readers.

Invitation to Wonder: Lessons begin with a model sentence or page from the mentor text. Students are invited to wonder about the choices the writer or illustrator made. The focus phrase emerges during these conversations as students answer the questions "What do you wonder? What do you see? What do you notice? What else?"

Invitation to Compare and Contrast: After you and your students have explored the mentor text together, a second example is introduced to continue the conversation through an exploration of how the two samples are alike and different. This example may be another page from the mentor text, a page from another text, or even something created by the teacher.

---

240   *Patterns of* **Wonder**

Invitation to WONDER

Choose any page from Jenkins's *Move!* labeled with a verb to display. When reading the sentence aloud, it will be helpful for context to read the previous page leading into the page you're displaying. Honor all wonderings and discuss the author's or illustrator's choices. This may be the first time your students see ellipses, so don't be surprised if these three dots bring on a lot of conversation. When the students notice the largest word on the page, stop to act out the word and discuss why Steve Jenkins and Robin Page chose to make that word bigger. Then match the verb to the picture to show how they support each other. Share the focus phrase: *I write words to show action.*

If students ask about the ellipses, explain to them that they can be used to make the reader pause, indicating an unfinished thought or a leading statement. Discovering ellipses usually sparks a lot of energy in emergent writers as they enjoy experimenting with them to build suspense, knowing the reader must pause and continue reading to find out what comes next.

Invitation to COMPARE and CONTRAST

Choose another page from Jenkins's *Move!* to share with your students, or use a page from one of the alternative texts listed. After reading the page aloud, ask, "What do you see is the same? What is different?" When your students notice the action in each sentence, stop to briefly act out the movements and revisit the focus phrase: *I write words to show action.* At some point, highlight that nothing would ever happen without verbs. "All sentences have verbs."

Invitation to IMITATE TOGETHER

Interactive Writing

Brainstorm a list of verbs and add them to an ongoing anchor chart "I Write Words to Show Action." Together, choose a verb to illustrate, label, and write a sentence like Steve Jenkins and Robin Page did in *Move!*

Wonder Note: Throughout the lessons, look for question mark icons where we include extra coaching information you may need or clarify common misunderstandings you might encounter.

Invitation to Imitate Together: Here, young writers imitate or try out the pattern from the mentor text with the teacher through shared or interactive writing. The process of writing gives writers firsthand experience playing with author's purpose, craft, effect, and meaning. This is the ultimate in practical application.

Patterns of Wonder **Time**

Using the anchor chart to help them, students choose a verb to illustrate and label. Encourage them to also write a sentence; it's OK if the sentence doesn't have conventional spacing or capitalization in this phase.

Writing Workshop

Writers add words to show action to the books they make by labeling their pictures and writing approximated sentences. When conferring with your writers, ask them to point out where they write about the action in their books.

> **Invitation to Play:**
> Practical application continues through various forms of play, giving students time to approximate and explore the focus convention in their writing. This play may happen during the *Patterns of Wonder* block, independent writing, literacy station rotations, small-group time, writing workshop, or even individual choice time.

Invitation
to
PLAY

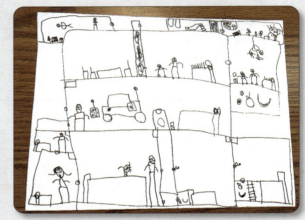

Homero drew a detailed picture of his house and thought about the action going on inside. As he pointed to each part of his picture during oral rehearsal, he said, "This is the rooms in my house. My mom is cooking in the kitchen and my twin sisters are playing together. My dad is fixing my remote car."

Moving Through the Hallway

Movement and action go hand in hand, so add some action to your typical walk down the hallway to lunch or recess. As a class, decide on a movement to demonstrate while walking, like moving your arms like a long-legged spider or flying with your arms sprawled like an eagle. Students have so much fun with this that they actually move more quietly through the halls. After returning to class, debrief your actions and remind the students that they can also write about these experiences.

Invitation to Share and Celebrate: Writers need an audience. Taking time to celebrate their creations and approximations gives emergent writers opportunities to share in different ways. Don't skip this joyful piece of the process.

Invitation to SHARE and CELEBRATE

To kick off this celebration, share an appropriate YouTube video of a song or rap about verbs. There are many to choose from! Afterward, students move about the room, sharing their imitations with one another and celebrating their verbs by acting them out.

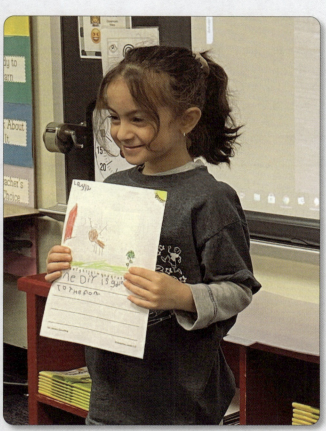

This young writer is eager to share her writing during the celebration. She chose to write a sentence and add some lines to show action to her picture, which she noticed many other authors do.

Patterns of Wonder Iconography

As you recall from Chapter 3, we unpacked the planning of the process, considering two, focused instructional goals—grammar or concepts about print—through three avenues of support: oral language, illustrating, and writing. With this in mind, each lesson in Part 2 includes correlating icons that designate the instructional goal for the lesson and highlight the most appropriate support for your young writers. Since our goals and avenues of support often blend and overlap, this nuance is implied in the layered icon placement throughout.

Concepts About Print: In lessons with a concepts about print focus, writers explore how print works, including principles such as the difference between pictures and words, that letters can be grouped to make words and words can be grouped to make sentences, space boundaries, upper- and lowercase letters, and the role of ending punctuation.

Grammar: With grammar as a focus, children learn to be clear with their message and to expand on it with details. Lessons with this icon will guide writers to use sentence structures and parts of speech such as nouns, verbs, adjectives, and prepositions to compose with subject-verb agreement and elaboration.

Oral Language: With this pathway of support, we encourage our writers to consider the focus phrase and tell about their picture in a way that their writing will eventually sound. These lessons will rely heavily on conversations that engage oral language when supporting writers.

Illustrating: With this pathway of support, we nudge our writers to add more to their illustrations to compose language, tapping into their developing proficiency with oral language. These lessons will invite writers to share meaning through their illustrations.

Writing: Lessons with this icon signal an avenue of support focused on the written language of the writer, moving from labeling pictures to writing sentences, expanding on those sentences, and intentionally using capitalization and punctuation.

A Guide, Not a Script

Before you dig into them, it's important to note that the lessons included in Part 2 were developed with flexibility in mind. To that end, some lessons will lend themselves perfectly to your whole groups' needs, while others might work better for a particular small group or even individually in a conference setting. We strongly believe that authentic teaching isn't scripted, and we're at our best when we're responsive to the children in front of us. With that, trust your intuition as a teacher. Take time to discover what your writers are doing, what your standards are expecting, and what the lessons in this resource explore. If needed, substitute the anchor text with an option from the alternatives we suggest, or pull your favorite picture books from your classroom or school library.

These lessons, outlined on the correlation chart that follows, are only a beginning sample—a place to start. Once you've worked through a handful of them, you'll have the familiarity and confidence with the *Patterns of Wonder* process to start crafting your own lessons, extending well beyond what we offer here. And we encourage this. We see the lessons in Part 2 as your very own Choose Your Own Adventure story. We're giving you a starting point, but the direction you take it could be different each time.

Let your students lead you on that adventure.

Patterns of Wonder Lesson Correlations

Topic	Scribble Writing Phase Lesson Number and Focus Phrase	Symbol and Letter Writing Phase Lesson Number and Focus Phrase	Transitional Writing Phase Lesson Number and Focus Phrase	Conventional Writing Phase Lesson Number and Focus Phrase
Using marks, symbols, and letters to record language and make words	1.1 *I write with words and pictures.**	2.1 *I write with words and pictures.**	3.1 *I write with words and pictures.**	4.1 *I write with words and pictures.**
Letter-sound correspondence		2.2 *I write the letters of the sounds I hear.**	3.2 *I write the letters of the sounds I hear.**	Use any book to repeat Lesson 3.2 if needed.
Using words to make sentences	1.2 *I use words to make sentences.**	2.3 *I use words to make sentences.**	3.3 *I write words to make sentences.**	Use any book to repeat Lesson 3.3 if needed.
Spacing between words			3.4 *I use spaces between my words.**	Use any book to repeat Lesson 3.4 if needed.
Capitalization		2.4 *I begin my name with a capital letter.*	3.5 *I begin names with a capital letter.*	4.2 and 4.3 *I capitalize names.*
			3.6 *I start my sentence with a capital letter.*	4.4 *I start my sentence with a capital letter.*
				4.5 *I capitalize the pronoun I (no matter where it is).*
Nouns	1.3 *I tell about people, places, and things in my writing.*	2.5 *I show and tell about people, places, and things in my writing.*	3.7 *I write words that show people, places, and things in my writing.*	4.6 *I use nouns to show people, places, and things.*
				4.7 *I use a singular noun to show one person, place, or thing.*
				4.8 *I use plural nouns to show more than one person, place, or thing.*

*Concepts About Print

Pronouns			3.8 *I match stand-in words to tell who.*	4.9 *I use pronouns to stand in for nouns.*
Verbs	1.4 *I tell what is happening in my writing.*	2.6 *I show and tell about the action in my writing.*	3.9 *I write words to show action.*	4.10 *I use verbs to show action.*
End punctuation		2.7 *I end my sentences with a period.*	3.10 *I end my sentence with a period.*	4.11 *I use end marks to help my reader.*
		2.8 *I show strong feelings with exclamation marks!*	3.11 *I show strong feelings with exclamation marks!*	
		2.9 *I end my questions with a question mark.*	3.12 *I end questions with question marks.*	
Adjectives	1.5 *I tell what kind.*	2.10 *I show and tell what kind.*	3.13 *I write words that tell what kind.*	4.12 *I use adjectives to show what kind.*
	1.6 *I tell how many.*	2.11 *I show and tell how many.*	3.14 *I write words that tell how many.*	4.13 *I use adjectives to show how many.*
				4.14 *I use a or an to show how many or the to show which one.*
Prepositions	1.7 *I tell where.*	2.12 *I show and tell where.*	3.15 *I write words that tell where.*	4.15 *I use prepositions to show where and when.*
Conjunctions	1.8 *I tell more with and.*	2.13 *I show and tell more with words like but and and.*	3.16 *I write more with BOA: but, or, and.*	4.16 *I write more with BOAS: but, or, and, so.*
Transitions	1.9 *I tell my thoughts in order.*	2.14 *I show and tell my thoughts in order.*	3.17 *I write my thoughts in order.*	4.17 *I use order words like first, next, then, and finally.*

Scribble Writing

Scribble Writing Phase Behaviors	▶ Drawing to represent writing ▶ Relying heavily on oral language ▶ Using a variety of lines and dots to record language

1.1   Making Your Mark: Use Marks to Record Language

Standards and Connections	Teacher Considerations	Texts
Standard Intentionally use marks, symbols, and letters to record language and make words. **Companion Lessons** • Lesson 2.1 • Lesson 3.1 • Lesson 4.1 	While children are writing through illustration and oral rehearsal, this lesson is one of our first moves toward being intentional with marks on the page to represent writing and record language. Be sure to check out the following note to see how this lesson's goal and focus phrase connect to its companion lessons. As children share their stories, invite them to point to their pictures and any marks they have made. These marks might be lines, symbols, waves, or scribbles. Observe how writers point to their marks, noticing directionality as they move their finger across the page.	*A Squiggly Story* Written by Andrew Larsen and illustrated by Mike Lowery **Alternative Titles** *Accident!* Written and illustrated by Andrea Tsurumi *Can I Be Your Dog?* Written and illustrated by Troy Cummings *Ralph Tells a Story* Written and illustrated by Abby Hanlon

Focus Phrase   I write with words and pictures.

A note about focus phrase visuals . . .

Since this same goal looks different as emergent writers develop, you'll notice the focus phrase for this lesson repeats through its companion lessons—even as the type of writing shifts across their phases. We highlight this shift with accompanying visuals that represent the type of writing children do in each phase.

For example, the focus phrase visual for this lesson represents the writing children do in the Scribble Writing phase. Keep in mind that the words in this phase are actually marks, probably not letters and words, but rather the beautiful lines, waves, or scribbles. Notice that the visuals for future lessons in this thread (2.1, 3.1, and 4.1) will change to represent the type of writing students are progressing through.

Invitation to WONDER

Share the cover of *A Squiggly Story*, inviting your children to wonder about the pictures and words, and even the scribbles. When students mention the scribbles or writing the character does, remind them that this is the way some writers their age may write. "This is how this boy writes his words. Now he is probably going to add a picture next, because we write with both words and pictures." Reveal the focus phrase and repeat together.

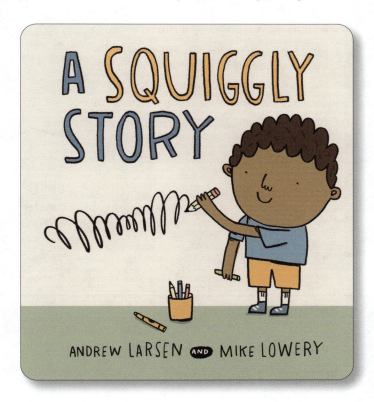

Invitation to COMPARE and CONTRAST

A Squiggly Story and each of the alternative titles listed include pages that demonstrate writing with both words (scribbles, waves, lines) and pictures. For example, the title page of *Can I Be Your Dog?* shows the dog writing with wavy lines. Choose a page to display alongside the mentor text cover, *A Squiggly Story*. When comparing and contrasting, students may notice that both have pictures. They may notice that one is the cover of a book and one is inside a book. Honor all of their noticings, and take the time to engage writers in conversation as they compare and contrast the two pieces. When students notice that both have marks that represent writing, revisit the focus phrase while inviting them to point to the marks on the page that represent words and then point to the pictures.

Shared Writing

Create a simple class story, choosing what the class wants each page to say and what should be included in both the picture and words. This piece of writing can be a made-up story, it can retell something that happened earlier that day, or it can tell all about something.

Even though this lesson is for writers in the scribble phase, in this shared writing imitation, you'll still write the words conventionally. Note, however, that your conversation will focus writers on the marks you're creating to leave your message, as opposed to the letters and sounds you might highlight in a more traditional shared writing experience.

This class decided to write about Theo on his skateboard because he shared his passion for it during the morning meeting that day.

Writing Workshop

Revisit the focus phrase as students make books each day. When talking with them about their books, invite them to point at their marks as they tell their stories.

Interactive Read-Aloud

While reading to students, stop to ask them what is happening in the story by examining the pictures closely. Invite some children to point to the marks the writer placed on the page that help tell the story.

In the scribbles phase, Aiden makes a book with both pictures and words during writing workshop.

Invitation to SHARE and CELEBRATE

Students sit in a whole-group circle, each standing up in turn to share one of their stories, pointing to their marks as they do so. This celebration may be spread across multiple days so that every child gets to share. Provide feedback during the share by highlighting when the writer used the focus phrase.

This superhero records his language with marks while writing in the kitchen at home.

1.2   What Could You Say? Use Words to Make Sentences

Standards and Connections	Teacher Considerations	Texts
Standard Recognize that sentences are comprised of words. **Companion Lessons** • Lesson 2.3 • Lesson 3.3	This lesson builds on writers' oral language, inviting them to move beyond one-word labels and into early attempts at sentences. Barney Saltzberg's *Inside This Book (are three books).* is a wonderful book for sharing what writing looks like at different ages, with the youngest writer drawing pictures and saying out loud what he means it to say in a way that many of our students also write their books.	*Inside This Book (are three books).* Written and illustrated by Barney Saltzberg **Alternative Titles** *The Word Collector* Written and illustrated by Peter H. Reynolds *One Day, The End: Short, Very Short, Shorter-Than-Ever Stories* Written by Rebecca Kai Dotlitch and illustrated by Fred Koehler *Wolf in the Snow* Written and illustrated by Matthew Cordell

Focus Phrase   ❝   I use words to make sentences.   ❞

A note about sentences and concepts about print . . .

Though the lessons presented throughout this thread focus mainly on using words to make up sentences, you'll notice an implied connection to other concepts about print conversations such as word boundaries and spaces from Lesson 3.4. You can make these natural connections explicit by circling back to those previous discussions as your students' needs dictate.

Invitation

to

WONDER

We recommend you share *Inside This Book (are three books).* with your students prior to this lesson so you can move quickly to the mentor page during this invitation. Share the page spread included at the end of this lesson with your students and read it aloud. It's amazing how such a simple picture can inspire so many thoughts. Let students wonder and notice for a bit, listening in, honoring, and asking, "What else?"

If they need some help moving closer to the focus phrase, you might prompt with, "What do you see on this page?"

They may respond with "Dinosaur!"

Continue this conversation, "Yes, this is a dinosaur. What else do you see?"

"Words!" Invite the student to come point to the words, as you move into the teaching point. You might say, "Wilbur made this book, and he drew a dinosaur on this page. Then he said, 'This is a dinosaur.' He could have just said, 'Dinosaur,' but he chose instead to say 'This is a dinosaur.' He used more than one word to tell about his picture. Let's count how many words he used." Count across your fingers as you orally say the sentence and then count the words again on the display, using a pointer. "Writers use words to make sentences, and you're writers, so you can do that, too!" Introduce the focus phrase, and invite your students to share another sentence or two about the picture, using words to make verbal sentences.

Invitation to COMPARE and CONTRAST

Choose a page from another book that has simple pictures with a short sentence. You'll find lots of possibilities listed in the alternative titles, or you may select a class favorite to explore with your students. Display the selected page alongside the dinosaur page from *Inside This Book (are three books)*. and ask, "What is the same on these pages? What's different?" As students begin to compare and contrast the illustrations and the words on the page, take the time to honor their thinking. When they bring up the words, discuss how both authors used the words to make a sentence about the picture, cycling back to the focus phrase. For an extension of oral rehearsal, you might ask, "What else might the author say about the picture?"

Invitation to IMITATE TOGETHER

Shared Writing

As a class, choose something in the classroom that you want to write about. Quickly sketch the item on chart paper and add some color. Remind students of the focus phrase and repeat it together three times. Together, orally rehearse several sentences about the picture, noting how you're using more than one word. Choose a few to write on the chart paper. Go back and reread the recorded sentences together, and count each word.

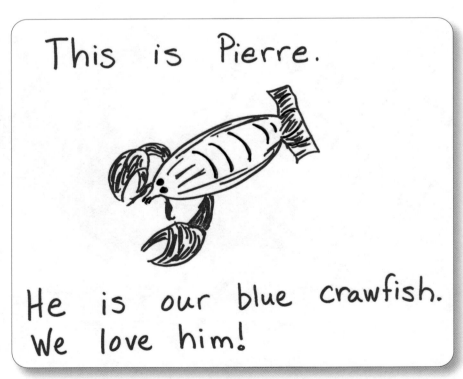

This kindergarten class chose to write about their class pet, Pierre.

Patterns of Wonder Time

Students walk around the room with a partner, telling each other about different parts of the room, using words to make their sentences. The partners help each other by counting across their fingers the number of words they put together to compose.

Writing Workshop

Revisit the focus phrase as students make books each day. At the end of each workshop, ask them to share their writing with a partner, using more than one word to tell about their pictures.

Mira created a piece of writing during writing workshop. When asked to share, she used more than one word to say, "My house has a lot of windows. All my friends are at my house. This tree is by my house."

Small-Group Writing

Share a wordless picture book, or one with few words like Matthew Cordell's *Wolf in the Snow* with your students. Invite them to orally rehearse sentences about each page, using Unifix cubes to visually show how many words they use in their sentences.

Invitation to PLAY

Invitation to SHARE and CELEBRATE

Students select one piece of writing they created any time during the Invitation to Play. As they share a sentence about their picture, count out how many words they used, and draw a line on your whiteboard to represent each word before writing them in and rereading the sentence.

1.3 Shake a Book and Nouns Fall Out: Nouns Show People, Places, and Things

Standards and Connections	Teacher Considerations	Texts
Standard Use frequently occurring nouns. **Companion Lessons** • Lesson 2.5 • Lesson 3.7 • Lesson 4.6 	Throughout the Scribble Writing phase, we build on students' oral language as they grasp fine motor skills and move from a variety of scribbling to some representational illustrations. In both reading and writing, we invite our young writers to tell *who* or *what* is in accompanying pictures. For this lesson on nouns, we chose *Shake the Tree!* because students enjoy repeated readings of it independently or as a group, and it's a great book for building fluency, storytelling language, and prosody of expression with dialogue.	*Shake the Tree!* Written by Chaira Vignocchi, Paolo Chiarinotti, and Silvia Borando and illustrated by Silvia Borando **Alternative Titles** *It's a Tiger!* Written by David LaRochelle and illustrated by Jeremy Tankard *Some Pets* Written by Angela DiTerlizzi and illustrated by Brendan Wenzel *Merry-Go-Round: A Book About Nouns* Written and illustrated by Ruth Heller

Focus Phrase I tell about people, places, and things in my writing.

A note about nouns and focus phrases . . .

Though the focus phrase, *I tell about people, places and things*, sounds like the traditional chant, remember the effect of using first person, or the *I*-voice. The focus phrase grows out of a convergence of the students' curiosity when we ask questions like, "Who's in this picture? Who's that? Is that you or somebody else? Tell me about that person (or place or thing). Where did this happen? What's this?" The questioning naturally, eventually arrives at the focus phrase: *I tell about people, places, and things in my writing*, or if you prefer, *My writing answers the questions who, what, and where?* Focus phrases may be adjusted as needed.

Invitation to WONDER

Choose a vertical page spread from this book to share with the class and ask, "What do you notice? What does that make you wonder?" Since the pictures are simple, students tend to note the animals, the tree, and the acorn, providing the opportunity to share the focus phrase. Students will share their thoughts as well, often around feelings of the characters because of their facial expressions and predictions or inferences they make based on what the pictures show. We honor and ride the wave of curiosity—stretching out those wonderings of relevance and interests.

Invitation to COMPARE and CONTRAST

Select a page from any picture book in your classroom that shows a variety of nouns (people, places, and things) in the picture. Display it side by side with the vertical spread of *Shake the Tree!* As students share what they notice is the same and different in the two examples, continue to honor their noticings as you highlight nouns throughout and revisit the focus phrase: *I tell about people, places, and things in my writing.*

This writer included people, places, and things in his writing.

Interactive Writing

Students turn to their partners and list out some of their favorite people, some of their favorite places, and some of their favorite things. Listen in on their conversations and share some of their favorites out loud. Distribute an index card to each child and ask them to draw one of their favorite people, places, or things and hand it back to you. Tape their pictures to chart paper titled "Our Favorite People, Places, and Things" and help them label it with the noun they choose.

Invitation
to IMITATE
TOGETHER

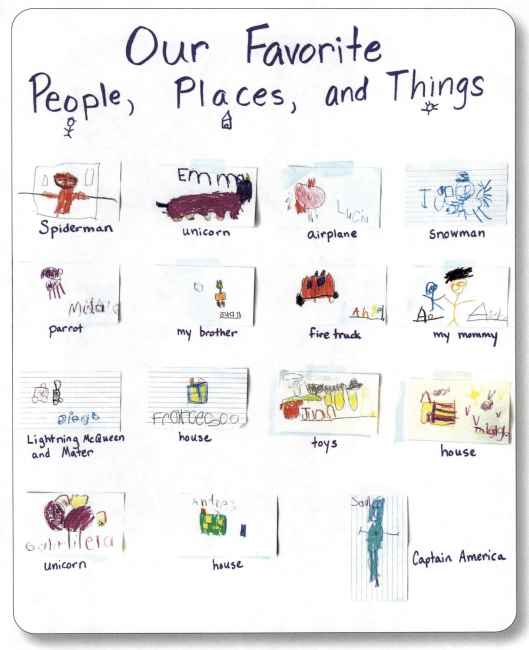

A PreK class created a list of their favorite people, places, and things together.

Invitation to COMPARE and CONTRAST

Patterns of Wonder **Time**

Students make a book to showcase their favorite people, places, and things, drawing a picture on each page. Encourage them to add words as well, knowing they will be in the shape of lines, scribbles, or waves. See the following note for tips on bookmaking. Include blank books in the writing center for those who want to make more.

Literacy Stations

Students sort picture cards into noun categories: people, places, things. In a bookmaking station, students add people, places, and things to their pictures.

This young writer uses nouns to show her favorite people, places, and things when bookmaking.

There are several ways to prepare for bookmaking. Some teachers prefer to make books ahead of time by stapling blank pieces of white paper together to make books, while others fold a few pieces of paper in half and staple them down the side. Other teachers leave staplers for their students to staple together depending on how many pages they want to include. Whichever way you choose, be consistent. When writers know the routines and expectations, they get to spend more time writing and less time trying to figure out what they are supposed to do.

Invitation to SHARE and CELEBRATE

Students sit in a circle on the rug. One at a time, go around the circle, pointing out the people, places, or things each writer had included in their pictures. To add some movement to this celebration, choose a sharing spot in the circle, perhaps next to the document camera. After each student shares, writers shift one place on the rug, getting closer to this sharing spot.

This four-year-old wrote about his family during bookmaking time.

1.4   We Nail Verbs: Verbs Show What's Happening

Standards and Connections	Teacher Considerations	Texts
Standard Use frequently occuring verbs. **Companion Lessons** • Lesson 2.6 • Lesson 3.9 • Lesson 4.10 	Because students are grasping fine motor skills and moving from a variety of scribbling to some representational illustrations, we build upon the foundation of oral language here. As young writers tell us about their pictures, we invite them to use words that tell *what's happening* or ask them questions like "What are you doing here?" or "Tell me all the things happening in your writing." These questions prompt students to share action-related details as they orally rehearse revision to their writing.	*Lucía the Luchadora* Written by Cynthia Leonor Garza and illustrated by Alyssa Bermudez **Alternative Titles** *Watch Me Throw the Ball!* (an Elephant and Piggie book) Written and illustrated by Mo Willems *I'm Not Scared!* Written and illustrated by Jonathan Allen *Stick and Stone* Written by Beth Ferry and illustrated by Tom Lichtenheld

Focus Phrase   ❝   I tell what is happening in my writing.   ❞

A note about showing action . . .

One major strength of the invitational process is the informal chats it sparks with young writers. When students working in the scribble phase read books, invite them to talk in detail about the pictures. For instance, in many books they explore, readers can tell what is happening in the illustrations because the illustrator uses action marks, or lines that show movement. You might use this opportunity to promote fun discussions around how writers show what is happening in pictures. Then, in a conversational way, you can casually remind students that they, too, can use those action marks or other strategies in their own books and daily writing.

Invitation to WONDER

Show the entire page spread from the mentor text (pictured) and read it aloud. After you read it, start the conversation: "Let's take a close look at these pictures. What do you wonder?" Students may wonder about the expressions on the faces of the characters. They may wonder about the setting: "Is it a park?" Honor their wonderings, engaging them in conversation about why the author and illustrator included the expressions on their faces or the details that show the setting. Continue to ask "What else?" or "What else do you notice or see?"

Some students may wonder about the white swirl lines, which we often refer to as action marks. When they do, honor their wondering—discuss why the action marks are used by focusing back on the picture and encourage them to talk about the action they see. When ready tie the action to the words used: *I dive. I spin. I dash up the dark, swirly slide.* Share the focus phrase when students discover actions: *I tell what is happening in my writing.*

This page spread from *Lucia the Luchadora* is included at the end of this lesson.

If showing the text under a document camera, the white lines and swirls that show action might be harder to see. Zooming in on the picture and inviting students to look closely at certain parts of the picture will help to guide their attention to the white swirls.

Invitation to COMPARE and CONTRAST

Choose a page from another book that shows action. You'll find lots of possibilities listed in the alternative titles, or you may select a class favorite to explore with your students. For example, we share a page from any of Mo Willems's Elephant and Piggy series. Mo often uses action lines to show action in his illustrations. As students begin to compare and contrast the pictures, help them to orally create sentences about the action in the picture and how they know. "Yes, both authors did use lines to show movement or action. What might we say to tell what is happening in this picture?"

Shared Writing

Refer to the model text, *Lucía the Luchadora*, and say the focus phrase together. Draw your students on the playground, adding lines or action marks to show movement in the picture. Orally rehearse some sentences that tell what is happening, and record a sentence or two under the illustration. Ride the wave of excitement and experimentation.

Patterns of Wonder Time

Students think about what they like to do and share this with a partner. After some oral brainstorming, writers create their own illustrations of themselves doing something they enjoy. For those having difficulty generating an idea, they can always refer to the shared writing as a model and choose something they do on the playground.

Bookmaking Literacy Station

Students add marks to their pictures to show action in their books. Then, in pairs, they tell their partners what is happening in their writing, pointing to the marks they've added and other strategies they use to show action.

Moving Through the Hallway

As a class, choose a movement to demonstrate while walking through the school to lunch or recess. This could be creeping on tiptoes like quiet mice or swaying an arm like the trunk of an elephant. Young children love to experiment with movement, and they tend to focus so much on the action that they move more quietly through the halls this way.

This writer added action marks to his writing and said, "There are four people jumping."

Invitation to SHARE and CELEBRATE

In a circle, students share what is happening or what they are doing in their pictures orally, revisiting the focus phrase: *I tell what is happening in my writing.*

PreK writers share their writing with each other during the celebration.

I dash up the dark, swirly slide that no one dares go near, but the boys pay no attention to me.

The boys try to jump off the monkey bars, but no one can do a high-flying leap from the top like I can. I dive. I spin. I nail my landing. Every! Single! Time!

1.5   What Color Is the Sky? Adjectives Tell What Kind

Standards and Connections	Teacher Considerations	Texts
Standard Use frequently occuring verbs. **Companion Lessons** • Lesson 2.10 • Lesson 3.13 • Lesson 4.12 	Because students are grasping fine motor skills and moving from a variety of scribbling to some representational illustrations, it's crucial to build upon their oral language in this lesson. As they tell us about their pictures, we invite them to use words that tell *what kind* in order to add details to this oral rehearsal of their stories. When students in the scribble phase are reading books, invite them to tell you about what kinds of things they see in the pictures.	*Snail and Worm: Three Stories About Two Friends* Written and illustrated by Tina Kügler **Alternative Titles** *The Airport Book* Written and illustrated by Lisa Brown *Freight Train* Written and illustrated by Donald Crews *Brown Bear, Brown Bear, What Do You See?* Written by Billy Martin Jr. and illustrated by Eric Carle

Focus Phrase 〝 I tell what kind. 〞

A note about adjectives that tell what kind . . .

Writers use adjectives to show what kind through colors and size. Both ways help to convey meaning more precisely. Writers also use adjectives that tell what kind to compare two or more nouns. This chart gives some examples of colors, sizes, and comparisons.

Possible Adjectives That Tell What Kind	
Colors	**Size**
green red orange blue pink	tall (taller, tallest) big (bigger, biggest) little (littler, littlest)

As students look over the red flower from the beginning pages of *Snail and Worm*, invite them to share their wonders and noticings. When students describe the flower as tall (or any other adjective), introduce the focus phrase: *I tell what kind.* Then ask, "What else do you notice?" This continued conversation leads to more adjectives that tell what kind. As they share, repeat student noticings in complete sentences (not to correct, but model). When someone notices the red flower, say, "Oh yes, what kind of flower?" The children shout, "A red flower!" "Now what could we say about the red flower? Maybe something like . . . The red flower grows high into the white sky, or Snail and Worm are looking up at the red flower." Students construct these sentences with you orally, generating as much talk about the picture as the class can, frequently circling back to what kind.

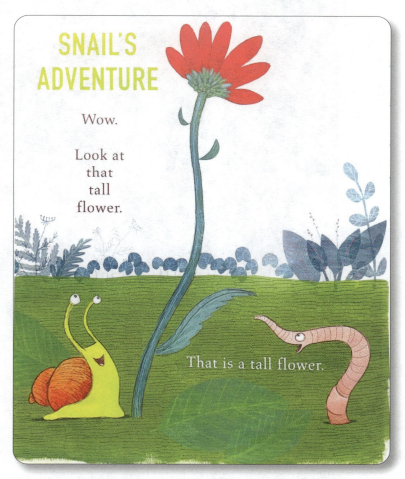

This page spread from *Snail and Worm* is included at the end of this lesson.

Invitation to COMPARE and CONTRAST

Select another illustration from *Snail and Worm* (or any other picture book) to share. With both pages displayed, ask, "What do you see is the same on both pages? What do you see is different?" As students begin to compare and contrast the pictures, support oral language development and knowledge of words that tell what kind by asking, "What kind of _____ is this?" Together, create an oral response to the prompt: "We could say . . ."

Students eager to share the similarities and differences between the two pages in *Snail and Worm*.

If you compare and contrast two pages from the same book, consider using two pages that are side by side, or if you have an interactive whiteboard or document camera, you can take a picture of the original page to display alongside the page with which you are comparing it.

Invitation to IMITATE TOGETHER

Shared Writing

As a class, brainstorm ideas for a picture and choose one to draw, focusing on the adjectives that tell what kind. Invite students to orally share sentences about the picture as you record their sentences. Don't forget to use color and size to tell what kind.

Patterns of Wonder Time

Distribute blank paper to students and invite them to draw—or even paint—pictures using adjectives that tell what kind. Encourage them to tell what kinds of things are in their picture. Students continue to use storytelling language as they talk about their creations.

Guided Reading or Reading Station

As students use pictures to comprehend the texts they are reading, reinforce the use of adjectives. When students explain what they see in the pictures, invite them to tell what kind of things they see.

Invitation to PLAY

Ewyn created this picture with paint. When asked about his picture, he said, "This is a beach with waves and storm clouds. There are cactuses on the beach, but they aren't the pokey cactuses." To help reinforce the use of adjectives, his teacher prompted, "Tell me more about what kind of things are in your picture." Ewyn replied by saying, "The beach is sandy and the waves are blue."

Invitation to
SHARE
and
CELEBRATE

Students sit in a circle and repeat the focus phrase a few times. They then share their pictures by placing them under a document camera or holding them up for everyone to see, telling about what kind of things they have in their pictures. Display student writing alongside the focus phrase in the classroom or hallway once sharing is complete.

This writer chose to write about firefighters putting out a fire. He used adjectives to tell what kind as he shared his story aloud.

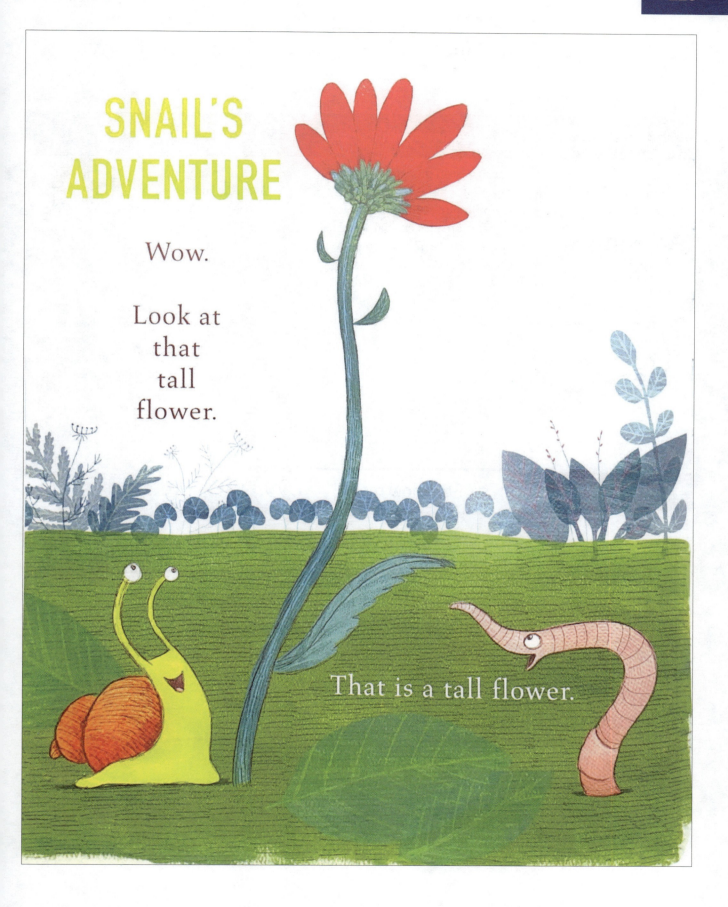

1.6   You Can Count on Me: Adjectives Tell How Many

Standards and Connections	Teacher Considerations	Texts
Standard Use frequently occurring adjectives. **Companion Lessons** • Lesson 2.11 • Lesson 3.14 • Lesson 4.13 	Because students are grasping fine motor skills from a variety of scribbling to some representational illustrations, it's crucial we use authentic questioning to support them. As they tell us about their pictures, we frequently ask "How many?" This enables writers to orally rehearse adding details that show quantity to their stories.	*The Little Red Cat Who Ran Away and Learned His ABC's (the Hard Way)* Written and illustrated by Patrick McDonnell **Alternative Titles** *Octopuses One to Ten* Written by Ellen Jackson and illustrated by Robin Page *Ten on the Sled* Written by Kim Norman and illustrated by Lisa Woodruff *The Very Hungry Caterpillar* Written and illustrated by Eric Carle

Focus Phrase   I tell how many.

A note about adjectives . . .

There are three kinds of adjectives—those that tell how many, what kind, and which one. This lesson focuses on how many; however, in students' conversations they're likely to throw in a color or a kind or a which one descriptor in conversation. Just accept the answers and don't feel you need to make the delineation unless a student asks.

Invitation to WONDER

We selected McDonnell's wordless ABC book as the mentor text for this lesson because it invites children to storytell through the pictures, like they would do with their own writing in the scribbles phase. Keep in mind that the marks in students' stories will not necessarily be letters and words, but rather beautiful lines, waves, or scribbles. Choose a page spread to share from McDonnell's book and ask, "What do you wonder?" As students share their thinking, honor what they say and name it by discussing what the author did and why he did it. When they notice the different animals in the pictures, ask them how many they notice. Change it up by rehearsing various sentences:

> "The dragon looks at four animals."
> "The chicken lays one egg."
> "A dragon has one eye open and one eye closed."

When ready, reveal the focus phrase and invite your students to say it with you.

In this phase, much of what your writers bring up will not be about adjectives that tell *how many.* Accept all answers. It's what they wonder. Engagement and attention are key. But when they do hit on the focus of the lesson, it's OK to stretch those conversations and do some responsive teaching.

Invitation to COMPARE and CONTRAST

Select a page from any picture book in your classroom that has countable illustrations. Ask your students to share what they see is the same and different. Support oral language development and prompt with "How many . . . ?" to begin rehearsal of sentences using adjectives that tell how many. Support their oral sentence construction by starting with, "We could say . . ."

Invitation to IMITATE TOGETHER

Interactive Writing

Prepare a bin with a variety of items inside. Together, discover what's inside and discuss different ways to group them such as by color, by shape, and so on. Write a sentence about at least one of the groups using adjectives that tell *how many.* Because the items are also grouped by attribute, the sentences will most likely also include adjectives that tell what kind. Bonus!

Patterns of Wonder Time

Students explore the classroom and choose something they can count and write and draw to describe their experience. When they tell about their picture, remind them of the focus phrase: *I tell how many*.

During remote learning, Ellie chose to write about her baby dolls. When she shared her writing with her teacher, she said, "These are my babies. I have four babies."

Invitation to
PLAY

Math Journals

Students explore bins of math manipulatives to form patterns. In their journals, they record their pattern and explain it using words that tell how many.

When asked to tell about her pattern, Maya says, "There are five red bugs and six blue bugs and six green bugs."

Invitation to
SHARE
and
CELEBRATE

Students share their pictures using the focus phrase to guide the language they use. Collect the pictures in a class book and place it in the classroom library for everyone to enjoy throughout the year.

Ja' Monique shared her story about playing with all of her friends. She added words during her oral rehearsal that told how many friends she played with.

1.7   Oh, Yes: Prepositions Tell Where

Standards and Connections	Teacher Considerations	Texts
Standard Use frequently occurring prepositions. **Companion Lessons** • Lesson 2.12 • Lesson 3.15 • Lesson 4.15 	As with all lessons in the Scribble Writing phase, we support and build upon oral language while writers tell about their pictures and thinking. To expand their sentences and add detail, we invite them to use words that tell where, such as "*under* the tree," "*by* the bed," or "*inside* the house," and then encourage them to add these details to their pictures.	*Oh, No!* Written by Candace Fleming and illustrated by Eric Rohmann **Alternative Titles** *The Napping House* Written by Audrey Wood and illustrated by Don Wood *Up, Down, and Around Big Book* Written by Katherine Ayres and illustrated by Nadine Bernard Wescott *There Might Be Lobsters* Written by Carolyn Crimi and illustrated by Laurel Molk

Focus Phrase   I tell where.

Because you are using pictures to support the use of prepositions orally, there's no need to search for the prepositions used in the print. However, when rereading the story to your children, stop and ask, "Where?" when you come across one. For example, after reading "Frog fell into a deep, deep hole" on the first page of *Oh, No!*, stop to ask, "Where did Frog fall?" These repeated reminders will help students hear how prepositions are used in print to tell where.

Invitation to WONDER

We love the patterned nature of Candace Fleming's *Oh, No!* We use it for shared reading because it repeats several prepositional phrases and adds meaning to them throughout the book. During the Invitation to Wonder, emergent writers play with its repetitiveness to think about the details in the pictures and their surroundings. Choose a page spread from the book, such as the one with the tiger looking down into the hole holding the other animals. "Let's take a close look at these pictures. What do you wonder?" Students may wonder about where the animals are or how they are feeling. No matter what they wonder, honor their thoughts and ask them to point out what makes them think this way. Discuss why the illustrator may have included what they note. When they discover the details that help tell where, share the focus phrase: *I tell where.* Continue the discussion, "What else helps us tell where in this picture? Let's use these details to tell more," building to statements like "The tiger's tail is hanging *below* the branch." Or "The tiger is *on* the branch." Or "The tiger is *above* the other animals." Then, if time permits, take this oral rehearsal from the book to their surroundings: "Who sees something that's on or below something else in the classroom?"

Invitation to COMPARE and CONTRAST

Create a picture that shows items in various places such as the example below, asking, "How is this picture and the page we studied from *Oh, No!* the same and different?" As emergent writers say sentences about location in the picture, continue reviewing the focus phrase: *I tell where.*

Possible sentences: The food is on the table. The cups are next to the food. The kids sit on the chairs. The kids sit at the table. The mountains are in the background. The flowers are in the middle of the table. The dog is under the table.

Invitation to

IMITATE

TOGETHER

Interactive Writing

Revisit both the model text and the comparison example and say the focus phrase together. On chart or butcher paper or another large surface, create a picture together. Students add details to the class illustration that help them tell where. Then, you record a sentence or two that tells where under the illustration.

PreK students worked with their teacher to add to this illustration before composing oral sentences about where things are in it.

Interactive writing is powerful for emergent writers because they get the chance to share the pen and be coauthors of whatever we write. To move the student additions a little faster, students tell you what they will add to the picture before adding it, and two students draw their parts at the same time. This can also be done in a small group where everyone gets to add to the picture and rehearse their writing orally and physically.

Invitation to PLAY

Patterns of Wonder Time

On large index cards or half sheets of paper, students create another imitation, choosing what to draw and what details to add that help them tell where. Create a gallery of their pictures to be shared during the celebration and beyond. As you revisit the gallery, make sure to revisit prepositions as a focused part of the conversation: "Geraldo's picture is under Alyssa's and next to DeVante's" and so forth.

Writing Workshop

When students share with others about their pictures, they include sentences that tell where. When conferring with students, ask them to tell you about their pictures using words that tell where.

Small-Group Instruction

Create word cards with sight words that are also prepositions like *in*, *to*, *by*, *at*, and *on*. Read and repeat the sight words. Display a picture from a familiar book—or a picture with plenty of details. We like this page from Carolyn Crimi's *There Might Be Lobsters*. Students pull random sight word cards and use them to tell about the picture. Add these word cards to your word wall.

This page spread from *There Might Be Lobsters* in included at the end of this lesson.

Invitation to SHARE and CELEBRATE

For this gallery walk celebration, half of the students stand by their imitations created during the Invitation to Play/*Patterns of Wonder* Time while the other half walk around to look at each one. The students standing by their pictures share the details that tell where with their peers. After a few minutes, switch roles. Yes, questioning and authentic conversation are encouraged.

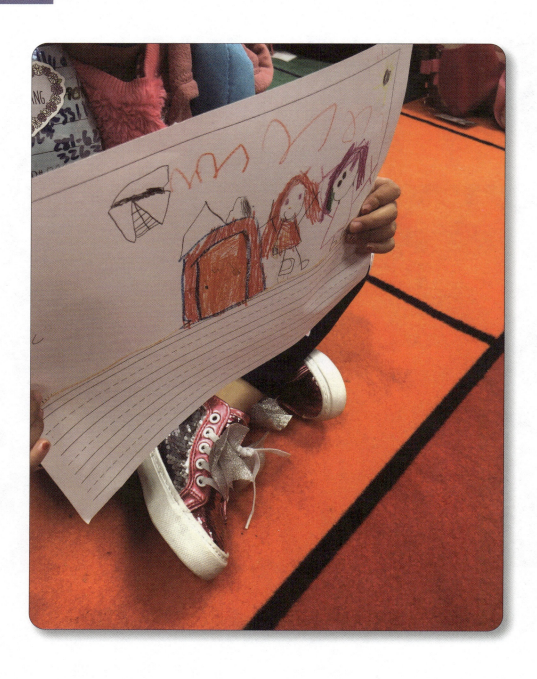

Sukie sat and watched beach balls bouncing and big boys running and umbrellas flapping and lifeguards blowing loud whistles and waves splish-splashing with Chunka Munka—

1.8   *And Adds More: Conjunctions*

Standards and Connections	Teacher Considerations	Texts
Standard Use frequently occurring conjunctions. **Companion Lessons** • Lesson 2.13 • Lesson 3.16 • Lesson 4.16 	In this phase, we rely heavily on students' oral language when they share their writing with us. As writers tell us about their pictures, this lesson shows them how the joining word *and* helps writers add details to tell more. Janet Stevens's *Tops and Bottoms* includes illustrations with a variety of things going on, so this picture book authentically lends itself to conversations that tell more using *and*. As students tell us more about their own writing, we invite them to consider trying out the joiner *and* to add those details to their pictures.	*Tops and Bottoms* Adapted and illustrated by Janet Stevens **Alternative Titles** *Pink Is for Boys* Written by Robb Pearlman and illustrated by Eda Kaban *The Wall in the Middle of the Book* Written and illustrated by Jon Agee *A Perfectly Messed-Up Story* Written and illustrated by Patrick McDonnell

Focus Phrase   ❝   I tell more with *and*.   ❞

A note about oral language . . .

Oral language helps us explore picture books. These authentic conversations allow students to naturally develop awareness and application. Once students know and understand the focus phrase, they can use it to tell more about the pictures in the books they read. In this way, we build on their production of sentences. Although we feel that requiring complete sentences isn't yet a developmentally appropriate or realistic expectation for emergent writers, we still introduce expanding their thoughts with conjunctions, or joining words, such as *and*. Through this introductory play, writers experiment with using complete sentences with a focus on volume of writing rather than correctness.

Share the page spread from *Tops and Bottoms*, which is also included at the end of this lesson. Ask, "What do you wonder?" Students share their thinking about the pictures that may include thoughts about the bear sleeping or the hares gardening. Honor their wonderings and extend them by inviting writers to share more.

"I wonder why the bear is sleeping," Jake shares.

"Let's think. *The bear is sleeping.* Why do you think he is sleeping?"

"*Because* he's tired." Piper explains. "Look! His shoes are untied!" (Notice how Piper just orally used the connecting word *because*. This is how the conversation and exploration builds on itself.)

"Oh yes! His shoes *are* untied. You know, we could say, 'The bear is sleeping *and* his shoes are untied.'

"What else do you wonder or notice?"

As students share more about the pictures, model the use of the joining word *and* to expand their sentences. When ready, reveal the focus phrase and repeat it together: *I tell more with* and.

Invitation to COMPARE and CONTRAST

Choose another page from this book (or another class favorite) that includes pictures with a variety of discussion entry points. As students share similarities and differences they identify in the two examples, continue to honor all contributions, helping them orally produce sentences using *and*. For example, if a student shares about two things and doesn't use the joiner *and*, you could say, "That's a great observation. Yes, they are climbing a ladder *and* looking up." Try continually stressing and in a tone that says more is coming: "Aaaaand." Repeat and point to the displayed focus phrase again and again throughout the lesson set.

Invitation to IMITATE TOGETHER

Shared Writing

Share a picture that lends itself to composing sentences with *and*. The picture we used here came from the image library on nasa.gov. Invite students to orally share sentences about the picture using *and*. Choose at least one sentence to write together.

The astronauts smile and play leap frog.

Students orally shared several sentences about the picture, eventually choosing one to write through shared writing.

Invitation to PLAY

Patterns of Wonder Time

Students build, act out, or draw something with a friend and tell each other about their masterpieces using the joining word *and*. You may wish to take a picture of their activity for celebration and display afterward. For a fun twist play the song, "Peanut Butter and Jelly" or play "Peanut Butter" by Barney. You can find videos of both on YouTube.

Writing Workshop

While making books, students add to their pictures and orally expand their sentences about them, using the joiner *and* to tell more. Look for points during your conferences where you might revisit the focus phrase to nudge writers to try it out.

A young writer made a book during writing workshop and used the word *and* to tell more on each page. This page says "My mommy and daddy is eating. And this is me."

Reading Workshop

Children explore a variety of picture books from their independent reading bundles. With a partner, they take turns orally sharing what the pictures tell them, making sure to use the joining word *and* to tell more as they discover new details.

Invitation to SHARE and CELEBRATE

Students sit in a circle and use the joining word *and* to tell about what they made or did during the Invitation to Play/*Patterns of Wonder* Time. Record sentences students share and attach the text to a photo of their item for an electronic display using Padlet or another online tool. In addition, students whoop when they see or use the conjunction *and*.

So Bear went back to sleep, and Hare and his family went to work. Hare planted, Mrs. Hare watered, and everyone weeded.

1.9   What's First? Use Transition Words to Share Thoughts in Order

Standards and Connections	Teacher Considerations	Texts
Standard Use frequently occurring transition words. **Companion Lessons** • Lesson 2.14 • Lesson 3.17 • Lesson 4.17 	Because writers use transition words in all types of writing, not just stories, our focus phrase in this lesson is about sharing their thoughts, which leaves room for both storytelling and informational writing. We chose Julie Downing's *No Hugs Till Saturday* because the wordless illustrations on pages 10–11 lend themselves to orally sharing thoughts, like events in order. This is a great lesson to repeat with wordless picture books, and you'll find some terrific examples in the alternative titles list.	*No Hugs Till Saturday* Written and illustrated by Julie Downing **Alternative Titles** *Wolf in the Snow* Written and illustrated by Matthew Cordell *Nope!* Written and illustrated by Drew Sheneman *Dandelion's Dream* Written and illustrated by Yoko Tanaka

Focus Phrase 66   I tell my thoughts in order.   99

A note about using oral language to plant time-order words . . .

When students are not using transitions or transition words to share their thoughts in order, we can model this language through our own sharing. You could practice during read-alouds or in small-group reading instruction as you retell a story or steps in a process. Invite students to retell with you, while you use starters like *first*, *next*, *then*, and *finally*. These are not the only transition words that children use, of course, but it is a start, and you can continue to model different transitions through any conversations that share information or retell books.

Common Transitions Used to Tell Something in Order		
First	Next	Finally
Once	Then	In the end
In the beginning	After that	Last

Invitation to WONDER

Show the illustrations on pages 10–11 from *No Hugs Till Saturday* in which the little dragon throws a fit. Although this picture includes no words, students share their wonderings and noticings. As they share their thoughts about the various scenes in the picture, help them to tell the story orally in order, prompting with some transition words.

"What happened first?"

"Felix blew fire."

"So we could say, First, Felix blew fire. Then, _____. Next, _____. After that, _____."

When students make books during writing time, they draw a picture on each page to represent the stories or information they share. Often their books will be composed with a different idea or event on each page. As you encourage them to share orally, they'll quite naturally use time-order words. You'll also find lots of opportunities to highlight such words in science, social studies, and math lessons.

Invitation to COMPARE and CONTRAST

Create an example of a wordless picture book that tells a simple story through pictures. Share the pages, and invite students to compare and contrast it with the page from *No Hugs Till Saturday*. When students notice that both texts tell a story or show what happens in order, ask them to repeat the focus phrase, *I tell my thoughts in order*. Though this preliminary exploration of transition words is all verbal, if writers are ready, you can extend it to include writing in the Invitation to Play.

Invitation to IMITATE TOGETHER

Shared Writing

Brainstorm ideas about something that has happened recently at school. It can be as simple as entering the classroom at the start of the day. Using these ideas, create a sketch for each part across pages to represent a book. Then, go back to each page and write a sentence through shared writing using a transition word on each page as students orally describe what happened.

To review transitions, a teacher records a sentence for each picture after the class orally rehearses how they began their day that morning.

Invitation to PLAY

Patterns of Wonder Time

Students use modeling clay to create an animal or other creature. Orally, they share a story about the creature, details about something it does, or the steps in how they made it. The choice is theirs, but they do need to go in order. If mobile devices are available, students may record themselves as they share their thoughts.

Small-Group Reading

Students retell their books in order. You may wish to give them sticky notes or note cards that have words like *first*, *next*, *then*, and *finally* written on each one to support ordered retellings.

Writing Center

Fill your writing center with premade blank three-page books. Display a teacher-created book that tells a story you've shared with the class as a model. Students share their thoughts through pictures and words (scribbles) in their own books and tell them in order to other classmates at the center.

It's helpful to have a personal story that you reference many times throughout the year. Over time, students get to know this story well as you expand it and share it in different ways. Create a sketch of it across a few pages that can be photocopied and used over and over to add details and writing to. Whitney's go-to story is about the time she ran into a huge snake on her walking path. Jeff's go-to story is about the things he'd do with his brother when their mother left them at home alone.

First, I walked on the path.

Then, I saw a snake. I was scared!

Finally, I ran away.

Invitation to SHARE and CELEBRATE

Students share their books from the writing center in small groups or with partners, using transitions to tell their thoughts in order. A few students share with the whole group. Invite the class to join you in restating the steps or order of what the writer shared as everyone moves across their fingers in order. Display student writing with the focus phrase when sharing is complete.

This young writer made a book in the writing center. When she shared it with the class, she read: "Once there was a princess who met a prince. Then they got married and danced. In the end, they moved to Texas."

Symbol and Letter Writing

Symbol and Letter Writing Phase Behaviors	<ul><li>Using mock letters or symbols</li><li>Including representational drawing</li><li>Using letter strings intended to represent writing</li><li>Exploring letter and sound correspondence</li><li>Experimenting with labeling</li></ul>

2.1   On Your Marks . . . Use Marks, Symbols, and Letters to Record Language

Standards and Connections	Teacher Considerations	Texts
Standard Intentionally use marks, symbols, and letters to record language and make words. **Companion Lessons** • Lesson 1.1 • Lesson 3.1 • Lesson 4.1	Our standard for this lesson is using marks, symbols, and letters to record language and make words. In the symbols and letters phase, the marks of lines, waves, and scribbles shift into a mix of approximated and conventional letters. We often find children recording language through letter strings and using initial sounds to label pictures. Students orally share their books across pages, reading the marks and approximated words they have made, including symbols and letters they have used. Be sure to check out the note on the next page to see how this lesson's goal and focus phrase connect to its companion lessons.	*Knot Cannot* Written by Tiffany Stone and illustrated by Mike Lowery **Alternative Titles** *A Squiggly Story* Written by Andrew Larsen and illustrated by Mike Lowery *Can I Be Your Dog?* Written and illustrated by Troy Cummings *What Can a Citizen Do?* Written by Dave Eggers and illustrated by Shawn Harris

Focus Phrase   ❝   I write with words and pictures.   ❞

A note about focus phrase visuals . . .

Since this same goal looks different as emergent writers develop, you'll notice the focus phrase for this lesson repeats through its companion lessons—even as the type of writing shifts across their phases. We highlight this shift with accompanying visuals that represent the type of writing children do in each phase.

For example, the focus phrase visual for this lesson represents the writing children do in the Symbol and Letter Writing phase, showing that all writers compose through both pictures and words. Keep in mind that the words in this phase are actually through symbols, single letters, and letter strings. Notice that the visuals for the companion lessons in this thread (1.1, 3.1, and 4.1) change to represent the type of writing students are progressing through.

Invitation to WONDER	Students enjoy when *Knot Cannot* is read aloud, because its patterns are full of wonder. Choose a page to share, inviting your students' curiosity around the author's craft by asking, "What do you wonder? What do you see? What do you notice?" Students comment on what the pictures include while others may notice the page includes words as well. When they comment on words or symbols, invite students to point to them, even if they don't yet conventionally read them. Ask them to reread the page with you as you point to the words. Introduce the focus phrase. Then, ask young writers what other letters they notice, showing them how writers in the symbol and letter phase might begin to record their language with letters.

Punctuation marks are symbols. When these little dots and lines are noticed, pause to wonder what the punctuation mark they've noticed does.

- Periods say stop.
- Commas say something else is coming.
- Exclamation marks say something is loud or important.
- Quotation marks mean someone is talking.

Invitation to COMPARE and CONTRAST

Share a piece of student writing with your class that uses symbols and letters to represent words. Not only will this be a conversation builder, it additionally values the writing students do in the symbol and letter phase. We've included an example piece here and at the end of this lesson that can also be used. Invite children to study the *Knot Cannot* page next to the student writing sample page and compare and contrast. "Writers, remember everything we noticed from *Knot Cannot* yesterday? William agreed to share his book that he made yesterday in writing workshop. We will use it to compare and contrast the two pieces of writing. Let's take a look at William's writing as he reads it to us." After the student shares, say, "Look at all of the choices William has made in his story writing. What do you notice that William did like Tiffany Stone? What do you notice is different?" Students share their thinking with their partner while you listen in on their conversations. What are they noticing? Bring them back to the whole group to share some of these noticings. Circle back to the focus phrase, reading it aloud together.

William wrote, "I'm riding a camel."

Many children get excited when asked to share their work, but it's important for your students to know how to respond in a positive manner. Before you choose to use a student example as a model in your lesson, think about how your students might respond and if more practice of positive responses needs to take place first.

Invitation to IMITATE TOGETHER

Interactive Writing

Share a picture you have taken of the class. Writers add words on sticky notes and attach them to the picture. The words they add may be made up of both symbols and letters and may not match every sound they hear. That's OK. Remember to celebrate their approximations as development in progress. If time permits, use some of the sticky notes to create a sentence or two through shared writing.

Young writers label a picture taken of their class during interactive writing.

Invitation to PLAY

Writing Workshop

Revisit the focus phrase each day as students make books: *I write with words and pictures.*

When talking about their books, writers point to their symbols, letters, and approximated words as they read their writing.

Literacy Station

Students use magnetic letters to make words and record the words they make on dry erase boards.

Tyler used words and pictures to make his book during writing workshop. This page says, "My and my friend were playing swordfight."

Invitation to SHARE and CELEBRATE

In a whole-group circle, each writer stands up to share one of their books, pointing to their words as they do so. Hang their piece of writing in a hallway display for others to enjoy.

2.2 The Sounds of the Sea: Letter-Sound Correspondence

Standards and Connections	Teacher Considerations	Texts
Standard Move from scribbles to some letter-sound correspondence using beginning and ending sounds when writing. **Companion Lesson** • Lesson 3.2 	You've probably been having concepts about print conversations about how letters make words, as your students learn more and more letters and their sounds. This lesson builds on these concepts with a developmentally appropriate dip into letter-sound correspondence, primarily initial and ending sounds. In this phase of writing, students write symbols and some letters they know how to form, and we celebrate this as we nudge them toward more precise use of letter sounds. Inviting them to use an ABC chart when writing is another way for them to begin thinking about letters and sounds.	*Swashby and the Sea* Written by Beth Ferry and illustrated by Juana Martinez-Neal **Alternative Titles** *Oops, Pounce, Quick, Run! An Alphabet Caper* Written and illustrated by Mike Twohy *I'm Not a Mouse!* Written and illustrated by Evgenia Golubeva *Lexie the Word Wrangler* Written by Rebecca Van Slyke and illustrated by Jessie Hartland

Focus Phrase I write the letters of the sounds I hear.

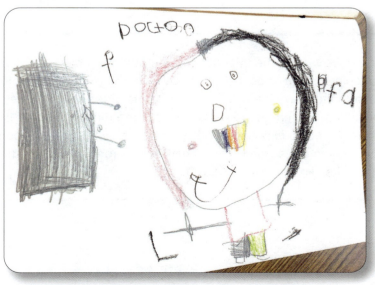

This PreK student writes the letters she knows with some initial letter-sound correspondence.

**Invitation
to
WONDER**

Display the page pictured here from *Swashby and the Sea* and invite your students to build curiosity around letters and words and pictures with the prompt, "What do you wonder?" Students comment on what the pictures include while others may notice the page includes words as well. When they discover the letters washed up by the sea, take a moment to make the sound of the *p*, and the *l*, and then the *ay*. Repeat the sounds together a few times and discuss how Beth Ferry used the sounds to help her write the letters. Remind your writers that they can do this, too, in their own writing using the focus phrase: *I write the letters of the sounds I hear*.

This page spread from *Swashby and the Sea* is included at the end of this lesson.

Don't stress over the phonogram, *ay*, in the word *play*. The lesson is about matching letters to sounds, and students will write whatever letters and sounds they have learned and understand. Possible ways they may write play include, *p*, *pla*, *pa*. All of these demonstrate the focus phrase: *I write the letters of the sounds I hear*. But sharing the *ay* through this conversation will invite some to use words they know how to read to help them spell words they write like *day*, *way*, and even *play*.

Invitation to COMPARE and CONTRAST

Share a labeled drawing you create like the example pictured here. Invite children to study the *Swashby and the Sea* page next to the teacher-created labeled picture and compare and contrast. "Writers, remember everything we noticed from *Swashby and the Sea* yesterday? Let's take a look at another piece of writing that I made. What do you see that I did that is like what Beth Ferry did? What do you notice is different?" Students share their thinking with their partner while you listen in on their conversations. What are they noticing? Bring them back to the whole group to share some of these noticings. Circle back to the focus phrase, reading it aloud together.

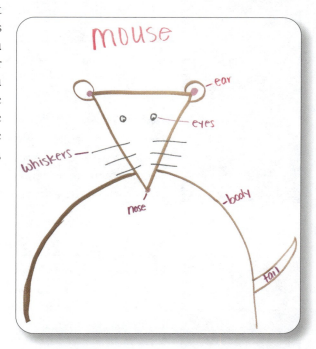

Invitation to IMITATE TOGETHER

Interactive Writing

Create another page for a class book that could follow the teacher-created piece used in the Invitation to Compare and Contrast. Invite students to help label the picture by writing the sounds they hear. "Writers, I was thinking about the labeled illustration we looked at yesterday, and I thought it would be cool to turn it into a class book that is all about animals. That could be one page in the book, and then together we could make another page for the book. So I drew this picture of a goat. Will you help me write the letters of the sounds we hear to add labels to this drawing?"

A kindergartner writes the letters of the sounds she hears during interactive writing.

Invitation to PLAY

Patterns of Wonder Time

Invite students to create another page for the book about animals. They draw a picture of an animal and label it, writing the letters of the sounds they hear. Create a class book with their pieces, and add it to the classroom library.

Writing Workshop

As you confer with students during independent writing, think about the letter sounds they control and look for places where you can leverage this alongside the focus phrase to encourage them to write the letters of the sounds they hear to add words to their pieces

Choice Time

Have paper, tablets, dry erase boards, or sticky notes available in all center areas for students to record writing any way they choose. For example, in the kitchen, they may decide to create a menu or write down a meal order. In the building center, they might label parts of their creations with sticky notes.

Invitation to SHARE and CELEBRATE

Play a favorite song of the class, and invite students to move around the room mimicking the animal they wrote about for the class book. When the music stops, they find the nearest classmate to share their page with. When the music starts back up, they begin moving as the animal would again. Stop the song several times to allow for multiple share sessions.

"*PL—AY!*" the girl sounded out, and did just that—with Swashby's shells and stones, with his buckets and shovels.

But her towers kept falling.

2.3   Jump into Sentences: Use Words to Make Sentences

Standards and Connections	Teacher Considerations	Texts
Standard Recognize that sentences are comprised of words. **Companion Lessons** • Lesson 1.2 • Lesson 3.3 	Writers in this phase begin to play with letters to make words, so we continue to support them in their oral language to produce sentences comprised of these words. We then nudge them to record their words in their own version of writing, whether it be a variety of symbols mixed with letters or strings of letters. *Jabari Jumps* is a beautiful story your students will want to spend lots of time with, so we suggest sharing it with them during a separate read-aloud time so you can pause to revisit it when it's time to teach this lesson.	*Jabari Jumps* Written and illustrated by Gaia Cornwall **Alternative Titles** *Brave* Written by Stacy McAnulty and illustrated by Joanne Lew-Vriethoff *Z Is for Moose* Written by Kelly Bingham and illustrated by Paul O. Zelinsky *Pete the Cat: Pete's Big Lunch* Written and illustrated by James Dean

Focus Phrase   ❝   I use words to make sentences.   ❞

Invitation to WONDER

Choose a page from *Jabari Jumps* to revisit with your students. We like the page near the end where Jabari hits the water with a splash, because it is simple and supportive for early writers. Display and read it aloud, giving your students a chance to look closely at the picture and how the words help to make meaning from it. Upon asking "What do you wonder?" honor and celebrate their thinking, building on their curiosity. They may wonder anything from if the water is cold to what the author means by "hit" the water. When they share a wonder, ask the students what they think and invite them to share their thinking with a partner. Then, turn their wonderings into composition and say, "Let's see what the author chose to say about this picture. 'Jabari hit the water with a splash!' Hmm. It looks like she chose lots of words to tell about the picture. You know what? Writers do this. They use words to make sentences. In fact, that's our focus phrase: *I use words to make sentences.* What other words could be put together into sentences to tell about this picture?" This oral rehearsal of further composition shows students that they can say a variety of things about the pictures they draw. As an author, they get to choose exactly what to say.

A note about concepts about print . . .

As your students learn that letters make words and words make sentences, you may consider having them help you create an anchor chart that highlights these conversations around concepts about print, building on to each concept as they come to it.

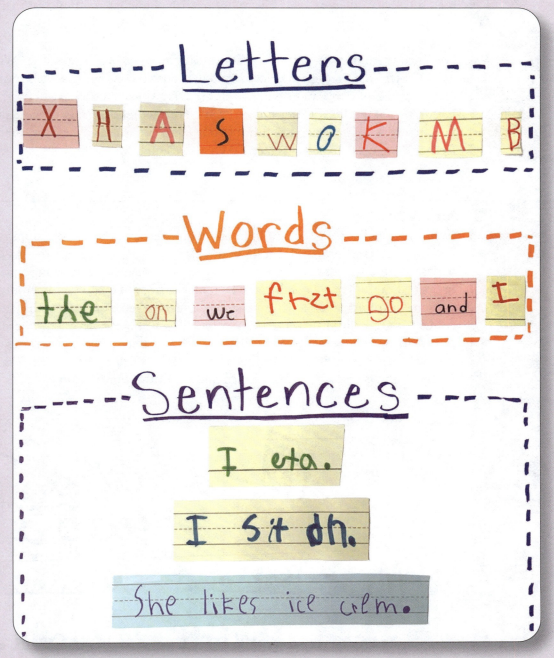

This interactive anchor chart, created over time, helps emergent writers remember the building blocks of letters, words, and sentences.

**Invitation
to
COMPARE
and
CONTRAST**

Choose a writer from your class to share a piece of their writing for this invitation, if they are comfortable. Keep in mind, this piece of writing probably includes a picture with a variety of symbols and letters rather than sentences. This is a time for comparing and contrasting, noticing what is the same and different about their piece of writing and the page from *Jabari Jumps*. So essentially, it's a celebration of this writer's work, and the child will feel honored to be the star of this invitation. As students notice what is the same in both and what's different, continue to honor their thoughts and build on their thinking.

A student might say, "Both pictures have a kid in it. Jabari is in that one and Michael is in this one."

A response and extension of the conversation might be, "That's true. Writers choose who will be in their stories and pictures. What does the author, Gaia Cornwall, say about Jabari? Yes, he hits the water with a splash! What does Michael say about himself here? That's right, he builds a tower out of Legos. Both writers use lots of words to tell about their picture, making sentences just like our focus phrase says. Let's say our focus phrase together: *I use words to make sentences*. What else could Michael say about his picture?"

**Invitation
to
IMITATE
TOGETHER**

Shared Writing

Jabari Jumps tells the story of a little boy who overcame his fear of jumping off a diving board. Use this mentor text during your shared writing experience to also tell a story as a class. It doesn't need to be about overcoming a fear, but something that has recently happened in class or school that can be told as a story. It could be something as simple as the time the principal visited the classroom. Quickly sketch one part of that story and invite students to verbally share sentences they would say about it, saying the words across their fingers to show how many words they use. Choose one sentence to write, saying it aloud first and then counting on your fingers how many words will be used. Then record the sentence and go back as a class to read and count the words again.

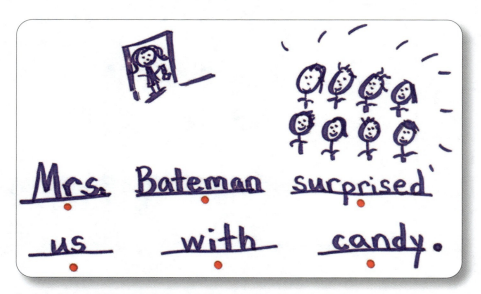

During shared writing, students retold a recent event and chose one sentence to write. After their teacher recorded their sentence, the class counted the words aloud while the teacher marked each one with a red dot.

Patterns of Wonder Time

Students draw a picture of something they like such as a favorite game or TV show. Then, they share with a partner what they will say about their picture, counting their words on their fingers. Finally, they write what they want to say in their own writing of symbols and letters.

Literacy Station

Stock a station with paper, crayons, and a couple of "mystery bags" that contain some trinkets. Students take an item from the bag and write about it using illustrations and their approximation of words. Station buddies can follow up by counting the words they included together.

Literacy Station

Create a few simple cut-up sentences made up of sight words and words with picture clues. Place them in individual baggies for groups to reassemble together. Some sentences they could build include:

> I like to run.
> I can see a horse.
> The ball is green.
> I am happy.

Students build sentences with words at a literacy station.

Invitation to PLAY

Invitation to SHARE and CELEBRATE

Students share their piece of writing created during the Invitation to Play/*Patterns of Wonder* time with a partner and then reread it, clapping to represent each word they use as they do. Choose one or two students to share their piece with the whole class. As students read their writing, count across your fingers how many words they use. Then, instead of clapping, they reread the sentence as students jump up and down for the number of words used.

2.4   Names from A to Z: Capitalize Names

Standards and Connections	Teacher Considerations	Texts
Standard Capitalize the first letter of names. *Companion Lessons* • Lesson 3.5 • Lesson 4.2 • Lesson 4.3 	Most students in this phase begin by writing with all capital letters. As they gain an understanding of the difference between a lowercase and uppercase letter, we explicitly show them how to write their names in a conventional fashion (which, of course, we've been doing all along). As a precursor to future lessons on capitalizing names in general, this lesson lays a foundation by focusing on capitalizing our own names.	*A Is for Audra: Broadway's Leading Ladies from A to Z* Written by John Robert Allman and illustrated by Peter Emmerich **Alternative Titles** *My Name Is Not Isabella: Just How Big Can a Little Girl Dream?* Written by Jennifer Fosberry and illustrated by Mike Litwin *My Name Is Aviva* Written by Lesléa Newman and illustrated by Ag Jatkowska *Thunder Boy Jr.* Written by Sherman Alexie and illustrated by Yuyi Morales

Focus Phrase 🙶   I begin my name with a capital letter.   🙷

A note about capitalization . . .

Have you ever heard the expression "all caps"? It means to capitalize everything. Curious young children are fascinated once they figure out how few letters in the books they read actually are capitalized. This is something you want to help them discover over time as they develop uppercase, or capital, letter awareness.

Invitation to WONDER

Take time to read and enjoy this book of names, immersed in the alphabet. Since the focus is on the convention of capitalization, invite your students to notice the sentence itself, in addition to the illustration. Write the following sentence from the first page of John Robert Allman's *A Is for Audra* on chart paper.

A is for Audra who awes and amazes.

Students may notice the letter *a*. When that happens, invite them to point out all of the *a*'s and discuss the difference between the uppercase and lowercase. At this point, focus on the capital *A* in *Audra*. "Let's look at this word. What do you notice about this word?" When a few students explain that it's a name, direct their focus to the first letter of the name. "Yes, it is her name! What do you notice about the *A* at the beginning of her name? What about the end of her name?" Through this conversation and discovery, reveal the focus phrase.

You may already have a class name anchor chart hanging in your room or a word wall with names included on it. In addition to using names to explore letter formation and print awareness, an alphabet chart of names is a fantastic tool for children to use when writing about others, and *A Is for Audra* shows some names for letters that might not be represented by children in the class. Add the names from the book as you see fit.

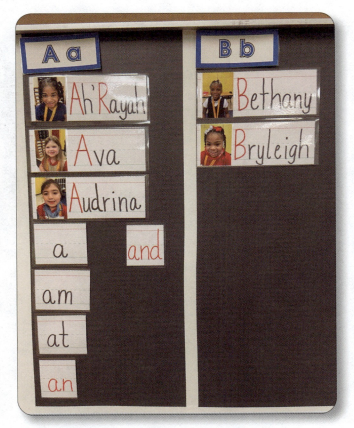

Names with pictures are added to the word wall.

Invitation to COMPARE and CONTRAST

Create an imitation sentence such as the following one and post it under the mentor sentence. Read each sentence aloud, inviting your readers to read with you, pointing to each word.

A is for Audra who awes and amazes.

K is for Keanu who giggles and plays.

Ask students to compare and contrast the choices the authors made with each sentence. When they notice the names, review the focus phrase.

When the students notice the name in each sentence, take a moment to clap or stomp the syllables in each name as another way to compare and contrast while bringing in some phonological awareness.

Invitation to IMITATE TOGETHER

Interactive Writing

As a class, compose a sentence about the teacher or class pet that imitates the pattern of the mentor sentence. If writers are interested in what the *and* does, explain how it allows our subject, who the sentence is about, to do more than one thing.

Juan begins the class pet's name with a capital letter during interactive writing.

Patterns of Wonder Time

Create an ABC class book of names. Each student writes their own imitation of the sentence using their name. Because students in this phase may not know how to write all of their letters yet, celebrate any approximations of their name as well as any in their illustrations showing what they do. A book page template is provided at the end of this lesson if needed.

Mia Bella's class book page reads, "M is for Mia Bella who likes to swing."

Literacy Station

Students play with plastic letters, matching the capitals to the names of their classmates. This can be done as shown here, or they can simply use name sentence strips at their tables.

Students match the uppercase magnetic letters to their classmates' names in a literacy station.

Share the class book during your read-aloud time, asking each student to read their page to the class. Add the book to your classroom library.

_____ is for _____

who _____

2.5   Can I Be Your Noun? Nouns Show People, Places, and Things

Standards and Connections	Teacher Considerations	Texts
Standard Use frequently occurring nouns. **Companion Lessons** • Lesson 1.3 • Lesson 3.7 • Lesson 4.6 	Although students in this phase are writing with both pictures and words, we continue to build on their oral language and support them through their illustrations because they're still writing with symbols and letters. When they add people, places, and things to their pictures, we ask writers to include words about them, knowing and honoring that their words may be a series of letter strings or symbols to represent letters they don't yet know how to form.	*Can I Be Your Dog?* Written and illustrated by Troy Cummings **Alternative Titles** *Hey, Water!* Written and illustrated by Antoinette Portis *Busy Creature's Day Eating!* Written and illustrated by Mo Willems *Sylvia's Bookshop* Written by Robert Burleigh and illustrated by Katy Wu

Focus Phrase ❝   I show and tell about people, places, and things in my writing.   ❞

A note about nouns . . .

The world is made of people, places, and things. Without nouns, our writing and world can't exist. We teach our students to add people, places, and things to their pictures to help them share their thoughts precisely, giving them the power to fill their writing with the stuff of the world. We continue to build on this both orally and in pictures as we move toward conventional writing.

Invitation to WONDER

Show an entire page spread from the book and read it aloud. We like the first page where the woman delivering the mail walks in front of a house with the children playing in the yard. When asked "What do you wonder?" students may notice all of the details in the picture such as the house, the children, the tree, or the woman with the mail. Write each person, place, or thing the group notices on a sticky note, adding it to chart paper. After several sticky notes have been collected, reveal the focus phrase.

Invitation to COMPARE and CONTRAST

Choose another page from this book (or another class favorite) that includes a variety of people, places, and things. We like some of the other pages in this book because the places on them have labels much like the environmental print children read every day, and this nudges them to add labels to their own pictures. As students begin sharing similarities and differences they notice in the two examples, continue to honor their contributions and add sticky notes of people, places, and things to the chart you started during the Invitation to Wonder.

I show and tell about people, places, and things.

People	Places	Things
lady	house	letter
woman	shop	mail
Postal worker	store	shorts
mailman		dog
kids		meat

Sticky note collection of people, places, and things students noticed during the Invitation to Wonder and the Invitation to Compare and Contrast.

Of course, since they are so excited about nouns, many students will simply list nouns and think no other words have any value. When a student plays around with including a verb with a noun, it makes perfect sense to take a moment to celebrate that, too.

Invitation

to

IMITATE

TOGETHER

Interactive Writing

Compose an illustration, showing people, places, and things that can be found in the classroom. You may start brainstorming some ideas with, "Let's think about our classroom. I'm going to draw some people, places, and things in it. What do you see in our classroom that I might draw?" As students give you ideas, add them to the picture until you have a variety of nouns represented. Then, write a sentence together about the classroom, inviting students up to contribute parts they know.

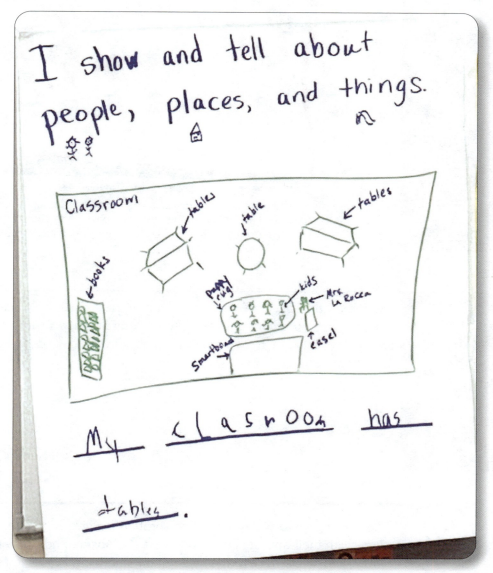

Students helped determine ideas and wrote some of the letters during interactive writing.

Patterns of Wonder Time

Students go on a noun hunt around the room, using sticky notes to label what they find to show people, places, and things. Leave labels up throughout your lessons on nouns.

Choice Time

Students create people, places, and things while building with blocks, drawing or painting, or manipulating modeling clay and talk about their creations with one another.

Writing Workshop

When conferring with writers throughout the week, invite them to share how they are showing and telling about people, places, and things.

Invitation to PLAY

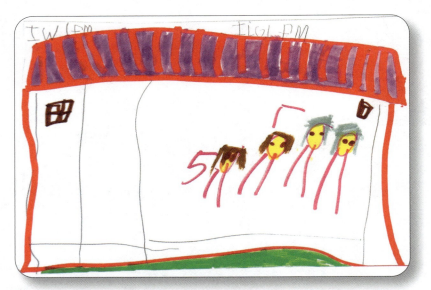

This child used *Can I Be Your Dog?* as a mentor text during writing workshop. When asked about her writing, she said, pointing to both her pictures and words, "It's my home. Mommy, Daddy, Carlos, and me. I have a house with my family. I live with my family."

Invitation to SHARE and CELEBRATE

To kick off this celebration, share an appropriate YouTube video of a song or rap about nouns. There are many to choose from! Students then sit in a circle on the rug and go around the circle, each child sharing a piece of writing where they showed and told about people, places, or things.

Continuing the play beyond the celebration will give writers more time to grow with their application of nouns. As you observe how they use nouns over time, circle back to the celebration as often as you see fit.

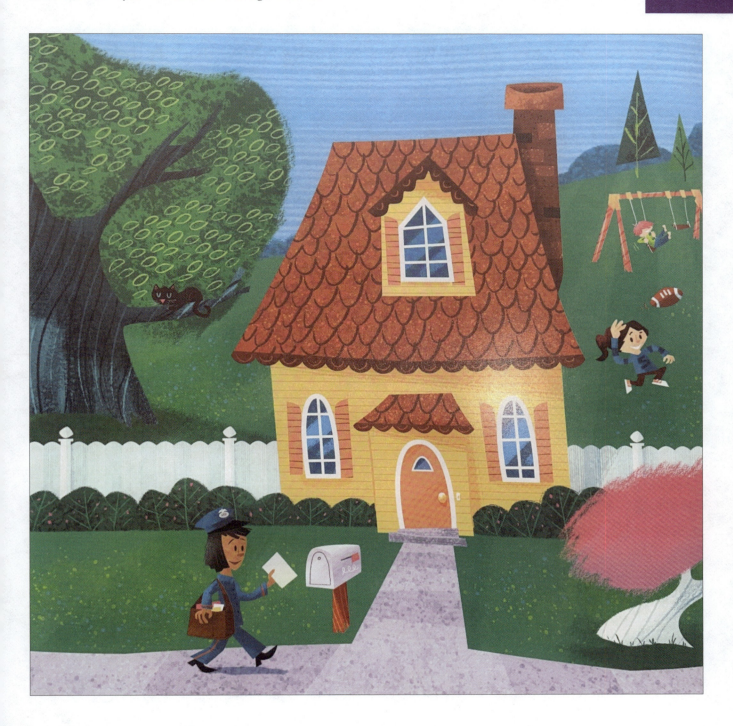

2.6 Writers Run into Verbs: Verbs Show and Tell Action

Standards and Connections	Teacher Considerations	Texts
Standard Use frequently occurring verbs. **Companion Lessons** • Lesson 1.4 • Lesson 3.9 • Lesson 4.10 	Students are learning that letters have sounds and are formed a certain way, so we still build on their oral language while also inviting them to add to their illustrations. As they tell us about their pictures, they add details that show action to their picture. Action may be shown through squiggles and lines. Our goal through modeling and attention is for young writers to begin to tell their audiences about action, both orally and in symbols and letters.	*Sorry (Really Sorry)* Written by Joanna Cotler and illustrated by Harry Bliss **Alternative Titles** *Shh! Bears Sleeping* Written by David Martin and illustrated by Steve Johnson and Lou Fancher *Skyscraper* Written and illustrated by Jorey Hurley *The Pigeon HAS to Go to School!* Written and illustrated by Mo Willems

Focus Phrase ❝ I show and tell about the action in my writing. ❞

A note about verbs and action . . .

Although verbs do indeed show action in a sentence like "I write," they can also show states of being with words often referred to as the *be* verbs: *is, are, was, were, be, been,* and *am*. For example, these sentences use *be*-verbs rather than action words:

I *am* a writer.
You *are* a writer
We will *be* writing today.

In this phase, the distinction doesn't matter. If students say a *be*-verb is a verb or an action, just accept it and move on. Now is not the time to delineate the types of verbs.

Invitation to WONDER

Display the page from *Sorry (Really Sorry)* that shows the goat running into the pig, and read it aloud. "Let's take a close look at these pictures and what the words say. What do you wonder?" Students may wonder about the expressions on the goat's and pig's faces. Honor their wonderings by engaging them in conversation about why the illustrator included the expressions on their faces and how we know how they are feeling. Students may also wonder about the smokelike lines and circles representing how fast Goat is running. We often refer to these as "action marks." When they do, honor their wondering, discuss why they are used, and tie the picture to the words used by the author: "Goat ran as fast as he could. He ran so fast, he ran right into Pig." This conversation may also lead to noticing other action marks in the picture of Goat running into Pig. Share the focus phrase when it's discovered.

Some students may note Goat and Pig are capitalized. If they do, ask, "What is the author telling us by capitalizing Goat and Pig?" Accept answers and say something like, "We don't capitalize many words, but the author capitalizing Goat and Pig shows that these are their names."

Invitation to COMPARE and CONTRAST

Select another page from *Sorry (Really Sorry)* (or from an alternative book listed previously) that includes an illustration with well-defined action to share with your students. If the sentences on the page include verbs to show action, read those sentences aloud to connect the sentence to the picture. As students compare and contrast the two illustrations, support their oral language development of using verbs by rehearsing several sentences together. Cycle back to the focus phrase, pointing out we show and tell about the action.

When pointing out the showing and telling of the action, stop to discuss how the action is detailed in the illustration and how we can tell about the action with words both orally and then in print. Students writing in the symbol and letter phase share sentences orally and write symbols and letters to represent their sentences in writing.

Interactive Writing

Revisit the model text *Sorry (Really Sorry)*, and say the focus phrase together. Students help you draw a dog or cat doing something, adding lines or "action marks" to show movement. Record a sentence together that tells what is happening or what the dog or cat is doing in the picture: *I show and tell about the action in my writing.*

A writer adds marks to show action during interactive writing.

Patterns of Wonder Time

Students create a page for a class book that shows action or something happening. They add to the pictures to show—and use their words to tell about—the action.

Hugo included action marks in his picture and wrote, "We are dancing to the music."

Invitation

to

PLAY

Dramatic Play or Recess

Repeatedly, ask students to tell what they are doing, emphasizing the words that show action.

Independent Writing

If writing stories, students add more to their pictures and words to show and tell action.

This writer adds more to her story to show and tell action.

Invitation

to

SHARE

and

CELEBRATE

Turn this celebration into an interactive read-aloud with your authors at the center. Read the class book together, acting out the verbs the writers use. One volunteer can act out the verb or the whole class can.

2.7   The Powerful Dot: Periods Start Clicking

Standards and Connections	Teacher Considerations	Texts
Standard Use end punctuation for sentences. *Companion Lessons* • Lesson 3.10 • Lesson 4.11 	This lesson extends the concepts about print conversations about recognizing and naming end punctuation you're already having with students throughout your school year. Here, we give writers a chance to play around with and explore end punctuation—even if they aren't yet writing full sentences—as they move from recognizing and naming to using periods at the end of their letter strings or whatever writing they're currently producing. Speech bubbles are an engaging way for students to add text to their pictures and, although we use them throughout this lesson, the primary focus is the period. Be sure to consistently cycle back to the focus phrase: *I end my sentences with a period.*	*My Name Is Elizabeth!* Written by Annika Dunklee and illustrated by Matthew Forsythe **Alternative Titles** *Today I Will Fly!* (an Elephant and Piggie book) Written and illustrated by Mo Willems *Lost. Found.* Written by Marsha Diane Arnold and illustrated by Matthew Cordell *Dare to Dream Big* Written by Lorna Gutierrez and illustrated by Polly Noakes

Focus Phrase   ❝   I end my sentences with a period.   ❞

A note about end punctuation and approximation . . .

Emergent writers often start playing with punctuation marks before they have received explicit instruction on them. Sometimes they place periods at the end of a line, even if it's in the middle of a sentence. Through our responsive instruction, these approximations move closer and closer to conventionality. We can support this experimentation with celebration instead of correction, as we nudge writers toward purposeful choices: "Tell me about why you placed a period here." or "Tell me about your choice to use a period here."

Invitation to WONDER

This model text, from Annika Dunklee's *My Name Is Elizabeth!*, uses a variety of punctuation within the speech bubbles. We demonstrate to students how speech bubbles work similarly to labeling, except speech bubbles tell what we and others say out loud. Display the page spread pictured from *My Name Is Elizabeth!* (also included at the end of this lesson), and read the speech bubble aloud. The richly detailed illustration will spark quite a bit of conversation as the readers get to know Elizabeth ("Her room is messy like mine"). If someone mentions the character's name, you might seize the opportunity and ask, "How do we know her name is Elizabeth?" ("We capitalize names." "That's what the girl says.") As the conversation moves to the information inside the speech bubble, call writers' attention to the speech bubble itself and how it connects to the speaker like a label. When writers notice the period, or dot, as they might call it, reveal the chosen focus phrase: *I end my sentences with a period.*

Invitation to COMPARE and CONTRAST

From another book in your classroom library or the alternate titles listed, select a page that includes a simple use of periods and, if you like, speech bubbles. Students compare and contrast the page from the mentor text with the second text. If students notice that both pages have speech bubbles, focus the children's attention on what is inside the bubble, inviting them to compare and contrast. When students notice that both pages have that dot, the period, make note of where the authors chose to use it and why. Revisit the focus phrase, repeating it several times together.

If it hasn't been discussed, make sure students explore how periods work when we read aloud, breaking up text and our talk. This discovery happens best when using texts with multiple sentences during shared or guided reading where students can clearly see the words on the page.

Invitation to IMITATE TOGETHER

Interactive Writing

Sketch a quick picture that would lend itself to speech bubbles or choose a picture from the Internet. As a class, draw a speech bubble for the picture and compose a sentence about the picture that requires a period. Ask a student to come up and add in the period as you come to it. When rereading the sentence, click your tongue when you come to a stop at the period. Your students will often repeat this gesture in their own writing as they come to a stop each time, reminding themselves to use a period.

Invitation to PLAY

Patterns of Wonder Time

Students draw a picture and add speech bubbles to show what someone says, adding periods to the end of sentences. Keep in mind the words inside the speech bubbles will most likely be represented through symbols and letter strings. Approximation is moving toward correctness and doesn't need to be incessantly corrected. Correcting is not teaching.

Writing Center

Fill the writing center with pictures that will inspire composing. On sticky notes, writers create sentences about the picture and post them around it. Celebrate student creativity and choice. Some may turn the sticky notes into speech bubbles while others will write letter strings to represent a sentence.

Writing Workshop

During writing workshop, encourage students to add periods to their writing to show the end of their sentences. Celebrate their attempts with an eye toward playful experimentation as opposed to complete accuracy.

Whitney confers with writers about their craft choices during independent writing.

Students share their writing with the class using the author's chair, clicking their tongue when they used periods. Repeat the focus phrase early and often as a celebratory chant: *I end my sentences with a period*. The idea of periods will really start clicking.

Saul used periods in some of his labels of the Avengers: Spiderman. Captain America. Thor. Thanos. Ironman. Hulk.

2.8 Yello! I'm So Excited! Exclamation Marks

Standards and Connections	Teacher Considerations	Texts
Standard Use end punctuation for sentences. **Companion Lessons** • Lesson 3.11 • Lesson 4.11 	As your background concept of print conversations around recognizing and naming punctuation blossom, it may be time for this lesson. Students in this phase write with a variety of symbols and letters, adding more to their illustrations, and children may also be playing with labels in their pictures. This lesson encourages them to add feeling to their labels with exclamation marks as they move through recognition and naming to more sophisticated use of end punctuation—even if they aren't yet writing full sentences. The simplicity of Adam Rubin's *High Five* invites writers to try out exclamation marks without the worry of writing complete sentences.	*High Five* Written by Adam Rubin and illustrated by Daniel Salmieri **Alternative Titles** *Hat Tricks* Written and illustrated by Satoshi Kitamura *This Is My Book!* Written and illustrated by Mark Pett *Perfect* Written and illustrated by Max Amato

Focus Phrase I show strong feelings with exclamation marks! (And yes, you can yell this focus phrase.)

A note about end punctuation and approximation . . .

Emergent writers tend to see and recognize the names of punctuation early on, but they often start playing with these symbols in this phase of writing. Beginning writers love using exclamation marks, and we celebrate their experimentation by prompting, "Tell me about why you used an exclamation mark here" or "Tell me about your choice to use an exclamation mark here."

Invitation to WONDER

Choose one of the pages from the book that says "**HIGH FIVE!**" to share with your students. Invite them to share their wonderings and noticings about the picture and the exclusive use of uppercase letters. Honor and name all that they share, and extend the conversation when appropriate. When their comments move to the use of the exclamation mark, discuss why Adam Rubin decided to use it and reveal the focus phrase. You may decide to share multiple pages in the book that use the same expression, reading it together with the strong feeling brought on by the exclamation mark.

Exclamation marks are a way to show yelling, and it can be fun to follow this lesson with books that have exclamation marks that prompt readers to yell its sentences to show extreme excitement. Allow some yelling fun for a time. Yelling can be joy! Always bring the conversation back around to the idea that we choose specific end marks to show our reader how to read out text.

Invitation to COMPARE and CONTRAST

Go grab a few of your class's favorite books and choose one that uses exclamation marks. We've also shared a couple of titles at the top of this lesson that work well. For example, in *Hat Tricks* by Satoshi Kitamura, almost every page has a sentence with an exclamation mark. Display a page from your book of choice and read it aloud. Then place it next to the page from the mentor text, and invite your students to notice similarities and differences. As they notice the exclamation marks in both texts, revisit the focus phrase, repeating it several times: *I show strong feelings with exclamation marks!* Go back and read each page together, showing a strong feeling with each.

Contrast is a great teacher, so remember to show and play with excitement/boredom, loud/quiet, fast/slow as well as the sound and purpose of each duality along with the punctuation that helps you know how the author intended you to read their writing.

Interactive Writing

As a class, compose a simple picture of kids playing and add words or phrases with exclamation points, similar to that in *High Five*. Remember in this lesson to prioritize the goal of using exclamation marks to show strong emotion over writing in complete sentences.

A writer adds an exclamation mark to the end of a sentence the class chose to write together.

Invitation to PLAY

Patterns of Wonder Time

Students draw a picture of themselves at play and use exclamation marks in their creations to show strong feelings. As emergent writers begin to play with exclamation marks, they'll likely overdo it. This is normal. Enjoy this playfulness while folding in interactions around the idea that one exclamation mark usually does the job.

Literacy Station

In the bookmaking station, remind students of the variety of punctuation marks by including a can containing a few craft sticks with punctuation marks on each end. As students make books, they use the sticks to help them decide how they want their readers to read their writing and make meaning from it.

Literacy Station

Students explore big books throughout the classroom, using highlighting tape to mark when they notice exclamation marks. For more advanced exploration, they mark any end punctuation mark they see.

Brain Break

Play "I'm So Excited" by the Pointer Sisters while your children get their wiggles out and dance.

Curiosity paired with playful activities breathe life into an emergent writer's day. Don't skimp on time in centers or stations, knowing that real, long-lasting learning takes place through rehearsal, experimentation, and invitations to take risks. Keep the play going!

Invitation to SHARE and CELEBRATE

Consider taking this celebration outside so students can shout at the top of their lungs when their writing shows strong feelings. Let students choose which piece of writing they want to share during this exciting and playful celebration. Have fun!

2.9   Are There Any Questions? Question Marks

Standards and Connections	Teacher Considerations	Texts
Standard Use end punctuation for sentences. **Companion Lessons** • Lesson 3.12 • Lesson 4.11 	While developing their writing through symbols, letters, and letter strings, this lesson moves writers towards using question marks to show questions and Ryan North's *How to Be a T. Rex* showcases question marks in a variety of creative ways that encourage exploration and wonder.	*How to Be a T. Rex* Written by Ryan North and illustrated by Mike Lowery **Alternative Titles** *Can I Play Too? (an Elephant and Piggie book)* Written and illustrated by Mo Willems *Night Animals Need Sleep Too* Written and illustrated by Gianna Marino *Which Is Round? Which Is Bigger?* Written and illustrated by Mineko Mamada

Focus Phrase   I end my questions with a question mark.

A note about question marks . . .

Though questions are often inverted sentences, students don't always notice. For example, "Dori is in the ocean" is a sentence, but if we flip it around it becomes "Is Dori in the ocean?" Or one might ask, "Where is Dori? Where does Dori live? Have you seen Dori?" You will note how unconsciously students make the inversion in multiple ways, without explicit instruction. Emergent writers don't need explicit instruction in this. Their natural exploration is plenty. Still, this is a great time to use oral language to model that the pitch of your voice goes up at the end of a question.

Invitation to WONDER

In this invitation, we mix things up a bit by lifting a specific part of the mentor text for closer study. Display the first page of *How to Be a T. Rex* that begins with "Hi, my name's Sal!" Read the page aloud for context, and ask, "What does the teacher ask on this page? Let me write her question down so we can look at that part more closely." Write the question on chart paper and invite students to look over it.

What do you want to be when you grow up?

Prompt the conversation with, "Let's talk about what Ryan North did here as a writer. Look very carefully at how he wrote this question. What do you wonder or notice?" When the punctuation mark comes up, extend the conversation by discussing its purpose. "Yes, there is that mark at the end of the question. We call that a question mark. Listen to my voice when I read this question aloud. What do you notice about it?" Reread the question together, paying attention to its end mark. Reveal the focus phrase, reminding students they can use questions in their own writing, too.

Invitation to COMPARE and CONTRAST

Find another question from a previous read-aloud, reread the page it's from, and write it underneath the question from *How to Be a T. Rex*. As students compare and contrast this lifted question to the original one from the mentor text page, stop to honor and celebrate their thinking. Here, we selected a question from *Night Animals Need Sleep Too* by Gianna Marino.

What do you want to be when you grow up?

Do you hear something?

"Both sentences have spaces between the words."
"That's true. We know to use spaces between our words when we write, too. What else?"
"They both have that mark we talked about yesterday."
"Hmm. Can you come point to the mark? Yes! We call that a question mark. Why do both sentences have question marks?"

When ready, revisit the focus phrase, repeating it together: *I end my questions with a question mark.*

Invitation
to
IMITATE
TOGETHER

Interactive Writing

Revisit the mentor text and read the question aloud together: "What do you want to be when you grow up?" Brainstorm a list of possible careers, and choose one to illustrate and surround with questions.

For example, if the class chooses a firefighter, draw the firefighter and record questions students might ask a firefighter:

- What do firefighters wear?
- Do you have a dog?
- Is your truck red?

Choose students to come up to add the question mark to the end of each question. This is a great activity to prepare for career day or a guest speaker.

A kindergarten class had lots of questions for a visiting firefighter!

Patterns of Wonder Time

On large piece of construction paper, students use the interactive writing piece as a model to continue with their own page about what they want to be when they grow up, surrounding their illustration with questions they would ask someone in that role.

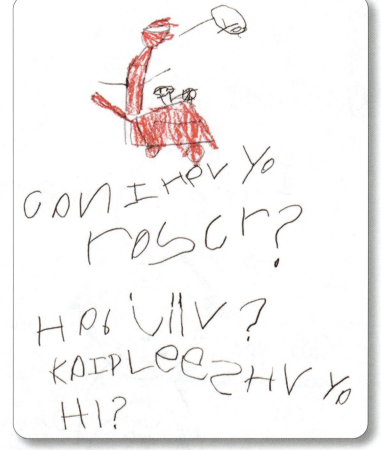

This young writer wants to be a race car driver when he grows up. Some questions he would ask a race car driver include: "Can I have your race car? How fast do you drive? Can I please try on your helmet?"

Literacy Station

Leave *How to Be a T. Rex* and other texts that use questions marks in the station for students to explore. They can use small sticky notes to mark the pages where they see question marks and discuss how the authors used these marks in both sentences and speech bubbles. Through this exploration, they are likely to discover other end marks as well.

Choice Time

Post chart paper near a window and title it "What Do You Wonder?" Students record their wonderings about the world on sticky notes and add them to the chart. Their wonderings can be in both pictures and words, using a question mark at the end.

For more ideas on using centers and areas in your room to hold wonder that inspires deeper meaning in both reading and writing, check out Georgia Heard's and Jennifer McDonough's professional text, *A Place for Wonder: Reading and Writing Nonfiction in the Primary Grades* (2009).

Invitation to SHARE and CELEBRATE	As partnerships of writers share their imitations they worked on during *Patterns of Wonder* time, the audience makes facial expressions that show what the question marks tell us as readers: questioning looks, looks of wonder, looks of confusion. For fun, encourage the group to use their whole body to accompany their questioning faces like shrugging their shoulders, bending forward, and spreading their arms out with palms up.

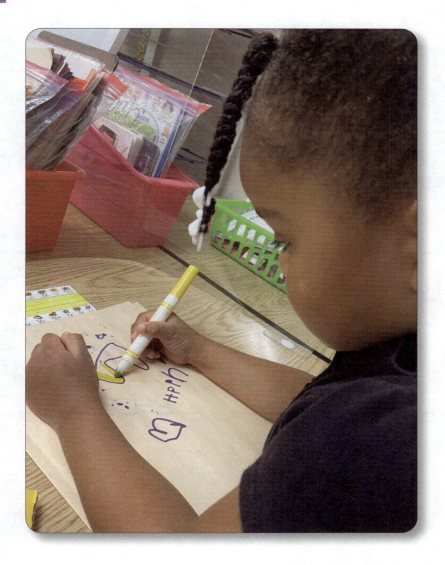

2.10 Are All School Buses Yellow? Adjectives Tell What Kind

Standards and Connections	Teacher Considerations	Texts
Standard Use frequently occurring adjectives. **Companion Lessons** • Lesson 1.5 • Lesson 3.13 • Lesson 4.12 	Because students are learning that letters have sounds and are formed a certain way, it's important that we still build on students' oral language while also inviting them to add to their illustrations. We invite them to include details that show what kind in their illustrations and tell what kind through their oral rehearsal. Many will likely attempt some writing as well, though their writing may not yet look conventional.	*The King of Kindergarten* Written by Derrick Barnes and illustrated by Vanessa Brantley-Newton **Alternative Titles** *Freight Train* Written and illustrated by Donald Crews *Truman* Written by Jean Reidy and illustrated by Lucy Ruth Cummins *Maybe Something Beautiful: How Art Transformed a Neighborhood* Written by F. Isabel Campoy and Theresa Howell and illustrated by Rafael López

Focus Phrase ❝ I show and tell what kind. ❞

A note about adjective stacking . . .

Sometimes, authors stack adjectives as Derrick Barnes did in his sentence about the big yellow carriage from *The King of Kindergarten.* When students figure this out, they may overdo it a bit. Relax. That's how they gain fluency. This is the time writers are allowed to overdo it in both oral and written language.

Invitation to WONDER

Show the entire spread from the page with the yellow school bus as you read it aloud: "Then a big yellow carriage will deliver you to a grand fortress."

It's important that students see the picture as you read, since this will support them in what they are doing in their own writing (adding to their pictures). Begin the discussion probing, "What do you wonder?" Students may wonder about the vocabulary such as *carriage*. Use this wondering to move into a conversation about the picture, "Hmm, what could be the carriage here? Oh, the bus! What kind of bus? Yes, a big yellow bus. The kids ride in a big yellow bus. What else do you notice in the picture? What kind of . . . ? We could say . . ." When the conversation leads to the focus phrase, reveal it and repeat it with students: *I show and tell what kind.*

Invitation to COMPARE and CONTRAST

Choose another page from *The King of Kindergarten* (or another class favorite) that includes a detailed illustration, possibly paired with a descriptive sentence, and share with your students. As they begin to compare and contrast the pictures, support their oral language development of using adjectives by asking, "What kind of . . ." and then create an oral sentence about the picture: "We could say . . ."

When comparing and contrasting two pages from the same book, you may consider taking a picture of one to display on your whiteboard, while holding the other page open in your hand for comparison. You might also choose a page from another book that has a picture that will invite conversation around adjectives that show what kind, holding both books up side by side. See the alternative titles at the beginning of each lesson for suggestions.

Invitation to IMITATE TOGETHER

Interactive Writing

As a class, brainstorm some possible people, places, or things and draw quick pictures of them. Then add details to the drawing that illustrate what kind. Label the picture or compose a sentence using adjectives that tell what kind.

A writer labels the picture with adjectives that tell what kind during interactive writing.

Patterns of Wonder Time

On blank paper, students draw pictures using adjectives that tell what kind. Encourage them to write what they might say about the pictures, knowing their writing will most likely be letter strings or symbols.

This student drew a red truck and wrote the letters of the sounds he heard in the word that tells what kind (red).

Writing Workshop

Revisit the focus phrase. Students revise their writing and pictures by adding details that show and tell what kind. During share time, students show a partner where they added these details.

Students share their pictures in small groups or with partners. Encourage them to use storytelling language to explain what is in the picture and the adjectives they included. Choose a few students to share their work with the whole group. Create a slideshow with images of everyone's writing for students to thumb through on their tablets during independent reading.

Invitation to PLAY

Invitation to SHARE and CELEBRATE

2.11 — *Five* Fingers, *One* Hand; *Ten* Toes, *Two* Feet: Adjectives Show and Tell How Many

Standards and Connections	Teacher Considerations	Texts
Standard Use frequently occurring adjectives. **Companion Lessons** • Lesson 1.6 • Lesson 3.14 • Lesson 4.13 	Since students are learning that letters have sounds and are formed a certain way, it's important that we still ground lessons in ample oral language, while also inviting students to add to their illustrations. We use details that show and tell how many in their illustrations as well as tell and show how many through their oral rehearsal as they read their words or symbols. In this phase, we also remind writers that how many can go beyond numbers to include adjectives like *many*, *few*, and *lots*.	*Bone by Bone* Written by Sara Levine and illustrated by T.S Spookytooth **Alternative Titles** *Chicken Break!* Written by Cate Berry and illustrated by Charlotte Alder *Bird Watch* Written and illustrated by Christie Matheson *Pete the Cat and His Four Groovy Buttons* Written by Eric Litwin and illustrated by James Dean

Focus Phrase ❝   I show and tell how many.   ❞

A note about adjectives . . .

Adjectives can show and tell how many, what kind, and which one. This lesson focuses on how many; however, students' conversations will likely include some other types of adjectives. Accept all answers and don't feel you need to make the distinction unless a student asks. "Wow! You just discovered another type of adjective."

Invitation to WONDER

This nonfiction book is useful as a mentor text because it uses adjectives that tell how many in a question-and-answer format. Thus, the book models how to use adjectives that tell how many, but it also gives writers an opportunity to play with a specific text structure. Choose a question-and-answer page spread to read aloud from this book. We like the one that asks, "What kind of animal would you be if you had only two fingers on each hand and two toes on each foot?" Students reveal their curiosity when you ask, "What do you wonder?" As they share their thinking about the pictures and the words, honor what they say, and name it by discussing what the illustrator or author did and why they did it. When students mention the number two either in the words or in the picture, invite them to hold up two fingers or find the two fingers or two toes in the picture. Reveal the focus phrase: *I show and tell how many.*

Invitation to COMPARE and CONTRAST

Create another question-and-answer page about an animal. Feel free to use the following example as a guide. Ask students to compare and contrast the two texts. They may wonder if the animal in the second example is real. Carry on the conversation of wonder: "Do you think it's real? Why or why not?" When they notice the compare and contrast example has a labeled picture, read the labels together and discuss the words the author used. Revisit the focus phrase when students brush against it.

**Invitation
to
IMITATE
TOGETHER**

Interactive Writing

Together, choose to create a real or made-up animal with a certain number of parts, and label the parts using words that show and tell how many. At the bottom of the picture, record a sentence that tells what the class wants to call the animal. This page will be the start to a class book. A template is available at the end of this lesson.

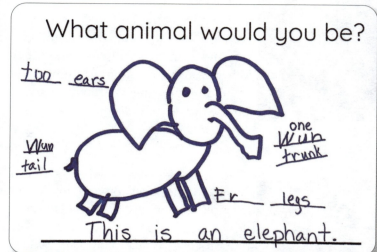

This class chose to write about an elephant, labeling its parts to tell how many.

Patterns of Wonder Time

Students make up their own animal and use the class book template—if they choose. They draw a picture and label it showing and telling how many. Some students may also choose to add a sentence to the bottom of the picture, using symbols and letters or whatever type of writing they demonstrate at this time.

Choice Time

Students count items in their workstations (e.g., pens in the writing station, cubes in the math station, blocks in the building station) and orally compose sentences about the items using words that show and tell how many.

**Invitation
to
PLAY**

This child chose to play with cubes in a math tub. When asked about his construction, he said, "I have eleven blocks."

Invitation
to
SHARE
and
CELEBRATE

Invite another class or the principal to listen in on the sharing of the class book, each writer sharing their page, focusing on the words and pictures that show and tell how many.

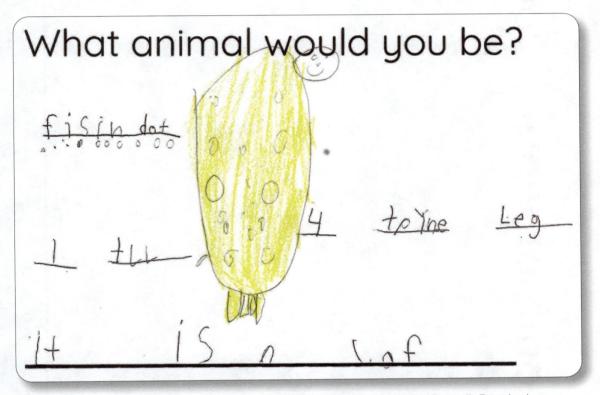

Cal chose to write about a giraffe, using words to tell how many: "Fifteen dots. One tail. Four tiny legs. It is a giraffe."

What animal would you be?

_____

2.12   In the Classroom: Prepositions Tell Where

Standards and Connections	Teacher Considerations	Texts
Standard	To continue our support in the Symbol and Letter Writing phase, we pay attention to the letters students use and what they do with those letters. Do they label their pictures with letters? Do they write sentences with those letters through letter strings? As we build upon their oral rehearsal toward transitional writing, the goal in this lesson is for writers to orally practice words that tell where, such as *under the tree*, *by the bed*, or *inside the house* and show these details in their illustrations.	*A Squiggly Story* Written by Andrew Larsen and illustrated by Mike Lowery 
Use frequently occurring prepositions.		
Companion Lessons		**Alternative Titles**
• Lesson 1.7		*Can I Be Your Dog?* Written and illustrated by Troy Cummings
• Lesson 3.15		*A New Home* Written and illustrated by Tania de Regil
• Lesson 4.15		*The King of Kindergarten* Written by Derrick Barnes and illustrated by Vanessa Brantley-Newton

Focus Phrase   I show and tell where.

A note about using your surroundings to teach prepositions . . .

When teaching prepositions, it's good to use your surroundings or a student as a reference for authentic conversations: "Where are we now?" (**on** the playground, **in** the library, etc.) Where is Jacob? (*He's* **at** home sick, **at** the end of the line, **next** *to me,* **by** *me, etc.*) Model as needed, especially to share new prepositions. If the kids are into it, teach them "Top of the World" by the Carpenters.

Display the pages from *A Squiggly Story* pictured here (and included at the end of this lesson) and read them aloud. It's important that students see the pictures as you read, since this will support them as they add to the pictures and words in their writing. Prompt the invitation with "Let's take a close look at this picture. What do you wonder?" No matter what they wonder, honor their thoughts, and ask them point out what makes them think this way. Discuss why the illustrator may have included what they note. When they discover the details that help tell where, share the focus phrase and continue the discussion ("What else helps us show where in this picture? Let's use these details to tell more"), leading to descriptions such as *The boy is sitting in Mrs. Singh's chair.* Or *The kids are on the rug.* Or *Mrs. Signh is standing next to the chalkboard.*

If you want to add the word *preposition* to the focus phrase, you can do so whenever you feel your students are ready. This is a teacher's choice. So feel free to shift over to *I show and tell with prepositions* as you feel comfortable. A word of caution, though. Try not to make this about memorizing the term. Instead, focus on the work prepositions do and the effect they have.

Invitation to COMPARE and CONTRAST

Select a page from another picture book that shows a setting with lots of possibilities for discussing where. We like to revisit the picture from Troy Cummings's *Can I Be Your Dog?* that we use in Lesson 2.5 about nouns in this phase.

As students compare and contrast the picture from *A Squiggly Story* to that of another book like *Can I Be Your Dog?* let their conversations lead the way to learning and discovery. They may notice the children or people in both pictures. They may notice that one example takes place *outside* a house or *in* the yard while the other takes place *at* school. Honor their noticings and name what they see. When the conversation lends itself to the focus phrase, move in that direction. "So, where are these children? *In* the backyard or *outside* the house? What about these children? *At* school? *In* the classroom? Yes! All of these phrases you're using tell where! Let's take a look at our focus phrase and read it together. What else shows and tells *where* in both of these pictures?"

Interactive Writing

Choose another picture from *A Squiggly Story* or a class favorite to display under a document camera or tape to chart paper. With their partner, students orally share some sentences that tell where things are in the picture, pointing them out as they do. Write some of the prepositions they use or point them out on your word wall to showcase them. Choose some students to come up and label the picture with some prepositional phrases on sticky notes or directly on the chart paper to show and tell where. In an interactive way, have students write the prepositions while you write the rest of the words in each label.

Invitation
to
IMITATE
TOGETHER

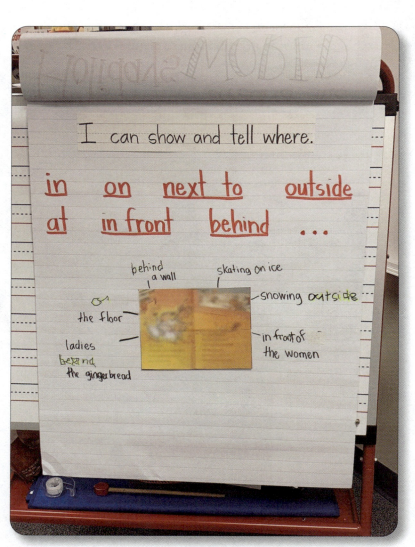

Ms. Peña taped a class favorite to chart paper and invited her students to show and tell where when labeling it.

Patterns of Wonder Time

On sentence strips, write some prepositions that are also sight words: *in, to, by, at, on, into.* Using these words as models, partners walk around the room making labels on sticky notes to show and tell where. For example, one pair of students might put a sticky note on the hall pass that hangs *on the hook*. Keep in mind that, beyond these sight word prepositions, their labels may show letter strings or a series of symbols rather than conventional spellings.

Writing Workshop

When checking in with writers, ask them to share with you how they show and tell where in their writing. Nudge them to include preposition words in their writing, pointing them out on your anchor charts or your word wall as you confer.

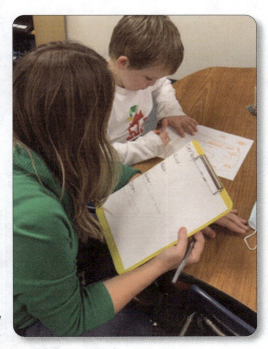

A student adds to his picture to show where during a writing conference.

Invitation to PLAY

Students choose a piece of writing created during writing workshop in which they added details to show and tell where. While sharing with the class, they point to their details. To provide positive feedback to each writer, name what they did to indicate where and talk about its effect. When we celebrate an effort with positive specific feedback like this, writers walk away with confidence to keep doing it.

A student shows and tells where as she shares her writing during the celebration.

Invitation to SHARE and CELEBRATE

2.13   Dare to Use Joining Words: Conjunctions

Standards and Connections	Teacher Considerations	Texts
Standard Use frequently occurring conjunctions. *Companion Lessons* • Lesson 1.8 • Lesson 3.16 • Lesson 4.16 	Students are beginning to add symbols to represent letters and words to their writing, so we continue to support their conversations and support the addition of details to their pictures to explain more. We invite them to *show* more by adding to their pictures and *tell* more by using joining words like *but* and *and* through oral rehearsal of their stories and other texts. This play with conjunctions gives emergent writers a chance to experiment with composing and expanding complete sentences orally, without demanding perfection.	*Dare to Dream Big* Written by Lorna Gutierrez and illustrated by Polly Noakes **Alternative Titles** *Scribble Stones* Written and illustrated by Diane Alber *Never Let a Unicorn Scribble* Written and illustrated by Diane Alber *The Magical Yet* Written by Angela DiTerlizzi and illustrated by Lorena Alvarez

Focus Phrase   I show and tell more with words like *but* and *and*.

A note about the conjunctions *but* and *and* . . .

Our focus in this lesson is to explore using *but* or *and* to add more detail. Both words may be conjunctions (joining or connecting words), but they serve two different functions. The joining word *but* shows contrast or opposition while *and* is adding on. Don't try to force this distinction. Some writers may note it, and you can talk about it, knowing that the end goal is function over identification.

Invitation to WONDER

Share the page spread seen here, also included at the end of this lesson, from *Dare to Dream Big*. Invite students to wonder and observe, nudging them to lead the conversation with their ideas. As individual students respond, encourage them to extend their comments with the use of conjunctions.

"I wonder if that little boy will pick that yellow flower."

"Hmm, what do you think his mom would say if he picked the flower?"

"She would tell him not to."

"Hmm, we could say, 'The little boy wants to pick the flower, *but* his mom will tell him no.' What else do you wonder or notice?"

"I see another little boy is sleeping in the stroller!"

"Oh, that's right. He does seem to be sleeping. How could we say more here? The little boy is sleeping in the stroller *and* . . . ?"

"The little boy is sleeping in the stroller, *and* he is dreaming."

After some time in this oral rehearsal, introduce the focus phrase: *I show and tell more with words like* but *and* and. Then continue with, "What else could we say about the picture?"

Create an example of writing, like the one pictured here, for your students to use during this invitation. Share it alongside the page spread from *Dare to Dream Big*, inviting writers to note similarities and differences between the mentor text and the additional example. When they notice that this example uses other words in the written sentence, read the sentence aloud again, and ask, "Are there any words here that you've seen before?" This conversation will most likely move into the excitement of finding sight words like *I*, *to*, or *the*. Celebrate this discovery and lead them toward the joining word *but*, with a prompt like, "Any other words that we've seen recently?" When discovered, circle the joining word and revisit the focus phrase. Encourage students to continue their comparing and contrasting, moving up and down, following their curiosity party.

 If the joining words *but* and *and* are not yet on your word wall, now would be a good time to add them, so students can start using these commonly used joiners immediately after learning about them.

Shared Writing

Every page in *Dare to Dream Big* lends itself to generating writing, so choose a new page to display. Students look closely at the picture and orally rehearse several sentences using *but* and *and*. Compose at least two sentences about the picture together, so you can model using a different conjunction in each.

> The kids are dancing **and** doing funny things.
>
> Some kids are wearing shoes, **but** others are in socks.
>
> Some of them are wearing long t-shirts, **and** some of them are wearing short t-shirts.

The teacher recorded sentences orally composed by her students about the picture of children dancing from *Dare to Dream Big*.

Patterns of Power Time

Distribute gloriously blank paper to students. They can make a book about whatever they choose, but invite them to try using joining words like *but* and *and* to tell more for their readers.

This writer wrote a book about baking cookies with her mom. She labeled the microwave, the cookies, and her dog, Max. When nudged to use *but* or *and* to tell more, she said, "Cookies are great, *and* I love eating them. The stool is high, *but* I have stairs for it. I like baking cookies with my mom *and* dad."

Writing Center

Stock the writing center with pictures to inspire ideas for bookmaking. Add a canister of craft sticks with a conjunction written on each end (*but, and*). Students choose a picture to orally tell more using the sticks to remind them of what words they can use to expand their sentences. You can easily add to this activity as you introduce more conjunctions later.

Mia Bella uses a craft stick with *but* on one side and *and* on the other to tell about a picture in the writing center. She then chose to write a book about a silly dog.

Invitation
to
PLAY

Students share their writing with each other, emphasizing they can use *but* or *and* to show and tell more. Change up the audience celebration depending on the conjunction:

- *And* = snap
- *But* = jazz hand wave

Dare to see
when others
don't...

2.14 Writers Use Tools: Transition Words to Share Thoughts in Order

Standards and Connections	Teacher Considerations	Texts
Standard Use frequently occurring transition words. **Companion Lessons** • Lesson 1.9 • Lesson 3.17 • Lesson 4.17 	In this lesson, writers move from orally sharing thoughts to making sure their pictures and words show and tell in order. Jamie L. B. Deenihan's *When Grandpa Gives You a Toolbox* is a delightful procedural text to showcase another way authors use transition words. It tells a story, but does so by giving readers ordered steps to follow. We encourage you to read the book prior to this lesson and revisit the first few pages during the Invitation to Wonder.	*When Grandpa Gives You a Toolbox* Written by Jamie L. B. Deenihan and illustrated by Lorraine Rocha **Alternative Titles** *How to Surprise a Dad* Written by Jean Reagan and illustrated by Lee Wildish *The Little Red Fort* Written by Brenda Maier and illustrated by Sonia Sanchez *When Grandma Gives You a Lemon Tree* Written by Jamie L. B. Deenihan and illustrated by Lorraine Rocha

Focus Phrase ❝ I show and tell my thoughts in order. ❞

A note about repeatedly modeling order words . . .

If it seems like you're continually prompting students to use order words for transitions, consider that may just be what it takes. We find creating a wall chart of time-order words and adding to it as we stumble across new ones in other subject areas to be an engaging way to raise awareness and usage. This constant exploration and repetition will pay off eventually.

Begin this invitation by rereading three pages from *When Grandpa Gives You a Toolbox* that show order:

> First, be patient . . .
> Next, compliment Grandpa . . .
> Once Grandpa runs out of stories . . .

Read the pages again, encouraging students to listen carefully to words the author used. Kick off the conversation with our standby, "What do you wonder?" Let the conversation flourish. Place the book under a document camera and zoom in on whatever students bring up. When they notice the word *first*, write it down on a sticky note and say, "Hmm. Let's look to see how the next page starts. Let me write it down for you." Record the sentence on the next page beginning with *Next*. When students notice this word, add it to another sticky note and place both on chart paper. Invite students to think about what both words, *first* and *next*, are telling us, the readers. When they discover that they help tell order in some way, reveal the focus phrase: *I show and tell my thoughts in order.* You may wish to add a few other transition words on sticky notes at this time to extend the conversation about order and establish the beginnings of an anchor chart like the one pictured here.

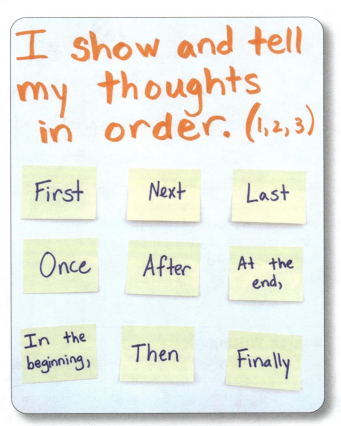

An anchor chart collection with transitions helps young writers think about how to share their thoughts in order.

Invitation
to
WONDER

Invitation to COMPARE and CONTRAST

Create an example piece of writing like the sample at the end of this lesson that shows the order of something such as planting a flower. Display your example underneath your lifted lines from *When Grandpa Gives You a Toolbox*, and invite your students to compare and contrast them.

First, be patient . . .
Next, compliment Grandpa . . .
Once Grandpa runs out of stories . . .

Depending on how many *Patterns of Wonder* lessons you've led with them, writers will most likely make connections to previous learning, like both examples have capital letters or both examples have end marks or periods. Honor these observations, reminding them that writers make these choices each time they write. When the students notice both examples use order words, have them point them out and add *then* and *last* to your anchor chart if they're not there already.

Invitation to IMITATE TOGETHER

Shared Writing

When Grandpa Gives You a Toolbox ends with plans for building a treehouse. Use this idea to compose a few steps together for building a treehouse. Ask students to tell across their fingers what they might say: *first, next, then, finally.* Enjoy their creativity on this one. Record four steps they share, underlining the transition words used.

<table>
<tr><td>

**Invitation
to
PLAY**

</td><td>

Patterns of Power Time

Students choose something they want to build or something they know how to do and create a book that shows a step on each page. They can use the anchor chart, which you've added to throughout this lesson set, to help them write the transition words.

Listening Center

Add index cards to your listening center with a transition word and visual on each card: *first, next, then, finally*. After listening to a book, students use word cards to help retell the story to a partner.

Writing Center

Post a list of transition words in your writing center, giving students easy access to them when making books or writing of any kind.

</td></tr>
</table>

Alex used transition words from the writing center to orally share his teleportation story in order.

<table>
<tr><td>

**Invitation
to
SHARE
and
CELEBRATE**

</td><td>

Students share the steps needed to build or do something that they wrote about during the Invitation to Play/*Patterns of Wonder* time. As they share, students count across their fingers in order each time a new transition word is used.

</td></tr>
</table>

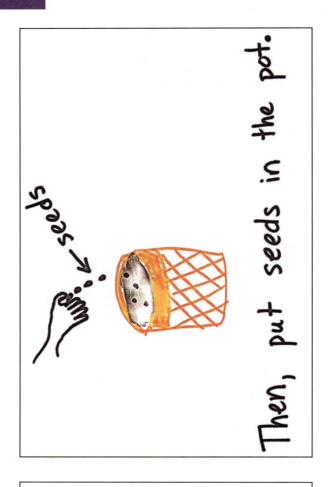

Then, put seeds in the pot.

First, put dirt in the pot.

Last, sprinkle with water.

Transitional Writing

Transitional Writing Phase Behaviors	◗ Labeling pictures using letter sounds ◗ Using letter sounds to write words with invented spelling ◗ Copying words from the room ◗ Beginning to use spaces as word boundaries in sentences ◗ Trying out capitalization and ending punctuation

3.1 The Sound of Words: Use Letters to Record Language and Make Words

Standards and Connections	Teacher Considerations	Texts
Standard Intentionally use marks, symbols, and letters to record language and make words. **Companion Lessons** • Lesson 1.1 • Lesson 2.1 • Lesson 4.1 	As children move from making letter strings in the symbols and letters phase into writing words that represent some letter sounds in the transitional phase, we continue to work with their concepts about print, using this lesson to focus on using letters to make words. The words they make can be found in the labels in their pictures as well as writing on lines in the form of a sentence, although they may not yet use spaces between those words. The reminder that we write with words and pictures still holds true, and we ask them to use both to make meaning for their readers. Be sure to check out the note on the next page to see how this lesson's goal and focus phrase connect to its companion lessons.	*The Box Turtle* Written and illustrated by Vanessa Roeder **Alternative Titles** *Lexie the Word Wrangler* Written by Rebecca Van Slyke and illustrated by Jessie Hartland *Quit Calling Me a Monster!* Written by Jory John and illustrated by Bob Shea *I'm Not a Mouse!* Written and illustrated by Evgenia Golubeva

Focus Phrase I write with words and pictures.

In this lesson, students get to explore how writing with words and pictures doesn't mean just sentences and pictures. The words can be included in speech bubbles and around the picture to denote sounds as in *The Box Turtle.* Labeling is another way to show words and pictures, which writers will discover in future lessons in this phase.

A note about focus phrase visuals . . .

Since this same goal looks different as emergent writers develop, you'll notice the focus phrase for this lesson repeats through its companion lessons—even as the type of writing shifts across their phases. We highlight this shift with accompanying visuals that represent the type of writing children do in each phase.

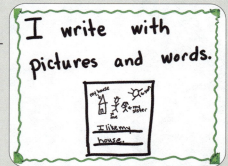

For example, the focus phrase visual for this lesson represents the writing children do in the Transitional Writing phase. Keep in mind that the words in this phase may be a mix of approximated and conventional spelling as students write the letters of the sounds they hear and copy words from around the room. Notice that the visuals for the companion lessons in this thread (1.1, 2.1, and 4.1) change to represent the type of writing students are progressing through.

Invitation to WONDER	Vanessa Roeder's *The Box Turtle* is full of pages with speech bubbles and sound words (onomatopoeia) as well as simple narration and pictures. Choose a page that you feel your students will enjoy and be eager to share their wonderings about. Display the page and enjoy the conversation that it prompts. When students notice the variety of words and pictures, reveal the focus phrase and repeat it together.
Invitation to COMPARE and CONTRAST	Choose a page with simple words and pictures from another picture book to display alongside the mentor text page. This second picture book can be a class favorite or one from the alternative titles. When comparing and contrasting, students may notice that the mentor text uses sound words and the other text does not. Or maybe both texts use speech bubbles. Whatever children notice, honor it and take time to engage writers in a conversation of curiosity and discovery. When the time is right to revisit the focus phrase, repeat it together.

Interactive Writing

Using the page you chose as your mentor text, brainstorm some ideas for a class piece of writing. Who will the characters be? Will there be speech bubbles, and if so, what might they say? Will there be sound words? After orally brainstorming some ideas, compose a page with both pictures and words, inviting children to write the words with you.

This writer begins to label the pictures in the class composition during interactive writing.

Invitation to PLAY

Writing Workshop

Revisit the focus phrase each day as students make books: *I write with words and pictures.* When talking about their books, writers point to their words as they read their writing.

Small-Group Instruction

Through interactive writing, create a book together using both words and pictures. It can be a simple story or an informational book teaching others about something your students know well.

Invitation to SHARE and CELEBRATE

Students sit in a whole-group circle, each standing up in turn to share one of their books, pointing to the words as they read them. This celebration may be spread across multiple days so that every child gets to share. Provide feedback during the share by highlighting when the writer used the focus phrase.

3.2 Letter Sounds Are No Accident: Letter-Sound Correspondence

Standards and Connections	Teacher Considerations	Texts
Standard Demonstrate and apply phonetic knowledge by identifying and matching the common sounds that letters represent. **Companion Lesson** • Lesson 2.2 	In this phase of writing, students continue to work hard to stretch out words, writing letters that match the sounds they hear. They also use words from around the room and ones they've locked into memory from reading. This lesson builds on this development with Andrea Tsurumi's use of single words in *Accident!* Making words is fun, and this lesson invites emergent writers' playful experimentation with spelling and stretching out words.	*Accident!* Written and illustrated by Andrea Tsurumi **Alternative Titles** *The Nuts: Keep Rolling* Written by Eric Litwin and illustrated by Scott Magoon *Jack Blasts Off!* Written by Mac Barnett and illustrated by Greg Pizzoli *LMNO Peas* Written and illustrated by Keith Baker

Focus Phrase ❝ I write the letters of the sounds I hear. ❞

A note about repeating this lesson . . .

The work children do with writing words is a process that grows as they learn more and more about letters, their sounds, and how letters work together to make more sounds. This lesson can be repeated as needed throughout the year. Just choose a different book from our alternative list or your classroom library and you're ready to go!

Invitation to WONDER

Display the page pictured here from *Accident!* and read it aloud together. Students will enjoy the playfulness of this text. As they begin to wonder, honor their thinking and let them lead your conversation about the choices Tsurumi made. When students bring the conversation to the words on the page, stop at the ones they point out and read them together again. Then stretch out each word as you read it, modeling the thinking you do when you read and write it. Repeat with a few other words from the book and reveal the focus phrase: *I write the letters of the sounds I hear.*

This page spread from *Accident!* is included at the end of this lesson.

Invitation to COMPARE and CONTRAST

Select a page from any book that uses sentences with words that are simple enough to stretch out. You might also consider words from your word wall or patterns your writers know or can relate to other words. We've shared a page from Tina Kügler's *Snail and Worm* here as an example, but check out our alternative titles for other recommendations. Display this page alongside the page from *Accident!* and invite your students to share with one another similarities and differences. They will probably notice that one text uses speech bubbles and the other doesn't. Remind them that this is the author's choice, and then ask, "What do you see is the same?" A common response is "They both have words!" Honor this, and continue the conversation around the words, stretching them out and making connections to the sounds, other words they know that sound like them, and even the sight words that may also be on your word wall. Cycle back to the focus phrase, "So writers, no matter how we write our words—in speech bubbles or in sentences or even labels—read it with me: *I write the letters of the sounds I hear.*"

This page spread from *Snail and Worm* is also included at the end of this lesson.

Invitation to IMITATE TOGETHER

Interactive Writing

Choose a toy, like a ball or stuffed animal, or even a game, for the class to write about. Orally brainstorm some things you could say about the toy or game, and choose one sentence to write together, focusing on stretching out the words and writing the letters of the sounds heard. On individual dry erase boards, have students write the words as they stretch them out with you.

Invitation to PLAY

Patterns of Wonder Time

Who doesn't love toys and games? Continue writing with students about toys or games. Students can bring them from home or show a picture. They'll have a lot to say about their favorites, so give them plenty of time to write it all down, listening for the sounds of the letters as they work.

Writing Workshop

In pairs, students go back over their writing, touching each word as they read their piece to their partner. Then they work together to pick a few words to stretch out, helping each other to check for the letters of the sounds they hear.

Literacy Station

Students create an ABC wall, choosing a letter and writing as many words as they can that begin with that letter. As they write each word, encourage them to do the best they can to stretch it out and write the letters of the sounds they hear. Though writers may not produce perfect spelling here, we celebrate their efforts and thinking!

A kindergartner writes words for her chosen letter on the ABC wall.

Invitation to SHARE and CELEBRATE

Students participate in a quick show-and-tell as they tell the class about the toy or game of their choice and then share their piece of writing about it. If the class has questions about the toy or game that aren't answered in the writing, encourage writers to add more during their next workshop time. Take a picture of the items and display them alongside their correlating pieces in the hallway.

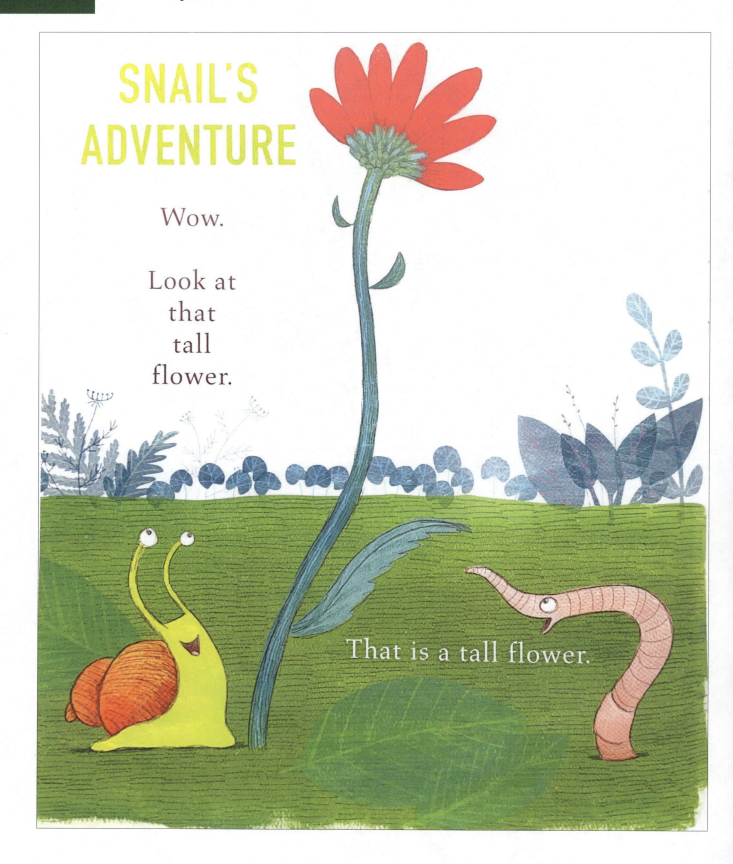

3.3   Be a Sentence Citizen: Use Words to Make Sentences

Standards and Connections	Teacher Considerations	Texts
Standard Recognize that sentences are comprised of words. **Companion Lessons** • Lesson 1.2 • Lesson 2.3 	As writers learn that letters make words and words make sentences, we continue to nudge our students to record their sentences on paper, and in this phase, their writing begins to include sentences that we can generally read without their help. We chose Dave Eggers's *What Can a Citizen Do?* for this lesson because the sentences are simple and can be imitated by emergent writers without too much support. Throughout the year, if students need additional work in using words to make sentences, repeat this lesson with another book of your choice.	*What Can a Citizen Do?* Written by Dave Eggers and illustrated by Shawn Harris **Alternative Titles** *Lexie the Word Wrangler* Written by Rebecca Van Slyke and illustrated by Jessie Hartland *The Itchy Book* Written and illustrated by Leuyen Pham *Rex Wrecks It* Written and illustrated by Ben Clanton

Focus Phrase   ❝   I write words to make sentences.   ❞

A note about complete sentences . . .

This lesson also lays the foundation for conversations your writers will have in the upper grades about complete sentences. Since the idea of complete sentences is a more sophisticated standard, we don't see it as appropriate for most emergent writers. If, however, your writers are ready to dip their toes into this water now or later in the year, check out the lessons in our companion book, *Patterns of Power* (2017).

Invitation to WONDER

Ahead of time, read aloud *What Can a Citizen Do?* and revisit this sentence during your Invitation to Wonder.

A citizen can plant a tree.

Read the sentence aloud together and ask your students to look closely at what the author did here. What do they wonder? What do they see? As students share their thinking, varying from mentioning sight words to wondering about the tree included in the accompanying illustration, enjoy their curiosity and conversations. Invite them up to point to the word, letter, or anything else that helps them share their thinking and consider together why the author chose to include it. When a word, any word, is noticed, bridge this into a conversation about words. "Do you see other words? How many? Hmm, let's count. This is a sentence. Writers use words to make sentences. How many words did Dave Eggers use to make this sentence? What words did he use?" After a study of words within the sentence, reveal the focus phrase, repeating it twice.

Invitation to COMPARE and CONTRAST

Choose another sentence from *What Can a Citizen Do?* or from another class favorite and record it under the mentor sentence used in the Invitation to Wonder. Read both sentences aloud and open the conversation up for exploration through comparing and contrasting the choices the author made in each sentence. As students note that both sentences use words, stop to count the words and revisit the focus phrase.

Invitation to IMITATE TOGETHER

Interactive Writing

This lesson is a wonderful opportunity to bring your class together as a group of citizens. Orally brainstorm what citizens of the classroom can do, and record students' thinking in a list on chart paper. Choose one thing from the list to write an imitation sentence of the mentor text. Say the sentence aloud, across your fingers, counting the words you will use. Add lines to your chart paper as place holders for the words, and chorally say the sentence again while you point to each line. Students help you compose the sentence by coming up to write the words while the others write the sentence on their dry erase boards.

Adding lines to hold the places of words helps students compose sentences during interactive writing.

A citizen can _____.

When the sentence is finished, read it aloud together, pointing to each word. Count the words one more time, and repeat the focus phrase: *I write words to make sentences.*

Invitation to PLAY

Patterns of Wonder **Time**

Students think about what they can do as a citizen of the classroom and compose a sentence about it on white paper. Invite them to illustrate it as well. These imitations can be displayed on a wall or even turned into a class book about citizenship.

Literacy Station

Select a page from a familiar book with a handful of simple sentences on the page. Students explore the page, counting how many words are in each sentence. As they work, they keep track of their counts, looking for the longest sentence.

Shared Reading

After reading a book, go back to explore how its words made sentences. What do you notice at the beginning of a sentence? At the end? Have individual students come up to model putting their left pointer finger at the beginning and their right pointer finger at the end to frame the sentence. Then count together how many words the author used to make this sentence. Repeat this process a few times. Once readers know how to frame a sentence, send them off to continue this exploration around the room or in other books.

Invitation to SHARE and CELEBRATE

Invite the principal or the custodian to sit in as students present their citizen writing from the Invitation to Play/*Patterns of Wonder* time. After each student has shared, revisit the focus phrase, showing the guest that we are celebrating how the words in our sentences tell about the responsibilities of citizenship.

3.4   Space Matters: Use Spaces Between Words

Standards and Connections	Teacher Considerations	Texts
Standard Understand that words are separated by spaces in print. **Companion Lessons** Repeat this lesson with another text at any time. 	As children begin to write words in a representational sentence, we introduce the convention of separating words with spaces. Most likely, you've already started talking with students about concepts about print during shared reading and writing experiences: letters make words, words make sentences, and those words and sentences have boundaries. We absolutely love B.J. Novak's *The Book with No Pictures* because it's interactive, silly, and just plain fun to read aloud to young children. We highly recommend you read aloud the entire book prior to this lesson.	*The Book with No Pictures* Written by B.J. Novak **Alternative Titles** *We Are in a Book* (an Elephant and Piggie book) Written and illustrated by Mo Willems *I Don't Want to Be Big* Written by Dev Petty and illustrated by Mike Boldt *Duck, Duck, Porcupine!* Written and illustrated by Salina Yoon

Focus Phrase   ❝   I use spaces between my words.   ❞

A note about repeating a lesson with a different mentor text . . .

Repeat this lesson as often as needed for students who need to revisit using spaces between their words or to support writers any time throughout the year. Just choose a different book from the list of alternatives or your classroom library and you're all set.

Your students will enjoy the interactive features and silliness of this read-aloud. You can choose a page to share or use the sentence we've chosen below and invite them to reread the sentence with you as you point to the words.

Yes, I am a monkey.

Observe your students' curiosity around the author's craft when you ask, "What do you wonder? What do you see? What do you notice?" Let your writers take you on the journey of their noticings. If they don't notice the spaces, you might ask, "How many words does this sentence have? How do you know? Let's count them again." As this conversation moves toward the focus phrase, be ready to reveal it: *I use spaces between my words.*

A kindergartner points to her noticing in *The Book with No Pictures.*

Invitation to COMPARE and CONTRAST

Choose another sentence from *The Book with No Pictures* to compare and contrast. We like the very next sentence because it's always fun to change our voices! If you have the book in your hands, show the two-page spread so students can also compare and contrast the shapes of the letters, as they represent a robot's voice in the second example.

Yes, I am a monkey.

Also, I am a robot monkey.

Students may notice that both pages use the color orange or both use the word *monkey*. They may even notice the slightest difference in the shape of the period on each page: one is a circle and one is a square. This could lead to the shapes of the words on each page with the second page's font representing a robot's voice. Take all of this conversation and curiosity in. Writers are learning craft moves that they might decide to try in their own writing. When they notice that both sentences use spaces between the words, revisit the focus phrase: *I use spaces between my words.*

Invitation to IMITATE TOGETHER

Interactive Writing

Choose a sentence to write together as a class. This sentence could be about something happening at school, something that you are learning about in science or social studies, or even a sentence about the student of the week. Rehearse the sentence aloud several times, counting each word across your fingers as you say it. As each student comes up to write a word of the sentence, model how to use your index finger to hold the spaces between the words you write. Students practice using their finger to hold spaces on their individual dry erase boards as well.

Ms. Anderson shows students how to use a finger as a space marker between words during interactive writing.

Patterns of Wonder Time

Give each student a popsicle stick to use as a space holder as another option to their finger. Students write in their freewrite journals, using spaces between their words.

Shared Reading or Reading the Room

Students use pointers to touch each word they read, noticing the spaces between them. They can also count each word they see as a way to highlight the purpose of spaces as word boundaries.

Writing Workshop

Revisit the focus phrase as students make books each day. Children will be excited to use their space holders. When conferring with writers, use the focus phrase as a conferring point rather than trying to tackle everything at once in the piece of writing. "Our focus phrase is *I use spaces between my words*. Will you show me where you've used spaces?"

Invitation

to

PLAY

This writer uses a space holder to help her put spaces between her words during writing workshop.

Students select one piece of writing where they have used spaces between their words and leave it on their desks or tables. Invite your writers to wander the room, noticing each student's writing and pointing to the spaces they see.

This writer shows his teacher how he used spaces between his words.

3.5 The Name Game: Capitalize Names

Standards and Connections	Teacher Considerations	Texts
Standard Capitalize the first letter of a name. *Companion Lessons* • Lesson 2.4 • Lesson 4.2 • Lesson 4.3 	As writers in the transitional phase move beyond capitalizing every letter refining their grasp of the difference between a lowercase and uppercase letter, we continue to show them how to write their names in a conventional fashion.	*Alma and How She Got Her Name* Written and illustrated by Juana Martinez-Neal **Alternative Titles** *My Name Is Not Alexander* Written by Jennifer Fosberry and illustrated by Mike Litwin *A Piglet Named Mercy* Written by Kate DiCamillo and illustrated by Chris Van Dusen *Hello, My Name Is Ruby* Written and illustrated by Philip C. Stead

Focus Phrase ❝ I begin names with a capital letter. ❞

A note about using capital letters . . .

As writers begin to differentiate between upper- and lowercase letters, it's good to start talking to them about the fact that most letters they write will be in lowercase. They will only use capital letters for a purpose, like capitalizing names or beginning a sentence. Eventually, after teaching your collection of capitalization standards, you may decide to shift your focus phrase to an inclusive one: *I only use capital letters when I need them.*

Invitation to WONDER

Prior to this lesson, read aloud and enjoy *Alma and How She Got Her Name*. This lovely book helps emergent writers think about the beauty of the stories behind names. Since the focus of this lesson is on capitalization, to prompt students' noticing of upper- and lowercase letters, rewrite the model sentence below on chart paper.

I am Candela!

When students notice the name, discuss the difference between the uppercase and lowercase letters. Through this discovery, reveal the focus phrase: *I begin names with a capital letter.*

Invitation to COMPARE and CONTRAST

Create an illustrated example of a person, with a sentence using their name included, like the example here, and display it next to the mentor text page. Read each sentence aloud with the students, pointing to each word. Invite students to compare and contrast the choices the authors made with each example.

I am Candela!

Because labeling is also a focus in this phase of writing, this compare and contrast piece includes labels along with its imitation sentence.

The compare and contrast example can be created on chart paper or an interactive whiteboard. For remote learning, it can be created on a whiteboard shared on the screen.

Interactive Writing

As a class, compose an "I am . . ." sentence about a book character, class pet, or school mascot using their first name and create a labeled picture to tell more.

This class composed a page about a favorite character.

Invitation to PLAY

Patterns of Wonder Time

Each student creates a class book page with their own imitation of the mentor sentence using their name. Encourage them to label their illustrations to nudge more writing. Although some writers may choose the safety and familiarity of the "I am . . ." format, they most certainly can innovate and write what they choose.

Writing Workshop

When including names in their writing, writers repeat the focus phrase, remembering to begin the names with capital letters. When conferring with writers, ask them to show you where they used names and discuss their decision to use capital letters.

Invitation to SHARE and CELEBRATE

Writers share a piece of writing where they wrote their name or the name of someone else, pointing out where they used capital letters. Classmates stretch to the sky whenever a capital letter is pointed out.

A note about upper- and lowercase letters . . .

Did you ever wonder where the terms *uppercase* and *lowercase* originated? Hundreds of years ago, printers of newspapers and books had to put every letter on a part of the printing press. The printers had a case of wooden or metal letters to use. The case was divided into two parts: the upper case and the lower case. The lower half housed the letters we know as lowercase, while the other half of the case, on the upper side, housed, you guessed it, capital letters. *Uppercase* and *capital* have become synonymous. There isn't a new balancing term for lowercase. We only have one term for the letters found in the lower case.

A printer's case housed capital letters in the upper section and lowercase letters in the lower section.

3.6   Off to a Good Start: Begin Sentences with Capital Letters

Standards and Connections	Teacher Considerations	Texts
Standard Capitalize the first letter in a sentence. **Companion Lesson** • Lesson 4.4 	Most likely, you've already been having conversations about the use of capital letters during shared reading and writing experiences around concepts about print. We use this lesson to move from recognizing capital letters in our reading to using capital letters intentionally in our writing. This lesson could be done with just about any book, but we really like Sherman Alexie's *Thunder Boy Jr.* because it also has a focus on names and culture, something that your emergent writers are probably now very familiar with. We recommend reading this book in its entirety during your read-aloud time prior to focusing this lesson on one sentence from it.	*Thunder Boy Jr.* Written by Sherman Alexie and illustrated by Yuyi Morales **Alternative Titles** *Mommy's Khimar* Written by Jamilah Thompkins-Bigelow and illustrated by Ebony Glenn *Words and Your Heart* Written and illustrated by Kate Jane Neal *The Word Collector* Written and illustrated by Peter H. Reynolds

Focus Phrase   I start my sentence with a capital letter.

A note of capital importance . . .

When we capitalize the first word of a sentence, we telegraph to our reader visually that something new is starting. That uppercase letter that starts names and sentences is usually where young children start exploring capitalization. Thus, we tend to focus on these more than other capitalization skills as they are both used most every time an emergent writer composes.

Invitation to WONDER

Write the following mentor sentence on chart paper so writers can focus on one sentence rather than the entire page with several sentences and an illustration.

My dog likes to chase his tail.

Read the sentence aloud together and ask, "What do you wonder?" As writers share their noticings, honor them and discuss the author's choices. When they notice that one letter is different from the rest, discuss what that capital letter does, reveal the focus phrase, and repeat it together: *I start my sentence with a capital letter.*

Invitation to COMPARE and CONTRAST

For this invitation, we use another sentence from *Thunder Boy Jr.*, but this one also includes a name because we want to challenge writers to think more about capitals and their purpose. Record the new sentence below the mentor sentence and ask your students, "What do you notice is the same? What's different?"

My dog likes to chase his tail.

My mom wanted to name me Sam.

Through conversation and discovery, students discuss that both sentences use the sight word *my*. This is a great time to simply talk about how authors use this word to show something belonging to *me*. "My what?" Continue the discovery with "What else?" When students notice that one sentence has one capital letter and the other sentence has two, talk about the purpose of each. This discovery can lead to a possible review of an earlier focus phrase (*I begin names with a capital letter*) and the introduction of the current focus phrase, *I start my sentence with a capital letter*, as students begin to see that we use capital letters for different reasons.

Invitation to IMITATE TOGETHER

Shared Writing

Using the content from the mentor text as your model, orally brainstorm a list of things and animals that belong to you. The children will enjoy learning more about you this way. Choose one to write about starting the sentence with *My* and making the focus the capital letter at the beginning. If your students decide they also want a name included and it fits, honor their choices as writers.

Invitation to PLAY

Patterns of Wonder Time

Students think of things that belong to them and choose one to write a sentence about, checking to make sure that the sentence begins with a capital letter. They compose their sentence on sentence strips and then use a marker, the color of their choice, to trace over the capital letter at the beginning of the sentence.

Morning Message

Rather than creating a morning message that is incorrect and asking your student to fix it, try leaving a blank line at the beginning of each word, omitting the first letter. Read the message aloud as it is supposed to sound, and have the class help you determine the first letter for each word and if it should be capitalized or not.

Writing Workshop

Writers developing in the Transitional Writing phase might still be mixing their use of uppercase and lowercase letters. Keeping this in mind as you confer with your writers, work with them to think about when they choose to use capital letters and when they don't. Focus more on beginning each sentence with a capital letter and that writers mostly use lowercase letters.

Invitation to SHARE and CELEBRATE

Students visit upper-grade classrooms to share their sentences from the *Patterns of Wonder* Time/Play, pointing out their capital letters. Front-load these visits by letting the older students know ahead of time your students are coming so they are prepared to be very impressed with the choices the writers make. After giving the young author a compliment, the older writer shares a quick sentence from their writing notebook that they wrote, also pointing out the capital letter at the beginning.

A kindergartner points out her capital letters to a fifth-grade buddy.

3.7 Map Maker, Map Maker, Make Me a Map: Nouns Show People, Places, and Things

Standards and Connections	Teacher Considerations	Texts
Standard Use frequently occurring nouns. **Companion Lessons** • Lesson 1.3 • Lesson 2.5 • Lesson 4.6 	Writers in this transitional phase move into labeling pictures with letters or words that match the sounds they hear. Since they're still approximating spellings, we encourage writers to use words around the room combined with letter-sound correspondence to create the words they are so desperately trying to communicate. Sara Fanelli's *My Map Book* is filled with labels and demonstrates how writers use labels to show people, places, and things in their pictures. This is a fun book to explore multiple times when playing with labels in different ways.	*My Map Book* Written and illustrated by Sara Fanelli **Alternative Titles** *Swing, Sloth! Explore the Rainforest* (National Geographic Kids) Written by Susan B. Neuman *My Pet Wants a Pet* Written by Elise Broach and illustrated by Eric Barclay *A Mink, a Fink, a Skating Rink: What Is a Noun?* Written by Brian P. Cleary and illustrated by Jenya Prosmitsky

Focus Phrase 66 I write words that show people, places, and things in my writing. 99

A note about the craft of nouns . . .

Nouns are the stuff of the world; therefore, they are the stuff of writing. The nouns writers use help readers create images in their mind's eye, and the more specific we can be, the more clearly we can express our ideas or explain concepts. As appropriate, pepper the craft of using specific nouns (e.g., *Target* versus *store*) across your lessons in this thread.

Invitation to WONDER

Choose any page spread from *My Map Book* to display. After reading all of the labels aloud, say something like, "Look what Sara Fanelli did here. What do you wonder?" When the conversation leads to how the labels show the reader people, places, and things, reveal the focus phrase, rereading it together several times.

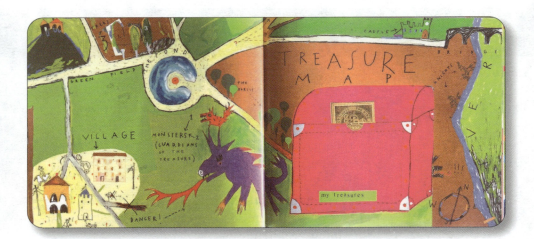

 Any page spread from *My Map Book* could easily be used as a mentor text for this lesson. We like this Treasure Map page because the labels show all three: people, places, *and* things. If you have a document camera, display the page under it, so you can zoom in on some of the smaller labels, like *knight*s.

Invitation to COMPARE and CONTRAST

Choose another page from *My Map Book* to display and read aloud, pointing to each label. Afterward, invite your students to compare and contrast the page with the mentor text, honoring what they notice. When they mention that labels are included on both pages, ask, "What do the labels show us here? What about here?" Repeat the focus phrase often.

 When comparing and contrasting two pages from the same book, consider taking a picture of each to display side by side on your whiteboard.

Invitation to IMITATE TOGETHER

Shared Writing

Together, using *My Map Book* for inspiration, brainstorm some ideas for maps you might make, like a map of your library or a map of your playground. Use *My Map Book* for inspiration. Students turn and talk about what people, places, and things might go on that map. Listen in on their conversations, and when ready, create an imitation, using those ideas and titling it "A Map of My _____." Label the picture with words that show people, places, and things.

Invitation to PLAY

Patterns of Wonder Time

Students create their own imitation maps, labeling them with words that show people, places, and things. Create a class *Book of Maps* with their imitations or hang the imitations in the hall.

Writing Workshop

While bookmaking, children label their pictures with words that show people, places, and things. They may choose to work with a partner, crafting labels for their pictures together. When conferring with writers, ask them to show you where they used words to show people, places, and things.

Choice Time

Students wander the room with sticky notes in hand, crafting labels for the people, places, and things they find, making the classroom into a live map.

Invitation to SHARE and CELEBRATE

Students choose a piece from writing workshop where they added words that show people, places, and things. They share under a document camera, pointing to their words. As they highlight each noun they used, the class celebrates with claps and snaps.

Taylan chose to draw his bedroom and label all of the things inside it.

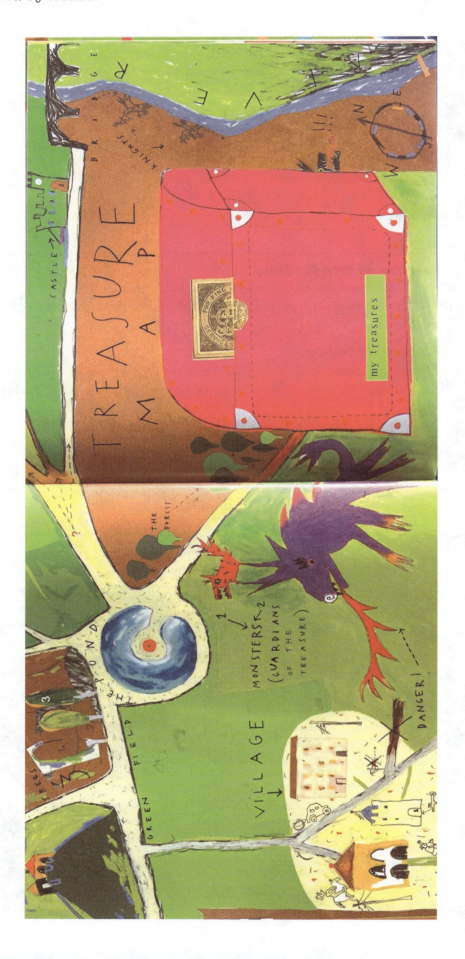

3.8   The Replacements: Pronouns

Standards and Connections	Teacher Considerations	Texts
Standard Use pronouns. *Companion Lesson* • Lesson 4.9 	Because pronouns are used so frequently in spoken English, your children most likely already use a variety of them in their own writing and speaking. For this introductory lesson about using pronouns, we emphasize some common pronouns (*he*, *she*, *they*, *we*, and *I*) that stand in for nouns that *tell who*. Here, we focus on this simple list of five so we can keep the heaviest emphasis on the idea that pronouns stand in for nouns. See Lesson 4.9 for a deeper dive into using pronouns beyond the five introduced in this lesson.	*Not Norman: A Goldfish Story* Written by Kelly Bennett and illustrated by Noah Z. Jones **Alternative Titles** *Jabari Tries* Written and illustrated by Gaia Cornwall *Vinny Gets a Job* Written and illustrated by Terry Brodner *I and You and Don't Forget Who: What Is a Pronoun?* Written by Brian P. Cleary and illustrated by Brian Gable

Focus Phrase   ❝   I match stand-in words to tell who.   ❞

A note about pronouns and gender . . .

In the past, singular nouns matched singular pronouns. Pronouns were based on number and person. *Person* meant that if the *preceding noun* were *female*, the stand-in words would be *she* or *her*, and, if it were male, the pronoun would be *he* and *his.* Recently, it has become standard to use the nongendered plural pronoun *they* as a stand-in to refer back to preceding singular nouns.

Invitation to WONDER

Display these two sentences from *Not Norman* on chart paper and invite your students to wonder about the choices Kelly Bennett, the author, made.

Norman!

He isn't scared.

These two sentences are plump with wonderings for young children. Enjoy the exploration. Feed their discoveries with little convention nuggets authors use to show meaning. "Yes, that's an exclamation mark. How does Kelly want us to read this sentence? Let's read it together using the exclamation mark to help us." After some discussion, ask, "What else do you wonder about?" Since names are a big deal in emergent classrooms, students notice that *Norman* is a name. Honor noticings and let them lead to the focus phrase. "So Norman is the *who* in this sentence. What about this sentence?" Point to the second sentence. They will likely say that *Norman* is the *who* in that sentence as well. Ask, "How do we know that? I don't see his name here." Students eagerly share their thinking. Treat them like the experts when they tell you *he* means *Norman*, adding, "You're so smart! Yes, *he* means *Norman*, so we say *he* stands in for *Norman*. Writers use stand-ins all the time, so they don't have to repeat the name or who they're talking about over and over again. We could say 'Norman! Norman isn't scared,' but instead, we use a stand-in like *he*. 'Norman! *He* isn't scared." Reveal the focus phrase now and repeat it together: *I match stand-in words to tell who.*

Students may comment on that "swirl in the air" or call it a "comma." It's perfectly OK to take a moment to explore this with them. "Oh, that mark! Yes, it looks like a comma, but when it's up higher, we call it an apostrophe. Say it with me: *apostrophe*. Kelly used an apostrophe here to push two words together. Instead of saying *is not*, she used the apostrophe to smush the two words together to say *isn't*."

Invitation to COMPARE and CONTRAST

Prepare an imitation sentence like the one from *Not Norman*, but use a different pronoun. Post it under the mentor sentences on your chart paper.

Norman!

He isn't scared.

Emily!

She is funny.

Students compare and contrast the two models with a partner first and then with the whole group. When they mention that one sentence says *he* and the other says *she*, clarify *who* they represent (*Norman* and *Emily*), and revisit the focus phrase: *I match stand-in words to tell who.*

Shared Writing

Together, create an imitation following the pattern of the previous model. Use the focus phrase to decide which pronoun you'd like to try as a class and then *who* that pronoun stands in for. Nudge students to use a pronoun that hasn't been used yet like *I*, *we*, or *they*. It would help to make a chart with the basic pronouns that *tell who* under the focus phrase. Record the sentence the class composes, and then craft another using another pronoun, and then another one. This will quickly give the children a model for each pronoun that *tells who*.

Invitation
to
IMITATE
TOGETHER

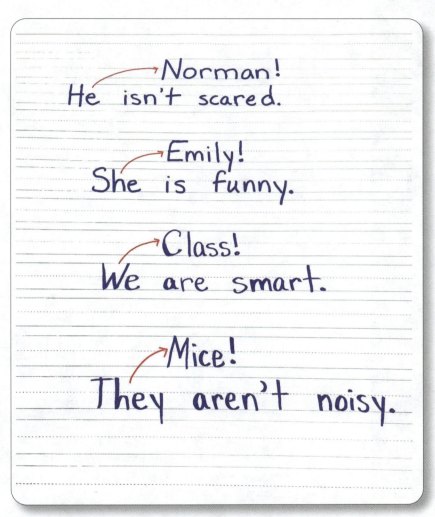

Using her students' ideas, this teacher recorded two more imitation sentences using the pronouns *we* and *they*. After the class discussed the nouns each one stands in for, they drew arrows to connect the two.

Patterns of Wonder Time

Students compose an imitation of the mentor sentences using one of the pronouns you have listed on chart paper under the focus phrase. Encourage them to illustrate their sentences for display.

Literacy Station

Write each pronoun on an index card and place the cards in a station for students to access. Students use Wikki Stix or magnetic letters to make a pronoun, and then they use the pronoun when they write sentences on a dry erase board.

Invitation to PLAY

Aubrey chose to write about her sister for this imitation. She wrote, "Lucy! She just turned two."

Invitation to SHARE and CELEBRATE

Repeat the focus phrase and have the students call out the spelling of each pronoun as you write in on the whiteboard. (They can of course use the chart you already made for support: writers use references.) Students stand in front of the whiteboard to share their writing and point to the pronoun they chose to use.

3.9   Verbs Gotta MOVE: Verbs Show Action

Standards and Connections	Teacher Considerations	Texts
Standard Use frequently occurring verbs. **Companion Lessons** • Lesson 1.4 • Lesson 2.6 • Lesson 4.10 	In this lesson, we move from adding action to our pictures to writing words to show action. *Move!* by Steve Jenkins and Robin Page labels each page with a verb and uses it in a sentence to show that animals move in different ways. When sharing the text with your students multiple times, invite them to read and act out the verbs with you. You might even collect these verbs on an ongoing "I write words to show action" anchor chart to be used in writing workshop.	*Move!* Written by Steve Jenkins and Robin Page and illustrated by Steve Jenkins **Alternative Titles** *Some Pets* Written by Angela DiTerlizzi and illustrated by Brendan Wenzel *An Island Grows* Written by Lola M. Schaefer and illustrated by Cathie Felstead *It's Hard to Be a Verb!* Written by Julia Cook and illustrated by Carrie Hartman

Focus Phrase 〝   I write words to show action.   〞

A note about verbs . . .

Sentences wouldn't *do* or *be* much without verbs. Verbs activate sentences, bringing them to life, identifying actions, setting a mood, or telling time. Quite simply, verbs help us *do* and *be*. That's right. In addition to action, verbs also signal a state of existence, linking nouns or pronouns to a description: you *are* a magnificent writer. They even help out other verbs from time to time. When working with young writers, we needn't worry whether they know the difference between a *be* verb or an action verb or a helping verb, or even if they are using past, present, or future tense. Instead, we want them thinking about how the actions in their writing help to create meaning for their readers.

Invitation to WONDER

Choose any page from Jenkins's *Move!* labeled with a verb to display. When reading the sentence aloud, it will be helpful for context to read the previous page leading into the page you're displaying. Honor all wonderings and discuss the author's or illustrator's choices. This may be the first time your students see ellipses, so don't be surprised if these three dots bring on a lot of conversation. When the students notice the largest word on the page, stop to act out the word and discuss why Steve Jenkins and Robin Page chose to make that word bigger. Then match the verb to the picture to show how they support each other. Share the focus phrase: *I write words to show action.*

If students ask about the ellipses, explain to them that they can be used to make the reader pause, indicating an unfinished thought or a leading statement. Discovering ellipses usually sparks a lot of energy in emergent writers as they enjoy experimenting with them to build suspense, knowing the reader must pause and continue reading to find out what comes next.

Invitation to COMPARE and CONTRAST

Choose another page from Jenkins's *Move!* to share with your students, or use a page from one of the alternative texts listed. After reading the page aloud, ask, "What do you see is the same? What is different?" When your students notice the action in each sentence, stop to briefly act out the movements and revisit the focus phrase: *I write words to show action.* At some point, highlight that nothing would ever happen without verbs. "All sentences have verbs."

Invitation to IMITATE TOGETHER

Interactive Writing

Brainstorm a list of verbs and add them to an ongoing anchor chart "I Write Words to Show Action." Together, choose a verb to illustrate, label, and write a sentence like Steve Jenkins and Robin Page did in *Move!*

Patterns of Wonder Time

Using the anchor chart to help them, students choose a verb to illustrate and label. Encourage them to also write a sentence; it's OK if the sentence doesn't have conventional spacing or capitalization in this phase.

Writing Workshop

Writers add words to show action to the books they make by labeling their pictures and writing approximated sentences. When conferring with your writers, ask them to point out where they write about the action in their books.

Homero drew a detailed picture of his house and thought about the action going on inside. As he pointed to each part of his picture during oral rehearsal, he said, "This is the rooms in my house. My mom is cooking in the kitchen and my twin sisters are playing together. My dad is fixing my remote car."

Moving Through the Hallway

Movement and action go hand in hand, so add some action to your typical walk down the hallway to lunch or recess. As a class, decide on a movement to demonstrate while walking, like moving your arms like a long-legged spider or flying with your arms sprawled like an eagle. Students have so much fun with this that they actually move more quietly through the halls. After returning to class, debrief your actions and remind the students that they can also write about these experiences.

To kick off this celebration, share an appropriate YouTube video of a song or rap about verbs. There are many to choose from! Afterward, students move about the room, sharing their imitations with one another and celebrating their verbs by acting them out.

Invitation
to
SHARE
and
CELEBRATE

This young writer is eager to share her writing during the celebration. She chose to write a sentence and add some lines to show action to her picture, which she noticed many other authors do.

3.10   At Lasso's End: Periods

Standards and Connections	Teacher Considerations	Texts
Standard Use end punctuation for sentences. **Companion Lessons** • Lesson 2.7 • Lesson 4.11 	This lesson builds upon recognizing and naming end punctuation and shifts more attention to using periods purposefully to end sentences. Because the transitional phase involves students combining words to make sentences, we chose this specific page from *Lexie the Word Wrangler* in which the same words are lassoed up, but in different orders. The goal is for students to continue their play with sentence creation; end punctuation will still be experimental and exploratory, as children try it out in different ways, experiencing the effects of its placement.	*Lexie the Word Wrangler* Written by Rebecca Van Slyke and illustrated by Jessie Hartland **Alternative Titles** *Loose Tooth* Written by Lola M. Schaefer and illustrated by Sylvie Wickstrom *Bird Builds a Nest* Written by Martin Jenkins and illustrated by Richard Jones *How to Read a Story* Written by Kate Messner and illustrated by Mark Siegel

Focus Phrase   I end my sentences with a period.

A note about end marks and focus phrases . . .

Eventually, students will use all three standard end marks with flexibility. So, though this lesson's focus phrase speaks to periods, it will remain true and useful, as writers take on additional focus phrases for questions (*I end my questions with question marks*) or exclamation points (*I show strong feelings with exclamation marks!*). At some point, the three can be combined into *I use end marks to help my reader.*

Invitation to WONDER

Display the last page of *Lexie the Word Wrangler* in which Russell creates a sentence from jumbled words on the left-hand side of the page. On the right-hand side of the page, read aloud the sentence inside the lasso circle. As students discuss the two lassoed circles, ask them to look closely at them. Some will discover that both lassoes contain exactly the same words, but one is out of order—a mess of words that don't make sense—while the other lasso surrounds those same words in an order that makes a sentence. When writers note the period, reveal the focus phrase: *I end my sentences with a period.*

There are a lot of things to note in *Lexie the Word Wrangler*: apostrophes, contractions, plurals, compound words. It's not only OK for young writers to wonder about anything on the page, we encourage this. Just make sure the opportunities for wonder come from the kids and not our wish to cram in as much as we can. Sometimes less is more. Let your young writers guide the way.

Invitation to COMPARE and CONTRAST

Write the sentence from *Lexie the Word Wrangler* on chart or butcher paper. Underneath it, write another sentence, like the imitation below, for the students to compare and contrast.

Let's ride to the treehouse and swing on the rope.

Let's read a story.

As students note the author moves that are the same and different, take time to honor their noticings and wonderings and discuss the choices the writers made. They might say one is long and one is short. They might count words in each sentence. Again, our task is to allow, honor, and then decide which ideas are developmentally appropriate for stretching out with direct instruction. When the period is noticed as a similarity, revisit the focus phrase, repeating it together: *I end my sentences with a period.*

Patterns of Wonder Time

Students work with partners to help each other add periods to the ends of their sentences. You may decide to give each student a punctuation stick (a craft stick with a period on it) to use as they write. If writers find this scaffold useful, you can add other ending punctuation marks to it in future lessons. Writers in this phase may not yet use spacing accurately, and that is OK.

Invitation

to

PLAY

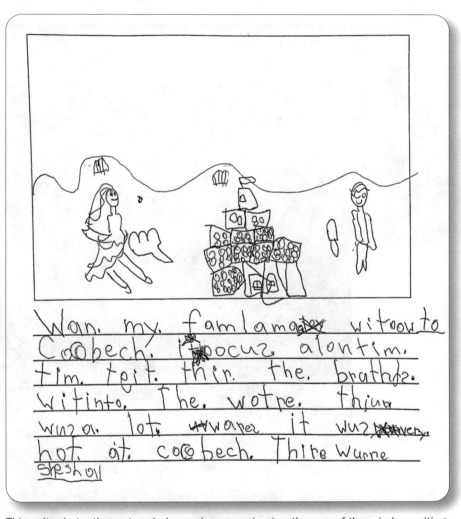

This writer is testing out periods as she approximates the use of them in her writing.

Literacy Station

Students explore some familiar books together to see how many periods are used. Through this exploration, they may begin to notice and wonder about the other end marks used as well. Encourage them to tally on a sticky note how many periods they find and how many other marks they find for each book.

Small-Group Writing

Give students a few minutes to create something with modeling clay or plastic bricks. Guide them through writing a sentence about their creations and put both on display in an honored space for the remainder of the week. Perhaps call it the End Mark Museum or Hall of Fame.

Approximation is the pathway toward convention. When possible, ask students questions about the choices they've made in their writing and resist the urge to fix every little mistake. To nudge them toward more conventional choices, ask them to tell you more about the choices they're making as a writer or call their attention to the accurate pattern modeled in text rather than fixing their approximations. Correcting is not teaching.

Invitation to SHARE and CELEBRATE

Each child chooses a piece of writing to share, pointing out the periods used. You may wish to have them click their tongues when they use a period. (They love it.) Once everyone has shared, display their writing on a wall or door or in the hall with the focus phrase.

3.11 Maybe Something Exciting: Exclamation Marks

Standards and Connections	Teacher Considerations	Texts
Standard Use end punctuation for sentences. **Companion Lessons** • Lesson 2.8 • Lesson 4.11 	This lesson helps writers transition from recognizing and naming punctuation to intentionally using it as we explore exclamation marks and how they help writers show excitement or other strong feelings. We use F. Isabel Campoy and Theresa Howells's *Maybe Something Beautiful* because we love how each page shares expressions that use exclamation marks.	*Maybe Something Beautiful: How Art Transformed a Neighborhood* Written by F. Isabel Campoy and Theresa Howell and illustrated by Rafael López **Alternative Titles** *I'm Not a Mouse!* Written and illustrated by Evgenia Golubeva *Exclamation Mark* Written by Amy Krouse Rosenthal and illustrated by Tom Lichtenheld *That Is Not a Good Idea!* Written and illustrated by Mo Willems

Focus Phrase ❝ I show strong feelings with exclamation marks! ❞

A note about end marks and focus phrases . . .

Eventually, students will use all three end marks. So although the current focus phrase for exclamation marks will remain true and useful—even after writers go through a series of lessons with focus phrases for questions (*I end questions with question marks*) or periods (*I end my sentence with a period*), at some point, the three will be combined into *I use end marks to help my reader.* Writers eventually learn to choose specific end marks based on their purpose in writing.

Invitation to WONDER

Display the vertical page spread from *Maybe Something Beautiful* that shows the artist painting and the words *BAM! POW!* mixed in with the rest of the text. Read the entire page aloud and ask, "What do you wonder?" Because exclamation marks are in color and paired with capitalized text, students are likely to wonder why the author made that choice. This provides the opportunity to share the focus phrase: *I show strong feelings with exclamation marks!* Students share other thoughts as well, often around what the picture shows. Honor their curiosity and surf the wave of wonder—stretching out that which is relevant and useful to learners.

Although exclamation marks, sometimes called exclamation points, show excitement and yelling, they also indicate strong emotions that may not always be yelling or excitement. Though we begin with yelling and excitement as a way to engage students in a study of these powerful punctuation marks, many emergent writers will soon show they are ready for a deeper understanding. If so, be ready to follow their lead.

Invitation to COMPARE and CONTRAST

Choose another page from *Maybe Something Beautiful* (or another class favorite) that includes the use of exclamation marks. As students begin sharing similarities and differences they notice in the two examples, continue to honor their contributions and read aloud the phrases or sentences they point out, paying attention to the end marks used and their effect on how they're read (prosody).

Interactive Writing

Together, brainstorm some other phrases or expressions that writers might include with exclamation marks. Make a list of the phrases they share like this poster shows:

Invitation
to
IMITATE
TOGETHER

Choose an expression to include in a piece of writing created together. As you craft other sentences to go with it, ask students which end mark they think would work best. Maybe all three will end with exclamation marks, or perhaps you'll end up with a mixture of end punctuation. Writers make choices.

Patterns of Wonder Time

Using the chart created during the Invitation to Imitate Together as a guide, students create a piece of writing, which includes exclamation marks. They may choose to draw a picture and add an expression from the chart or include an exclamation of their own. Some writers may even write a sentence to go with the picture that doesn't end with an exclamation mark. Allow for this. The choice is theirs.

Literacy Station

Students work with partners to read individual sentences in a pocket chart, changing out the end punctuation with each reading. An example of sentences that could be used for this station is included at the end of this lesson. Encourage a range of volume and expression and include only the end marks children know.

Writing Workshop

Students continue adding punctuation to their writing as a way to help their readers. During conferences, ask writers why they chose to use particular end marks. If you notice writers overusing exclamation marks, for instance, this is a great way to build awareness around author's purpose. "Talk to me about how you used exclamation marks here. You sound really excited the whole time. Is that what you meant?"

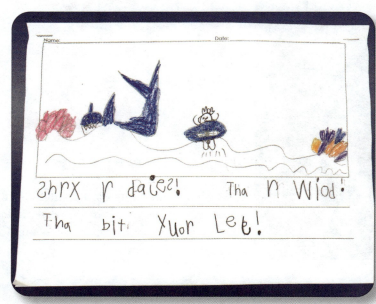

This young writer composed a book about sharks during writing workshop. On this page, he plays with exclamation marks to show his excitement.

Students pretend to be superheroes as they share their writing with exclamation marks under a document camera, adding strong feeling to their oral reading. Emergent writers love to dress up, so get those capes and power rings ready!

?

.

!

It is cold outside

They went to the pool

My mom is here

Pizza is for lunch

You have a puppy

3.12   Going Up? Question Marks

Standards and Connections	Teacher Considerations	Texts
Standard Use end punctuation for sentences. **Companion Lessons** • Lesson 2.9 • Lesson 4.11 	As students in the transitional phase write approximated sentences with intentional use of letters and words, question marks become another one of their purposeful choices. Yamile Saied Méndez's book *Where Are You From?* helps us focus on the purpose of this end mark while showing a variety of ways to begin questions. Because it's a bit longer, we suggest reading aloud the entire book before the lesson, perhaps during a read-aloud time.	*Where Are You From?* Written by Yamile Saied Méndez and illustrated by Jaime Kim **Alternative Titles** *Who Is the Mystery Reader?* Written and illustrated by Mo Willems *Snail and Worm: Three Stories About Two Friends* Written and illustrated by Tina Kügler *Cat the Cat, Who Is That?* Written and illustrated by Mo Willems

Focus Phrase ❝   I end questions with question marks. ❞

A note about other question words . . .

Although knowing the five Ws is a great help for writing, reading, and life, other question words that don't begin with *W* can generate conversation and writing. For example, the word *how* is quite useful: How many . . . ? How often . . . ? How do you . . . ? How old . . . ? Don't forget the lesser-known sixth *W, which*, which will often make you use adjectives: Which . . . is yours? (The yellow one.) Which is your favorite? Which one do you want? (I want the one with extra cheese and black olives.) The point is that questions are about more than what word you start with.

Invitation to WONDER

On chart paper or another large surface, record the following sentence from *Where Are You From?* Read the sentence aloud, making sure to model how your voice changes because of the question mark. Invite students to read it aloud again with you, practicing fluent reading, while reinforcing what question marks do to our voice.

Where am I from?

Even though this sentence—or this question—is short, students will wonder and notice so much. When they notice the capital letters or spaces, celebrate this. They are making connections to both reading and writing they do, and they're doing it through discovery. Of course, when your writers wonder about that mark at the end of the sentence, discuss why the author chose to use it, what it signals our voices to do, and reveal the focus phrase: *I end questions with question marks.*

Choral and repetitive reading can do wonders for students' understanding of syntax (word order and flow) and how punctuation affects our voice when we read aloud or in our head. When students notice a question mark, go back and read the question together, focusing on the intonation of your voice, making it go up in pitch a little.

Invitation to COMPARE and CONTRAST

Underneath the mentor sentence, write another question, like the one below.

Where am I from?
Will we go outside for recess today?

As students share with their partner their noticings about the similarities and differences, listen in on their conversations and choose a couple of students to share their thoughts with the class. Through this conversation, the question mark will be a similarity, bringing the group back to the focus phrase. Extend the conversation by asking, "What else?" Students may notice that the words are different. When they do, ask them to tell you more and point to the words that are different, like the beginning word. Before concluding the lesson, students read both sentences aloud with you, paying attention to how their voices sound when question marks are present.

Invitation to IMITATE TOGETHER

Interactive Writing

Young children love to ask questions. Use your interactive writing time to compose some of their questions together. Students share questions, any questions, with their partners. Listen in and choose one student to share a question. Write the question together, adding the question mark to the end. Then choose another student to share a question, and repeat the process. Write as many questions as time allows, while continually calling back to the focus phrase: *I end questions with question marks.*

Patterns of Wonder Time

Writers generate questions on sentence strips or index cards. Create a great wall of questions to display them. Invite students to continue to add to it whenever they have a question they want answered. Revisit it often and they'll keep adding to it. Wonder? Curiosity? You bet.

Writing Workshop

Writers use questions in all types of writing, and they can make for engaging headings or titles in nonfiction. If students are writing nonfiction, show them how they might choose to start each page with a question before sharing their information about the topic.

Choice Time

Partners explore the classroom library books and big books in search for question marks and point them out to each other when they find one. They can also make tally marks on a sticky note to keep track of how many they find.

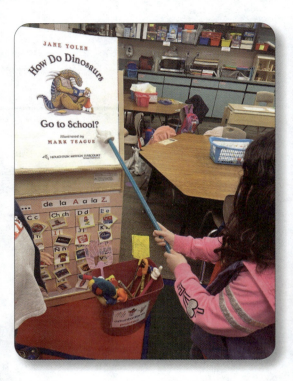

This young writer points out a question mark she discovered on the title page of a big book.

Line Up/Transition Time

While waiting in line or between lessons, say a sentence out loud using vocal expression to represent the end mark you would use. Students listen to the sentence and draw in the air the appropriate end mark. Repeat with the same sentence using a different end mark or add a new sentence each time. Soon, you'll be able to let volunteers model a question while you just listen and breathe.

Invitation to PLAY

Invitation to SHARE and CELEBRATE

Gather your students around the question wall you created during your Invitation to Play and *Patterns of Wonder* time. Writers read their questions aloud, focusing on what the question mark does with their intonation. Audience members draw a question mark in the air at the end of each question shared.

3.13   More to a Label Than a Noun: Adjectives Tell What Kind

Standards and Connections	Teacher Considerations	Texts
Standard Use frequently occurring adjectives. **Companion Lessons** • Lesson 1.5 • Lesson 2.0 • Lesson 4.12 	This lesson builds on the labeling writers do in their pictures to show more details. Most of these labels are one word, most likely nouns. Here, our goal is to teach students to elaborate on their details. Adding these words to their labels will help them move from oral rehearsal to written language. Some writers will add these words to elaborate their written sentences as well.	*The Bear in My Family* Written and illustrated by Maya Tatsukawa **Alternative Titles** *Quit Calling Me a Monster!* Written by Jory John and illustrated by Bob Shea *One Fox: A Counting Book Thriller* Written and illustrated by Kate Read *See the Cat: Three Stories About a Dog* Written by David LaRochelle and illustrated by Mike Wohnoutka

Focus Phrase   I write words that tell what kind.

A note about adjectives that tell what kind . . .

Writers can use adjectives to show what kind through colors, sizes, and traits to help to convey meaning more precisely. Writers also use adjectives that tell what kind to compare two or more nouns. This chart gives some examples.

Possible Adjectives That Tell What Kind		
Colors	**Size**	**Traits**
yellow red orange blue purple magenta	large (larger, largest) big (bigger, biggest) short (shorter, shortest) small (smaller, smallest)	mean (meaner, meanest) friendly (friendlier, friendliest) kind (kinder, kindest) happy (happier, happiest) sad (sadder, saddest) strong (stronger, strongest)

Invitation to WONDER

Show the entire page spread (included at the end of this lesson) of the labeled bear from *The Bear in My Family* while reading it aloud. As students notice the labels, read them again and ask, "What are these labels telling us?" "Yes, the bear has big ears. What kind of ears? Big ears." Repeating this with each label leads to the focus phrase.

 After it's unveiled, remember to invite more conversation beyond the focus phrase by asking, "What else do you wonder?" or "What else do you notice?"

Invitation to COMPARE and CONTRAST

Create a labeled picture to share with your students, or use the labeled picture of the monster on the second page of Jory John's *Quit Calling Me a Monster!* Read the labels aloud, pointing to the words. Then ask, "What do you see is the same? What is different?" When your writers notice the labels, prompt them further by asking, "What do the labels tell us?" Be sure to continue to explore this comparing and contrasting: "What else do you see is the same? What else is different?"

Invitation to IMITATE TOGETHER

Interactive Writing

As a class, brainstorm some possible people, places, or things, and draw quick pictures of them. Then choose one to label together using adjectives that tell what kind.

The class chose to label a flower with words that tell what kind during interactive writing.

Invitation to PLAY

Patterns of Wonder Time

Students choose something to draw and label with adjectives that tell what kind, creating their own imitation of the mentor text. Compiling their drawings into a class book will give students an opportunity to celebrate each other and revisit adjectives throughout the year.

This writer chose to draw herself and label "black and white (picture), pretty dress, skinny legs."

Writing Workshop

Students share their writing with a partner and help each other add more detail by asking, "What kind of _____?" When writing independently, they continue to think about how they show *what kind* to expand their sentences.

For some beginning writers, their labels might just include one letter, usually the initial sound, or they represent the sounds they hear through invented spelling. As students move through these approximations, you might show them how to use an alphabet chart for help. Value and celebrate where they are in their developmental process.

Invitation
to
SHARE
and
CELEBRATE

After students share their labeled pictures with each other, collect the pictures in a class book and place it in the classroom library for everyone to enjoy throughout the year.

Student-created page for the class book. Labels read: "big blue sky, long big stem, long giant trunk."

3.14   I Ate Three Snacks in Two Hours, But I'm Still Hungry: Adjectives Tell How Many

Standards and Connections	Teacher Considerations	Texts
Standard Use frequently occurring adjectives. **Companion Lessons** • Lesson 1.6 • Lesson 2.11 • Lesson 4.13 	Students in this phase of writing approximate words and sentences as they write the letters of the sounds they hear, copy words from around the room, and write sight words they know. We can teach them to tell more by writing words that tell how many in both their labels and their sentences. We chose this well-known book, *The Very Hungry Caterpillar*, because of its pattern of writing using numbers, similar to the reading the students may be doing on their own. If this is not a familiar book yet for your students, we suggest reading it ahead of time to them, so they know the pattern of the book.	*The Very Hungry Caterpillar* Written and illustrated by Eric Carle **Alternative Titles** *One Fox: A Counting Thriller* Written and illustrated by Kate Read *Bird Watch* Written and illustrated by Christie Matheson *Bone by Bone* Written by Sarah Levine and illustrated by T.S Spookytooth

Focus Phrase   " I write words that tell how many. "

A note about adjectives that show how many . . .

Adjectives that show how many go beyond just exact numbers. Here are a few examples.

Possible Adjectives That Show How Many	
Exact	**Approximated**
one	several
four	many
twenty	some

Choose a page to reread aloud from Eric Carle's *The Very Hungry Caterpillar* such as:

On Thursday he ate through four strawberries, but he was still hungry.

Invitation to WONDER

Students reveal curiosity after you ask, "What do you wonder?" As they share their thinking about the pictures and the words, honor what they say and name it, discussing what Eric Carle did and why he did it. When students mention the number four either in the words or in the picture, invite them to find the word *four* in the sentence and count the four strawberries on the page. Reveal the focus phrase.

You aren't limited to this one-page spread; if the kids are loving it, read the whole book again. Keep asking the questions, "What do you wonder? What do you notice? What else?" and do the rest of the lesson, arriving at the focus phrase, the next day. Repeated readings often unlock reading and writing for emergent writers.

On chart paper, add the imitated sentence below the original and read it aloud to your students, inviting them to read it again with you. Note we changed the sentence pattern. We added another word that tells how many, since this is the focus of the lesson.

On Thursday he ate through four strawberries, but he was still hungry.

On Saturday Morgan made six bracelets and seven necklaces.

Invitation to COMPARE and CONTRAST

Ask, "What did these two authors do that was the same? What did they do differently?" As students share what they notice, honor what they say and discuss the author's purpose and craft behind each move. "Yes, words that show how many are used in both sentences. Let's read the words that show us how many. Why did the authors choose to use these words? Yes! They wanted to help their readers picture how many in their minds." Revisit the focus phrase when ready.

When students compare and contrast, they see all sorts of things. Often they surprise us. Remember the conversation is meant to generate wondering and noticing based on the texts—not just to discuss adjectives. But, when your writers do mention adjectives, s-t-r-e-t-c-h it out and be the responsive teacher you are.

Invitation to IMITATE TOGETHER

Interactive Writing

Compose a sentence that relates to your school day using a word or two that tells how many. Together, choose which structure from the examples you want to try: "Do we want to use one word to tell how many or two words to tell how many?" An example might be:

On Monday we counted twenty cubes and four buckets.

Invitation to PLAY

Patterns of Power Time

Students think about something they ate or made recently. They then create their own imitations of the model either with partners or independently, focusing on telling how many.

This writer composes a sentence explaining what he ate on Monday, including six Skittles.

Writing Workshop

Students add words that tell how many to their writing. During conferences, invite writers who are labeling pictures to add these words to their labels where they see fit.

Literacy Station

Partners read through a stack of word cards, finding the words that tell how many and add them to a pocket chart with the focus phrase at the top. A set of word cards is included at the end of this lesson.

Invite each student to share one place in their writing where they used words that tell how many. Create a slideshow with images of everyone's writing for students to thumb through on their tablets during independent reading.

Young writers point to the words they used to tell how many while sharing with partners during the celebration.

Word Cards for Sorting Literacy Station

four	the	some
play	two	many
one	ten	like
look	am	was

3.15   Where Is the Monster? Prepositions Tell Where

Standards and Connections	Teacher Considerations	Texts
Standard Use frequently occurring prepositions. **Companion Lessons** • Lesson 1.7 • Lesson 2.12 • Lesson 4.15 	The goal of this lesson is to teach writers how to ground a reader in space by writing words that tell where. We love the fun nature of Jory John's *Quit Calling Me a Monster!* because it has so much to offer as a mentor text for emergent writers. Read this book aloud in its entirety ahead of time, so you can revisit the page and focus on prepositions during this lesson.	*Quit Calling Me a Monster!* Written by Jory John and illustrated by Bob Shea **Alternative Titles** *How to Read to Grandma or Grandpa* Written by Jean Reagan and illustrated by Lee Wildish *In a Jar* Written and illustrated by Deborah Marcero *Yellow Ball* Written and illustrated by Molly Bang

Focus Phrase   ❝   I write words that tell where.   ❞

A note about prepositions evolving . . .

During this lesson set, some writers may start to note that prepositions do more than ground our reader in space. They also tell *when*. Don't push this conversation, but a child may note, for instance, that we say *in*, even when we don't mean *where*. ("I'll be with you in a moment.") Though we add *when* to the focus phrase in companion Lesson 4.15, don't feel like you have to hold back until then if students are ready to explore. The invitational process quite naturally invites students to wonder. Let them. Adjust. Enjoy the journey as both a leader and a learner.

Invitation
to
WONDER

Display and read the page spread here (also included at the end of this lesson). Invite students to reread it with you a few times, building fluency and paying attention to punctuation. "Let's look at both the pictures and the words on these pages. What do you wonder?" Enjoy the conversation while leading writers to connect the words to the pictures and eventually to the focus phrase.

Just because I hide under the bed . . .

. . . or behind the shower curtain . . .

. . . or at the back of the closet . . .

. . . or in the glove compartment.

If students ask about the ellipses, tell them what they are called and explain that writers use ellipses to cause a pause, build suspense, or trail off. Ellipsis can also indicate an unfinished thought. Writers who discover ellipses enjoy experimenting with them to build suspense, knowing the reader must pause and . . . see what comes next.

Invitation to COMPARE and CONTRAST

On chart paper, create a scene that could be labeled with prepositions. An example might be a park with a squirrel in it. Label the picture with a variety of prepositional phrases and display it alongside the original pages from *Quit Calling Me a Monster!* Ask, "What is the same in these two pieces of writing? What is different?" Through conversation, students discover that both pieces of writing use words that tell where. When they do, repeat the focus phrase together: *I write words that tell where.*

During your invitations to compare and contrast, remember, you decide which noticings need to be explored deeper, looking for opportunities to spotlight the focus phrase. Ask questions. Listen. But try not to judge or force. Allow your students to come to know over time.

Invitation to IMITATE TOGETHER

Interactive Writing

Using the content from the mentor text as your model, brainstorm a list of places where someone might hide. Choose one to use in a sentence and then write that sentence together. While you call individual students up one at a time to write part of the sentence, everyone else writes the entire sentence on their own dry erase boards.

Ezzat wrote the imitation the class composed together on her dry erase board during interactive writing.

Patterns of Wonder Time

Students think of where they might hide in the classroom to surprise someone walking in. After some sharing of ideas, they craft their own imitation sentence using the interactive writing imitation as a guide. Have them illustrate their sentence and display their piece of writing near the area of the classroom they chose to write about or compile their imitations into a class book.

Writing Workshop

Repeat the focus phrase often. When conferring with students during independent writing, encourage them to study their pictures looking for places they might add more to show where or add words to tell where, or both.

This writer works on telling where in a book she made during writing workshop. On this page, she wrote, "I walked my dog to my mailbox."

Brain Break

Stop to play a quick game of I-Spy, giving clues that use prepositions to tell where. For example:

- I spy something over the window.
- I spy something below the computer desk.
- I spy something on the rug.

Invitation to PLAY

Invitation to SHARE and CELEBRATE

It's always fun to bring music and videos into a celebration, and a quick YouTube search of preposition songs for preschool or kindergarten will bring up several videos that are about two minutes long. Choose one that your students will enjoy watching and singing along to before sharing their imitations composed during the Invitation to Play. Some of our favorites are from Maple Leaf Learning.

3.16   BOA Connectors: Write More with Conjunctions

Standards and Connections	Teacher Considerations	Texts
Standard Use frequently occurring conjunctions. **Companion Lessons** • Lesson 1.8 • Lesson 2.13 • Lesson 4.16 	In this lesson, students move from showing and telling more in their pictures to writing words to tell more. Here, writers explore common conjunctions like *but, or, and,* which make for a helpful mnemonic: *BOA.* We chose to revisit Steve Jenkins's book *Move!* because it includes the use of all three conjunctions throughout the book, giving students a model for each.	*Move!* Written by Steve Jenkins and illustrated by Robin Page **Alternative Titles** *A Perfectly Messed-Up Story* Written and illustrated by Patrick McDonnell *A New Home* Written and illustrated by Tania de Regil *Dream Big* Written by Kat Kronenberg and illustrated by Stephanie Dehennin

Focus Phrase   〝   I write more with BOA: *but, or, and.*   〞

A note about BOA . . .

We like the mnemonic BOA because it is simple and fun and can be repeated easily. When introducing each conjunction, make the first letter bigger and bolder to help the letter of the mnemonic stick out. In addition to adding these words to your word wall, hang them in your writing center or write them on popsicle sticks for students to use frequently.

Invitation to WONDER

To prepare for this invitation, write the following sentence from *Move!* on chart paper.

A gibbon swings through jungle trees or walks on two back legs.

Reread the first three pages of the book for context, showing the picture of the gibbon monkey. Then, direct your students' attention to the sentence you've recorded on chart paper, inviting them to share their curious thoughts about Jenkins's choices. When they notice the gibbon does two things, use it to glide into the focus phrase with a discussion around how *or* connects to the two possibilities.

Invitation to COMPARE and CONTRAST

On your chart paper, add a sentence you compose that shows a different BOA. We chose one that uses *but*.

A gibbon swings through jungle trees or walks on two back legs.
A frog jumps into the water but not a toad.

As your students compare and contrast the two, honor what they bring up, and take the time to discuss the choices the writers made. When students recognize the difference in the conjunctions used, discuss how both words help to tell more, and revisit the focus phrase: *I write more with BOA:* but, or, and.

Invitation to IMITATE TOGETHER

Shared Writing

Use the school breakfast or lunch menu to compose several sentences that use different conjunctions. Have fun with sentence creation, writing statements, questions, and exclamations. The joining word *or* is used often in questions like, "Are you going to get a hamburger or pizza?" Invite individual students up to circle or highlight the BOA word in each sentence to help the group make the connection back to the focus phrase: *I write more with BOA:* but, or, and.

This class chose two things from the school breakfast menu and composed sentences about them using BOA words.

> I like cereal, but
> I love muffins!
>
> cereal   muffin
>
> I like to eat cereal and a muffin.
>
> Do you like cereal or muffins?

Patterns of Wonder Time

As a class, orally brainstorm some other foods that you would find on a menu. Record some of these ideas on a chart to get students' thinking started. You may even choose to look at a few online children's restaurant menus that include visuals like Olive Garden or Chili's. With partners, students create their own menu and write a sentence about it, using one of the BOA joining words: *but, or, and*.

Invitation
to
PLAY

This young writer created her own menu and wrote sentences about it using BOA words. Her sentences say, "I want a hot dog and I want apple juice. I want raspberries or lemonade. I like lettuce but I want a hot dog."

Writing Workshop

Revisit the focus phrase and repeat it several times: *I write more with BOA:* but, or, and. When students use joining words like *but, or,* and *and* in their books, invite them to circle or highlight those words in some way.

Literacy Station

Stock a station with a variety of pictures, including photographs and illustrations. Students orally tell each other more about the pictures of their choice using BOA words. Then, they choose one to write about, composing it on a sentence strip using one of the BOA words.

Invitation to SHARE and CELEBRATE

Kick off this celebration with a joining word chant:

We use BOA to tell more
Joining ideas is what it's for!
But
Or
And
BOA! BOA! BOA!

After students share their menus and their BOA sentences with the class, do a final celebration dance to the BOA chant.

This kindergartner writes more with *and*.

3.17   Transitions Are Directions: Using Transition Words to Write Order

Standards and Connections	Teacher Considerations	Texts
Standard Use frequently occurring transition words. **Companion Lessons** • Lesson 1.9 • Lesson 2.14 • Lesson 4.17 	Writers use transitions to share their thoughts in a specific order. We often teach children to use time-order words like *first*, *next*, *then*, and *finally* to retell stories they read and when sharing their thoughts in order during writing. But transitions go beyond these four words. In this lesson, we create a chart of frequently occurring transitions for children to try out in their own writing and speaking.	*Bird Builds a Nest* Written by Martin Jenkins and illustrated by Richard Jones **Alternative Titles** *How to Raise a Mom* Written by Jean Reagan and illustrated by Lee Wildish *When Grandma Gives You a Lemon Tree* Written by Jamie L. B. Deenihan and illustrated by Lorraine Rocha *My First Soccer Game* Written by Alyssa Satin Capucilli and photographed by Leyah Jensen

Focus Phrase ❝   I write my thoughts in order.   ❞

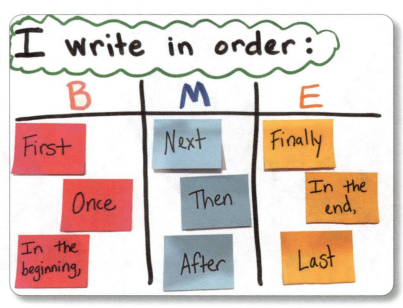

This is a final version of a chart you willl begin during the Invitation to Wonder, and complete throughhout the lesson.

Invitation to WONDER

Record the sentence below from *Bird Builds a Nest* on chart paper. Read the first three pages of the book for context, and then share the sentence on the chart paper to begin the invitation.

First she needs some breakfast.

Students may wonder what comes next (after *first*). If they do, use this as an entry point to a conversation about order. "How do you know something will happen next? What clue do you have in this sentence?"

When students discover the transition word, reveal the focus phrase, and begin creating an anchor chart like the one pictured here to ground a discussion of order words. "Martin Jenkins used the word *first* to write in order. What other words have we heard before that can come at the beginning?"

Stop after listing a few beginning transitions. You will continue to build on this chart during the Invitation to Compare and Contrast.

Invitation to COMPARE and CONTRAST

Compose two more sentences that show a middle and an end of a day in the life of a bird or simply retell the content of *Bird Builds a Nest* like we include below. Read all three sentences aloud, inviting the students to read them with you. As students compare and contrast, continue to explore the purpose and effect of time-order words, building your transitions anchor chart as each part comes up in conversation.

First she needs some breakfast.

Next Bird gets twigs.

Finally she builds her nest.

Invitation to IMITATE TOGETHER

Interactive Writing

Brainstorm some recent events that have occurred at school, like a fire drill or an author visit or pizza day in the cafeteria. Choose one to write about in order, deciding which transition to use for the beginning, middle, and end. Choose which words you will write and which words you will invite students up to write. When you've finished, invite individual students up to locate and circle one of the transition words you used.

A possible story might be:

First the fire bell rang.
Then we lined up.
Finally we walked out of the school.

**Invitation
to
PLAY**

Patterns of Wonder Time

In groups of three, students brainstorm something else that has happened at school and think about how they would retell it in order. Once they settle on the exact order of events, they take turns writing it out. On a sentence strip, one student records what happened in the beginning, using a transition word to signal the beginning. Another records what happened in the middle on another sentence strip, using a transition word, and the third writer records what happened at the end on another sentence strip, using an ending transition word. Check out the picture in the Invitation to Celebrate for an example of what this might look like.

Reading Response

Students choose a book from their independent reading bag to retell. On a piece of construction paper folded into thirds, they write three events that happened: beginning, middle, end. They may choose to use both pictures and words to retell.

Writing Workshop

As students write in any genre, they use the order anchor chart to play with ways to write in order. When conferring with students, ask them to share their writing with you in order, encouraging them to use transitions.

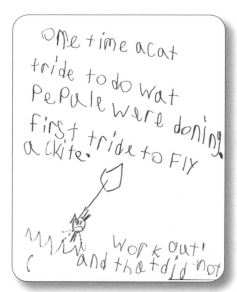  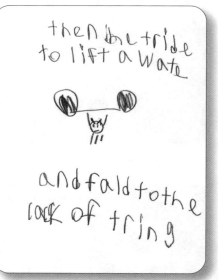

Zander wrote this book during writing workshop. Notice the way he played with transitions as he told his story in the first three pages of his book: "One time a cat tried to do what people were doing. First he tried to fly a kite. And that did not work out. Then he tried to play the piano. And he lacked success. Then he tried to lift a weight and failed to the lack of trying."

Display the letters *B*, *M*, and *E* in large font on butcher paper or a whiteboard to use as a backdrop for this celebration. Trios from the Invitation to Play/*Patterns of Wonder* time stand in front of the *B*, *M*, and *E* to share their sentence strips in order with the class. For further extension, bundle the sentence strips by trio and place them in a literacy station for students to practice putting in order, using the transitions for support.

A trio of kindergartners share their sentences in order about lunch time: "First I get my lunch. Next I sit down. Finally I eat."

Conventional Writing

Conventional Writing Phase Behaviors	◗ Conventionally spelling common words
	◗ Approximating spelling of less common words using letter sounds
	◗ Using spaces between words in sentences
	◗ Using ending punctuation, may be approximated
	◗ Using both uppercase and lowercase letters intentionally

4.1 A Journey Through Words and Pictures: Use Letters to Record Language and Make Words

Standards and Connections	Teacher Considerations	Texts
Standard Intentionally use marks, symbols, and letters to record language and make words. **Companion Lessons** • Lesson 1.1 • Lesson 2.1 • Lesson 3.1 	Now that students have a better understanding of letter sounds and using those to make words, we can continue that work as we move into putting words into sentences. The focus of this lesson is the act of making words, but it could be paired with Lessons 3.3 and 3.4 to connect this work to sentence creation. The reminder that we write with words and pictures still holds true, and we ask writers to use both to make meaning for their readers. Be sure to check out the note on the next page to see how this lesson's goal and focus phrase connect to its companion lessons.	*Do I Have to Wear a Coat? A Journey Through the Seasons* Written and illustrated by Rachel Isadora **Alternative Titles** *What Can a Citizen Do?* Written by Dave Eggers and illustrated by Shawn Harris *Lexie the Word Wrangler* Written by Rebecca Van Slyke and illustrated by Jessie Hartland *This Is My Book!* Written and illustrated by Mark Pett

Focus Phrase ❝ I write with words and pictures. ❞

Invitation to WONDER

Share the page from *Do I Have to Wear a Coat?* that shows the children playing baseball at the park and drawing on the sidewalk. We like to use this page as a mentor text because there is a simple sentence that goes with each picture, and the sentence represents the type of writing children may be producing at this time. Display the page and enjoy the conversation that it prompts. When students notice the variety of words or sentences and pictures, reveal the focus phrase and repeat it together.

A note about focus phrase visuals . . .

Since this same goal looks different as emergent writers develop, you'll notice the focus phrase for this lesson repeats through its companion lessons—even as the type of writing shifts across their phases. We highlight this shift with accompanying visuals that represent the type of writing children do in each phase.

For example, the focus phrase visual for this lesson represents the writing children do in the Conventional Writing phase. Keep in mind that the words in this phase may be a mix of approximated and conventional spelling as students write the letters of the sounds they hear and copy words from around the room. Notice that the visuals for the companion lessons in this thread (1.1, 2.1, and 3.1) change to represent the type of writing students are progressing through.

Invitation to COMPARE and CONTRAST

Display the two-page spread from the original page studied in the Invitation to Wonder so that it is side by side with the next page showing the children playing hopscotch and riding bikes. Ask the students what they notice is the same and different about the two pages. These pages are very similar, but students will notice a variety of differences as well. Honor their noticings and extend on them as you see fit. Remind the writers that they, too, can try these same things they are noticing. Revisit the focus phrase and repeat together when the students notice both the words and the pictures.

While exploring *Do I Have to Wear a Coat?* students may notice the words written in pink font, representing an internal voice. In other books, we sometimes see internal voices represented with thought bubbles.

Invitation to IMITATE TOGETHER

Interactive Writing

Using the pages from *Do I Have to Wear a Coat?* as your mentor text, brainstorm some ideas for a class piece of writing. What are some things we do? After orally brainstorming some ideas, compose a page with both pictures and words, inviting children to write the sentence with you.

Patterns of Wonder Time

With a partner, students brainstorm something they do and create their own imitation of the mentor text on a large piece of construction paper.

Writing Workshop

Revisit the focus phrase each day as students make books: *I write with words and pictures* When sharing their books, writers point to their words as they read their writing and discuss their pictures.

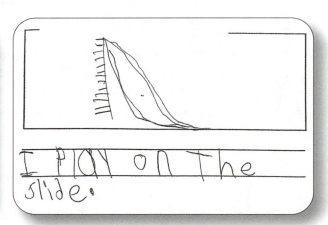
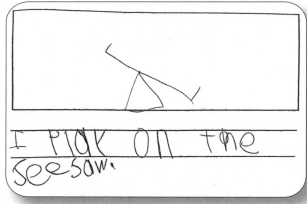

This student wrote a book about what he does on the playground, choosing a different focus for each page.

Partners share the imitations they wrote together during the *Patterns of Wonder* time, explaining their pictures and reading their sentences. Display all of the imitations on a wall alongside the focus phrase.

4.2 Splitting Hairs: Capitalize Names of People

Standards and Connections	Teacher Considerations	Texts
Standard Capitalize names of people. *Companion Lessons* • Lesson 2.4 • Lesson 3.5 • Lesson 4.3 	In this phase of writing, students generally become more automatic with their name and begin to master the difference between uppercase and lowercase letters. As they write more conventionally, we invite them to use names in various places within sentences to continue practicing appropriate capitalization use.	*Hair Love* Written by Matthew A. Cherry and illustrated by Vashti Harrison **Alternative Titles** *Hello, My Name Is . . .* *How Adorabilis Got His Name* Written by Marisa Polansky and illustrated by Joey Chou *I'm Not a Mouse!* Written and illustrated by Evgenia Golubeva *Catch That Chicken!* Written by Atinuke and illustrated by Angela Brooksbank

Focus Phrase ❝ I capitalize names. ❞

A note about *Hair Love* . . .

Hair Love has also been made into a short film that your students will enjoy. A simple YouTube search will bring you to the Sony Animations video.

Invitation to WONDER

Share the first sentence of Matthew A. Cherry's *Hair Love* with your students. You may choose to write it on chart paper for easy viewing.

My name is Zuri, and I have hair that has a mind of its own.

Invite them to notice and wonder about the choices the author made. Honor and name all of their noticings. When students bring up the girl's name, ask, "How do you know that is her name? What do you notice about the letters in her name?" Reveal the focus phrase when appropriate.

This character's name, Zuri, beginning with *Z* could be added to your class name chart or name wall, especially if you don't happen to have any names that start with *Z* in your learning community.

Invitation to COMPARE and CONTRAST

Create a sentence that mirrors the pattern of the mentor sentence, like the one below, and write both—one on top of the other—on your chart paper. Read each sentence aloud, pointing to each word. Students compare and contrast the choices the authors made with each sentence.

My name is Zuri, and I have hair that has a mind of its own.

My name is Carlos, and I have a puppy named Max.

Students may notice that both sentences have sight words in them. If they do, invite them to come up and point them out. Make reference to the word wall, if you have them posted there, and repeat reading them together. You may invite students to write one or two of them in the air. Then continue the conversation of comparing and contrasting with the prompt, "What else is the same or different?" They will likely get excited about the names and notice the second sentence has two names in it. When they do, ask, "How do you know those are names?" When the time feels right, repeat the focus phrase.

Invitation to IMITATE TOGETHER

Interactive Writing

Compose a sentence about a teacher or someone else in the building that's similar to the mentor sentence. Include an item the person usually has with them. When brainstorming interactive writing sentences with your students, try embedding early discussions about what makes up a sentence (subject-verb). "Who will be in our sentence?" "What will they have?" Count the words across your fingers as you repeat the sentence together. It's also helpful to draw lines on the chart paper to hold spaces for each word, as in the picture below.

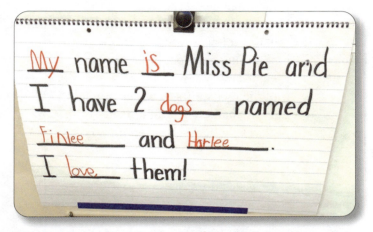

This class wanted to write about their teacher's two dogs, using both their names in their imitation.

Invitation to PLAY

Patterns of Wonder Time

Students create their own sentence and illustration about themselves, capitalizing their name. Display them on the door, in a paper quilt pattern.

Literacy Station

Students continue to play with names. They collect other names found in books, around the room, or within the building, paying attention to uppercase and lowercase letters. Perhaps they'll write the names they find on sticky notes for the teacher to post under the focus phrase. These can be used for list-group-label activities later.

Invitation to SHARE and CELEBRATE

Invite the principal, librarian, or instructional coach into your classroom for your students to share the door chart with, giving each student an opportunity to read their page. Students share and point to where they capitalized names, reinforcing the focus phrase.

4.3   Place Time: Capitalize Names of People and Places

Standards and Connections	Teacher Considerations	Texts
Standard Capitalize names of people and places. **Companion Lessons** • Lesson 2.4 • Lesson 3.5 • Lesson 4.2 	Now that students understand their name and the names of other people, places, and things begin with capital letters, this lesson continues that focus, adding in names of places. Note the portability of the focus phrase, which applies to any name, including names of places, holidays, or even brands.	*A New Home* Written and illustrated by Tania de Regil **Alternative Titles** *Norman: One Amazing Goldfish!* Written by Kelly Bennett and illustrated by Noah Z. Jones *Can I Be Your Dog?* Written and illustrated by Troy Cummings *Me on the Map* Written by Joan Sweeney and illustrated by Qin Leng

Focus Phrase   I capitalize names.

A note about capitalizing relatives' names . . .

When using someone's given name, we always capitalize it. However, even many adults wonder why words like Mom, Dad, Grandpa, and Grandma are capitalized. The difference maker is when the name is preceded by a *possessive pronoun* or *any possessive*—*my* mom, *Chris's* dad, *her* grandma, *their* grandpa—the word isn't capitalized. Though most emergent writers aren't developmentally ready for this conversation, some may be ready to dig into this curiosity.

Invitation to WONDER

Display the following sentence on chart paper or under a document camera.

Mamá and Papá told me that we are moving to New York City.

As students share their wonderings and noticings, honor and name what they say. Students will probably notice the accents on *Mamá* and *Papá*. To extend on this noticing, explain, "Sometimes we use symbols to help us know how to say words. Spanish words often have accent marks to let a reader know how to say a word. These two words are in Spanish, and these accent marks let us know how to read the words aloud. What else do you notice about these two words: *Mamá* and *Papá*?"

When children point out the capital letters throughout the sentence, discuss why each word is capitalized, discovering that they are all names. Reveal the focus phrase and repeat together: *I capitalize names.*

Some observant students may notice that *City* is capitalized in this sentence but not in other books they've read. When *city* stands by itself, it is a common noun rather than a proper noun, or name, and therefore, not capitalized—though most emergent writers will be satisfied with the explanation that, in this example, *City* is part of the name, so it begins with a capital letter.

Invitation to COMPARE and CONTRAST

Display the following sentences for students to compare and contrast.

Mamá and Papá told me that we are moving to New York City.
Zayne visited his friend in California.

When considering what is the same and different, students may notice only one person is named in the second sentence or the name of the place is only one word. Encourage this curiosity and discuss what makes them names. This leads to the focus phrase, showing a variety of ways to capitalize names.

Invitation to IMITATE TOGETHER

Interactive Writing

Together create a list of names of people and of places in two columns on chart paper. Choose some names from this list and compose an imitation of the mentor sentence, focusing on capitalizing them. For the sake of time, you might split this activity into two parts, interactive writing to create your lists of names and shared writing to write about them.

Patterns of Wonder Time

With a partner, students write their own imitation of the mentor sentence on construction paper, capitalizing names of people and places. If needed, they can use the list they generated as a class during interactive writing to come up with places. They may also choose to write more than one imitation sentence.

Literacy Stations

Students go on a name hunt, searching for names in books they read. When they find one, they write it on a sticky note, making sure to capitalize it, and post it on a chart in the station. Later, as an additional station, students can sort the sticky notes into places and people.

Students share their imitation sentences. After pairs read their sentence twice, the class calls out the names the writers used. Display student writing alongside the focus phrase in the classroom or hallway once sharing is complete.

A young writer visits the school library to share his writing.

4.4   Capitals Begin: Begin Sentences with Capital Letters

Standards and Connections	Teacher Considerations	Texts
Standard Capitalize the first letter in a sentence. **Companion Lesson** • Lesson 3.6 	Most likely, you've already focused attention on capitalizing names, and now that your students may be independently playing with the intentional use of spaces between words and even end marks, it's time to expand their intentional choices with capitalization. This lesson adds beginning sentences with capital letters to students' growing repertoires, as we inch closer to a broader understanding that we only use capital letters when we need them.	*Saturday* Written and illustrated by Oge Mora **Alternative Titles** *What If . . .* Written by Samantha Berger and illustrated by Mike Curato *The Magical Yet* Written by Angela DiTerlizzi and illustrated by Lorena Alvarez *Goodbye Summer, Hello Autumn* Written and illustrated by Kenard Paks

Focus Phrase   ❝ I start my sentence with a capital letter. ❞

A note about repetition of instruction . . .

Quell your expectation that you won't have to repeat the message to begin sentences with capital letters again and again to your emergent writers. At this point in student development, this is such a crucial skill that it could become a roadblock later in their writing progression if it isn't taught fully and well to automaticity. Overteach it!

Invitation
to
WONDER

Write the following mentor sentences from *Saturday* with a space in between them on chart paper and read them aloud.

The day would be special. The day would be splendid.

As students share what they wonder, feed into their curiosity with a discussion about Oge Mora's choices as a writer. Students will most likely wonder why she started both sentences with the same words. Talk about possible reasons why she may have done that. They may wonder why two sentences are there since we normally don't use two sentences in our Invitation to Wonder. This discovery is a wonderful segue into sentence boundaries. Ask, "How do you know there are two sentences?" As the conversation turns to where one sentence ends and another begins, introduce the focus phrase.

In this Invitation to Wonder, we use two sentences for students to see when one sentence ends and another begins, causing the need for a capital letter. So, be sure to place them one after the other as you conventionally would (as opposed to one on top of the other or spread apart).

Invitation
to
COMPARE
and
CONTRAST

To deepen the conversation around capital letters, we chose another sentence from *Saturday* to compare and contrast that also includes the day of the week. Record the mentor sentences shown here, and ask your students, "What do you notice is the same? What's different?"

The day would be special. The day would be splendid.
On Saturdays they zipped to the library for weekly story time.

Let your students' conversations lead the way through discussion for discovery and instruction. They may notice the spaces between words in both sentences or that both sentences use the high-frequency word *the*. They may also discover that you've added only one sentence to the chart paper as opposed to the two they are comparing it to. Students are likely to wonder why that word *Saturday* is capitalized. "It's not at the beginning." Feed into this curiosity, talk about the choices authors make (we use capital letters for a reason), and move toward the focus phrase. "You mentioned it's not at the beginning. What do you mean by that?" When students explain that the word *On* is at the beginning, continue this discussion, with a heavy focus on it beginning the sentence, therefore needing to be capitalized. Revisit the focus phrase when appropriate.

Invitation
to
IMITATE
TOGETHER

Interactive Writing

Compose a sentence or two together, focusing on using a capital letter at the beginning and lowercase letters everywhere else. If the class decides to use a day of the week in this sentence, honor it and include its capital. Writers have choices.

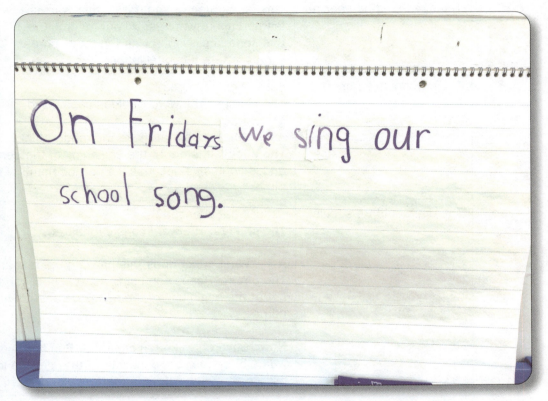

Since this first-grade class was also learning about days of the week, they decided to use a day of the week in their imitation.

Invitation to PLAY

Editing Conversation

In *Patterns of Power* (2017), we use an editing conversation during our Invitation to Edit. When children are ready to try some conventional editing, this is a great time to introduce this interactive activity that zeros in on author's purpose and author's craft as well as the effect our choices have on our readers. Display four versions of the mentor sentence; the first one is the original mentor sentence. The other three have one change each. As you review each version of the sentence, ask students what changed in each one and what effect that change has on the reader. We include a display for you to try with students at the end of this lesson along with some teacher considerations outlined below.

The day would be special.	This is the mentor sentence. Quickly review what we've learned about writing from our mentor, Oge Mora, and this sentence. Also, revisit the focus phrase: *I start my sentence with a capital letter.*
The day Would be special.	Ask, "What changed?" **The change**: The word *would* is capitalized. Ask, "What does that make the reader think?" **The effect:** It is not at the beginning of the sentence and is confusing because it's not the name of anything either.
The day would Be special.	Ask, "What changed?" **The change:** The word *be* is capitalized. Ask, "What effect does this have on the reader?" **The effect:** This is confusing as well, because *Be* is not at the beginning of the sentence and it's not a name. **Note:** Children will often capitalize *B* in the middle of words or sentences, especially if they get the lowercase *b* confused with other letters like *d*, *p*, and *q*.
The day would be special!	Ask, "What changed?" **The change:** The end mark is changed to an exclamation point. Ask, "What effect does this have on the reader?" **The effect:** We read it out loud in a different way, with excitement. Read the sentence out loud together, focusing on the end mark.

Writing Workshop

Writers read their pieces aloud to their partner to check for capitalization. In a selected piece of writing, they go back over the capital letters they used at the beginning of sentences with a colored pencil to make the capitals pop out further for their readers.

Invitation
to
SHARE
and
CELEBRATE

Invite students to wear a cap to school for this celebration. Students share the sentences they created during the Invitation to Play/*Patterns of Wonder* time wearing their CAPS. They may not get it, but you will, and it's always fun to wear a cap!

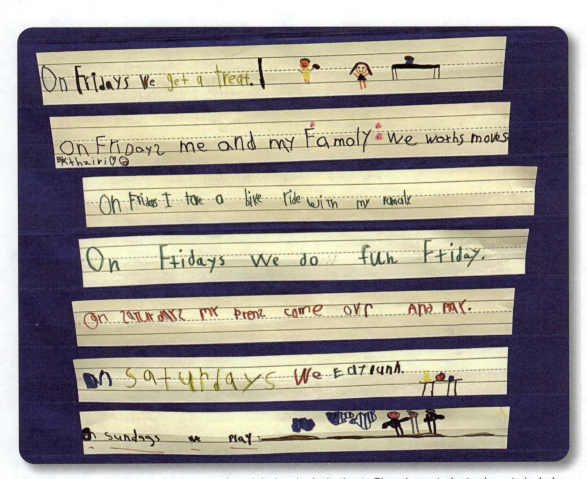

The imitating in this first-grade class continued during the Invitation to Play where students chose to include a day of the week in their imitations. After celebrating their use of capitalization, Mrs. Bleakley displayed their sentences for others to admire.

Editing Conversation

What did we learn about writing from Oge Mora?

The day would be special.

What changed? What is the effect of that change?

The day Would be special.

The day would Be special.

The day would be special!

4.5   Because I Say So: Capitalize the Pronoun *I*

Standards and Connections	Teacher Considerations	Texts
Standard Capitalize the pronoun *I*. **Companion Lessons** • Lesson 4.2 • Lesson 4.3 • Lesson 4.4 	Capital letters are used for a purpose, and this lesson explores the capitalization of the pronoun *I*, which we use to tell a story or share information in first person. Abby Hanlon's *Ralph Tells a Story* is told from Ralph's point of view, so the pronoun *I* is found on almost every page. This fun story is about a boy who can't think of anything to write about, but then he discovers that anything can become a story—a good message to students that they, too, can write about anything.	*Ralph Tells a Story* Written and illustrated by Abby Hanlon **Alternative Titles** *Memoirs of a Goldfish* Written by Devin Scillian and illustrated by Tim Bowers *What If . . .* Written by Samantha Berger and illustrated by Mike Curato *Little i* Written and illustrated by Michael Hall

Focus Phrase ❝ I capitalize the pronoun *I* (no matter where it is). ❞

A note about the pronoun *I* . . .

Pronouns aren't capitalized unless they are the first word of a sentence or in a title, so why is *I* capitalized? The pronoun *I* finds its origins in the Old and Middle English word *ic* or *ich*. When it was two and three letters, it wasn't capitalized. When the word evolved from three letters to one, typesetters and printers decided the lone lowercase *i* would get lost on the page, which is why we capitalize our only one-letter pronoun, *I* (Winter 2008).

Invitation to WONDER

Display the following sentence from *Ralph Tells a Story*, and invite students to wonder about Abby Hanlon's choices as a writer.

I closed my eyes and imagined I was at the park.

When students note that *I* is used twice, say, "Oh, you're right! *I* is used twice. Here and here. Hmm, what do you notice about this *I*? And this one?" When they note that the pronoun *I* is capitalized in both spots, ask if they see any other capital letters. After exploring who the *I* is referring to (the person who is telling the story) and discussing its purpose (to show writers are telling about what they know or experience), reveal the focus phrase: *I capitalize the pronoun* I (*no matter where it is*).

When repeating the focus phrase, we read the first part in a regular voice (*I capitalize the pronoun* I), but when we say the part enclosed in parentheses, we stage-whisper, like it's a secret (*no matter where it is*).

Invitation to COMPARE and CONTRAST

Create another sentence like the model, or use the following one, and display it under Hanlon's sentence.

I closed my eyes and imagined I was at the park.
I closed my eyes and imagined I was eating ice cream.

When comparing and contrasting, the students may notice both sentences begin the same way. Invite a student to come up and point how each sentence begins or which words are the same. When they point to one of the *I* pronouns, ask, "What else do you notice about that word?" As you look for and discuss the second *I*, tie the conversation back the focus phrase: *I capitalize the pronoun* I (*no matter where it is*).

Invitation to IMITATE TOGETHER

Shared Writing

Ask your students to close their eyes and imagine something. You could say, "Give me a thumbs up when you have something in mind" to let you know when they are ready. Students open their eyes and share with their partner what they imagined. Listen in on their conversations and describe a couple you hear. Then, share what you imagine to model an imitation of the mentor sentence. "Wow! You all were imagining so much! Let me tell you what I imagined when I closed my eyes." As you share what you imagined, record the sentence, mirroring the mentor sentence from *Ralph Tells a Story* and directing their focus to the capitalized pronoun *I*.

I closed my eyes and imagined I was a race car driver.

Invitation to PLAY

Patterns of Wonder Time

After exploring the pattern of the mentor sentence and seeing you imitate it, students will be ready to try their own independent imitations. Writers close their eyes for a minute, imagining something, anything. Then, they compose an imitation of the mentor sentence on a piece of blank paper, capitalizing the pronoun *I* no matter where it is. If this is their first attempt at independent imitation, writers may need some extra coaching.

This young writer focused on capitalizing the pronoun *I* in his imitation: "I closed my eyes and imagined I met Peppa Pig."

Writing Workshop

As students write personal stories, they'll repeatedly need to use the pronoun *I*. Personal stories present a perfect conferring opportunity to help writers check to make sure *I* is capitalized no matter where it is in their writing. When they read their stories aloud, students stop at the pronoun *I* to give a thumbs up and then turn their thumb so that it points to themselves as a reminder that *I* is always capitalized.

Invitation to SHARE and CELEBRATE

Students walk onto an imaginary stage made of a single piece of butcher paper laid out like a rug and hold a microphone as they share their imitations of what they imagined. You could even play some soft music in the background to take the audience into a feeling of imagination. As students read their pieces, the audience celebrates by pointing to them each time the word *I* comes up in their writing to signify who the word *I* represents.

4.6   Don't Cry over Spilled Crayons: Nouns Show People, Places, and Things

Standards and Connections	Teacher Considerations	Texts
Standard Use frequently occurring nouns. *Companion Lessons* • Lesson 1.3 • Lesson 2.5 • Lesson 3.7 	As we move into conventional writing, writers start to understand how parts of speech can be crafted to more effectively convey meaning. For example, the noun *group* is a perfectly good noun, but if you meant The Beatles, the exact name provides more detail. In this lesson, we turn our conversations toward the craft of nouns. We teach our students to use the people, places, and things from their pictures and their worlds to help them write precisely, giving them the power to make meaning for others.	*Love Is Powerful* Written by Heather Dean Brewer and illustrated by LeUyen Pham **Alternative Titles** *Mommy's Khimar* Written by Jamilah Thompkins-Bigelow and illustrated by Ebony Glenn *This Is Me: A Story of Who We Are and Where We Came From* Written by Jamie Lee Curtis and illustrated by Laura Cornell *A Lime, a Mime, a Pool of Slime: More About Nouns* Written by Brian P. Cleary and illustrated by Brian Gable

Focus Phrase   ❝ I use nouns to show people, places, and things. ❞

A note about the craft of nouns . . .

Who? What? Where? When writers craft nouns with precise language, they answer these questions to create images in their readers' minds. As writers are ready, you might choose to show them how crafting more and more precise nouns can affect the level of detail in their writing.

> person ➡ kid ➡ girl ➡ Aliyah
>
> animal ➡ dog ➡ poodle ➡ miniature poodle
>
> thing ➡ toy ➡ car ➡ Hot Wheels race car
>
> stuff ➡ balls ➡ baseballs ➡ Rawlings baseball
>
> place ➡ building ➡ school ➡ Williams Elementary School

Invitation to WONDER

Share Heather Dean Brewer's sentence from *Love Is Powerful* with students. Write it on chart paper, put it into a digital slide, or display the page from the book under the document camera.

Mari spilled her crayons onto the table.

Ask young writers to share their wonderings about what the author did as a writer in this sentence. Their wonderings might first be related to comprehension, like "I wonder why she spilled her crayons." Honor this wondering with further discussion, returning to the text and pictures for clarification. Then ask the students to consider what the author did in this sentence. "Let's think about the author's choices here. Look carefully at the words in this sentence. What do you wonder or notice about the words? What do they tell us?" As the conversation shifts in this direction, honor what they notice. "The words *do* show us what spilled. And what did spill? Which word? Yes, crayons. *Crayons* is the *thing* that spilled. Is there another word that shows us a *thing*?" Introduce the focus phrase when the time seems right.

Nouns often serve as the subjects of sentences—the *who* or *what* that does or is something. The subject of this sentence is *Mari*. When students wonder about this word, begin planting seeds about what makes up a sentence. "*Mari* tells who. All of our sentences have a who or a what, and that who or what does something or is something. Who? (Mari.) What did Mari do? (Spilled her crayons on the table.)" The concept of subjects and verbs don't need to be drilled home in kindergarten or even in first grade, but when emergent writers show wonder and curiosity around it, extend a little here and there as you begin to lay a foundation.

Invitation to COMPARE and CONTRAST

Prepare an imitation sentence that mirrors the original sentence and display it below the mentor text, inviting students to compare and contrast them.

Mari spilled her crayons onto the table.

The dog chased a frisbee at the park.

These two sentences are a perfect opportunity to reinforce noun categories again, such as the people (we choose to include our fur babies), places like the park, and things like crayons and frisbees. This conversation might also spark an exploration of plural versus singular. As students discuss what the words in each sentence show the reader, revisit the focus phrase, repeating it several times.

Invitation to IMITATE TOGETHER

Interactive Writing

The class brainstorms ideas for an imitation of the mentor sentence. Where will our sentence take place? Who will be in it and what will they do? What thing will they have? Draw a picture to visually show the planning that is happening. Craft the sentence together based on the people, places, and things found in the picture.

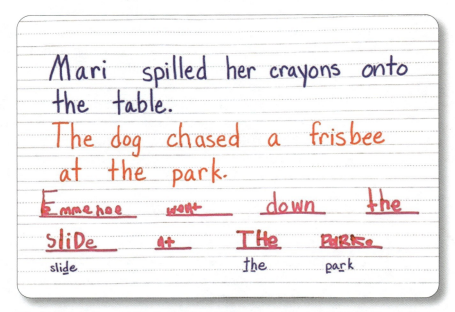

Mari spilled her crayons onto the table.
The dog chased a frisbee at the park.
Emmenoe went down the
slide at The Pirse
slide   the   park

When composing an imitation of the mentor sentence during interactive writing, this teacher focused on the use of nouns, inviting children up to add them to the sentence.

Invitation to PLAY

Patterns of Wonder Time

Students use sentence strips or blank paper to craft their own imitations of the mentor sentence, showing people, places, and things.

Writing Workshop

Repeat the focus phrase several times. Writers use their pictures in the books they are making to write sentences that use nouns to show people, places, and things.

Invitation to SHARE and CELEBRATE

Begin an anchor chart where students can share their imitations, adding the nouns they used as they do. Hang the chart in the reading center and leave lots of room for this class collection of nouns to grow as students discover more in writing they create and the books they read over the next week.

4.7 One Singular Sensation: Singular Nouns

Standards and Connections	Teacher Considerations	Texts
Standard Use singular nouns. *Companion Lesson* • Lesson 4.8 	The next two lessons take a deeper dive into nouns and may be paired together. In this lesson, we will use nouns to represent one person, place, or thing or the concept of singular. Next, in Lesson 4.8, we will explore nouns representing more than one (plural). It's important to note that the goal is using—as opposed to identifying—singular and plural nouns. When we craft our sentences with nouns that show people, places, and things, we think about the image we create for our readers. Do I want my reader to picture one dog in my story or more than one? The way we write our nouns matters.	*Lubna and Pebble* Written by Wendy Meddour and illustrated by Daniel Egnéus **Alternative Titles** *Milo Imagines the World* Written by Matt de la Peña and illustrated by Christian Robinson *My Pet Wants a Pet* Written by Elise Broach and illustrated by Eric Barclay *How Do Dinosaurs Show Good Manners?* Written by Jane Yolen and illustrated by Mark Teague

Focus Phrase 〝 I use a singular noun to show one person, place, or thing. 〞

A note about singular and plural nouns . . .

It's quite difficult for some learners to tell singular and plural nouns apart, unless you can compare and contrast one with the other. If you find the concept of plurals—more than one—flowing naturally into this lesson's conversations, as usual, go with it. If it's bubbling up from the students, don't be afraid to give plurals some play. Of course, it can make a great math connection and playing Three Dog Night's "One" will certainly tell you about the loneliest number.

Invitation to WONDER

As with some other lessons, we highly recommend you read *Lubna and Pebble* ahead of time. Write this sentence from it on chart paper or drop it into a PowerPoint slide.

She drew a happy face on her pebble.

Upon inviting students to wonder about this model sentence, continue to honor their thinking and build on what they say. One of them might say, "I wonder who *she* is." Or, if they don't, you might ask, "Does anybody wonder who *she* is? How can we find out?" However this occurs, open the book to the page spread that includes the sentence, and read the sentence that precedes it. "Let's see, before this sentence, it says 'In a big white tent, Lubna found a felt-tip pen.' This helps us figure out who *she* is. Who is she?"

"Lubna!" the class eagerly calls out.

"Yes, Lubna. She's the girl in this story. Hmm, so we have a person here, a girl. What else?"

Through conversation and your guidance, students will find the sentence includes a person and one thing (a happy face) and another thing (her pebble). When they do, extend the conversation and ask, "How many girls does this sentence refer to? Just one? Hmm. What about the other thing or noun, pebble? How many pebbles? Just one. If it were more than one, we would say *pebbles* with an *s* at the end. So, it looks like both nouns show us just one person, place, or thing. We call that singular. Say it with me: singular." Reveal the focus phrase: *I use a singular noun to show one person, place, or thing.*

For an added extension to this Invitation to Wonder, you might read the sentence from *Lubna and Pebble* about the big white tent and display it alongside the other singular nouns Wendy Meddour used, leading a discussion similar to this one.

Invitation to COMPARE and CONTRAST

Compose an imitation of the model to use for this invitation and post it under Meddour's sentence.

She drew a happy face on her pebble.

A boy found a caterpillar on the playground.

As students compare and contrast the two sentences, build on their conversation with discussions about author's purpose and craft. Why did the author use that word? How does it help us as readers? When they notice the person, thing, and place in the imitation, revisit the focus phrase, repeating it together: *I use a singular noun to show one person, place, or thing.*

Interactive Writing

Guide students through the construction of the imitation with oral brainstorming of singular nouns: Who will be in our sentence? What will the one character do? With what will the character do it? Where will the character do it? When the ideas come together, rehearse the sentence out loud twice together, saying it across your fingers. Then, write the sentence on chart paper while the class writes on individual dry erase boards. Invite students to come up to write the singular nouns used in the sentence while you compose on chart paper.

She drew a happy face on her pebble.

A boy found a caterpillar on the playground.

I made slime with colored water.

Students compose a sentence using nouns during interactive writing.

Invitation to PLAY

Patterns of Wonder Time

Students create their own imitation of the sentence, choosing who will be in their sentence and one thing the character will find or do with one thing. They may even choose to add a place to their imitation as well. That's their choice as writers.

Interactive Read-Aloud

While reading to students, stop from time to time when you come across a singular noun and point it out. "This author chose to use this singular noun to show us one thing, the yellow bus. This helps me see one bus in my head." This modeling of noticing helps children see the effects of an author's choice.

Writing Workshop

When conferring with your writers, pay attention to the nouns they use and how they use them. Do they help the reader create a mental image? Compliment the writer with naming what you notice: "I'm noticing you chose to say 'My mom drove the car.' You helped me picture who is in your picture by saying 'my mom.' Wow! And instead of just saying 'My mom drove,' you gave me more information with 'the car.' You know what? Those nouns you chose, *mom* and *car*, really helped me understand your story better. And they're singular. Keep it up!"

Math Connection

Represent the number one on a five frame or ten frame and discuss how many dots the students see. Orally rehearse sentences children can use:

- There is one dot on the five frame.
- I see one dot on a ten frame.

Revisit the focus phrase to connect the number *one* to the word *singular*. For even more fun, show Jack Hartman's "I Can Show the Number One in Many Ways" on YouTube. Your students will have fun singing along to this video.

Invitation to SHARE and CELEBRATE

As you play Jack Hartman's YouTube song about the number one, students sing along and move about the room. After calling out the number *one* in the song each time, pause the video. Students find a partner nearby to share their sentence with, pointing out where they use nouns to show *one* person, place, or thing.

4.8 More Than One Amazing Person, Place, or Thing! Plural Nouns

Standards and Connections	Teacher Considerations	Texts
Standard Form and use regular plural nouns. **Companion Lesson** • Lesson 4.7 	We use this lesson to leverage the use of nouns by zooming in on plural nouns. Students already use plural nouns naturally, but, here, we focus their attention on how authors craft nouns in writing. The standards call for forming regular plural nouns, so this lesson highlights those nouns ending in s when spelling these specific plural nouns.	*Norman: One Amazing Goldfish!* Written by Kelly Bennett and illustrated by Noah Z. Jones **Alternative Titles** *In a Jar* Written and illustrated by Deborah Marcero *Roy Digs Dirt* Written and illustrated by David Shannon *If You Were a Plural Word* Written by Trisha Sue Speed Shaskan and illustrated by Sara Jean Gray

Focus Phrase I use plural nouns to show more than one person, place, or thing.

A note about regular and irregular plurals . . .

To form regular plural nouns, add *s* or *es* to the end of the singular noun. However, there are a few ways to form irregular plural nouns, which you may discuss casually, knowing a deeper dive is beyond an emergent writer's priorities. For example, if someone writes about more than one foot, we bring the word *feet* into the discussion. "Yes, that does mean more than one. In the English language, we say *feet* instead of *foots*."

Make It More: Make It Plural		
Singular Noun (*one*)	**How to Make It More Than One**	**Plural Noun** (*more than one*)
dog	**+s**	dogs
pen		pens
pig		pigs
apple		apples
For words that end in *ch*, *j*, *s*, *sh*, *x*, or *z*		
dish	**+es**	dishes
box		boxes

For context and a richer conversation, we use two sentences in this Invitation to Wonder. Display the sentences on chart paper, a document camera, or a slide from your presentation software.

> ### The Pet-O-Rama line is super long.
>
> ### There are dogs, cats, birds, rabbits, snakes, and lots of other animals.

Invite students to wonder about the author's choices and enjoy the conversation that follows. When students notice the author refers to lots of animals, ask, "What does *lots* mean? One? More than one?" Then, invite the students to look closely at the animals listed. "How did Kelly Bennett choose to write each animal to show more than one? Dogs. Cats. Birds. Rabbits. Snakes. What do you notice about all of these words?" When they discover all of the nouns end with *s* and mean more than one, reveal the focus phrase and say the word *plural* together several times before repeating the entire focus phrase together: *I use plural nouns to show more than one person, place, or thing.*

Invitation to COMPARE and CONTRAST

Create another sentence like the model, or use the following one, and post it under Bennett's sentences.

The Pet-O-Rama line is super long.

There are dogs, cats, birds, rabbits, snakes,
and lots of other animals.

The art room is fun.

There are crayons, paintbrushes, markers,
and lots of other drawing things.

When comparing and contrasting, students may notice that both have two sentences. When they do, ask, "How do you know?" and let the concepts learned about capital letters and periods spiral back in. When they notice both sentences list things, zoom in on those things and how they are spelled. They all end with *s*. What can this mean? Yes, here they are plural or more than one!

Invitation to IMITATE TOGETHER

Shared Writing

Together, think about the playground or another area of the school that has a variety of things that show more than one. Choose one area to compose an imitation about. Because these sentences are a bit longer, the teacher does all of the writing while the children help orally. An example might be:

Our playground is big.

There are slides, swings, monkey bars, and basketball hoops.

Patterns of Wonder Time

Students, with paper and pencil in hand, travel to another area of the school like the library, music room, or science lab. With a partner, they observe the things in the area that show more than one. Partners make a list or draw the plurals out. Upon returning to the classroom, they individually compose an imitation using their notes. Students can use the models provided during the Invitations to Wonder, Compare and Contrast, and Imitate Together to help them use plural nouns to write about the area they visited.

A partnership visited the library and drew notes of some of the things they saw that represented plural nouns. Independently, each child wrote about what they saw; one imitated the mentor text, and the other labeled the books, computers, and bookshelves in his picture.

Literacy Station

Students sort word cards into singular and plural nouns, then write a sentence on the table with a dry erase marker that uses at least one plural noun. A reproducible of some word cards are included at the end of this lesson.

Students share their imitations about an area of the school with the class. Display their sentences in the area of the school they wrote about. After everyone has shared, each student writes the plural nouns they used on sticky notes to help create an anchor chart about singular and plural nouns. As each child adds their sticky notes to the chart, the class determines the singular form of the noun, and the teacher adds these words to the singular column of the chart.

Singular/Plural Noun Sort

dog	dogs
pen	pens
pig	pigs
apple	apples
day	days
box	boxes
stick	sticks

4.9   Match Game: Pronouns

Standards and Connections	Teacher Considerations	Texts
Standard Use pronouns. **Companion Lesson** • Lesson 3.8 	In addition to using nouns to show people, places, and things in their writing, we teach writers they can also use words to *stand in* for those nouns: *pronouns*. We chose Thyra Heder's *Alfie* because not only is the story from two different perspectives beautiful and worth sharing ahead of time with your students, but it also uses a wide range of pronouns.	*Alfie* Written and illustrated by Thyra Heder **Alternative Titles** *Giraffe Problems* Written by Jory John and illustrated by Lane Smith *Joey: A Baby Koala and His Mother* Written and illustrated by Nic Bishop *If You Were a Pronoun* Written by Nancy Loewen and illustrated by Sara Jean Gray

Focus Phrase   I use pronouns to stand in for nouns.

A note about pronouns and gender . . .

Just like new words are added to the dictionary over time, grammar patterns also evolve, giving us even more reason to call them *patterns* over *rules*. One recent evolution in grammar is using nongendered *they* to stand in for singular nouns. For example: "When I draw a name, that person can say what they want us to sing next."

For this lesson, it is helpful to display the picture that goes with the mentor text, so we find it useful to lift the first two sentences and write them on chart paper. In this way, students can zoom in as you hold up the illustration.

After a while, I kind of forgot about Alfie. He didn't do much.

Display the page shown here (and included at the end of this lesson) and read it aloud. Invite students to look closely at the words the author used along with the picture. Then, ask, "What do you wonder?" As students make the word-to-picture connection and point to Alfie, the turtle, in the picture, put a sticky note on the turtle that says "Alfie." Guide this conversation more and ask, "Look at the next sentence. Who didn't do much?"

The children answer, "Alfie!"

When they do, say, "But how do we know it's Alfie? I don't see his name in this sentence."

"Because it says *he* and that means Alfie!"

Act like this is an incredible discovery, and write the word *he* underneath the turtle's name on the sticky note. Then reveal the focus phrase: *I use pronouns to stand in for nouns*. Explain that *he* is a pronoun that stands in for the noun *Alfie*. If warranted, lead a larger discussion on what it means to "stand in" for something. Move to the discovery of one more pronoun in the sentence: *I*. Ask, "Who does *I* stand in for on this page?" or "Who can point to the person in the picture who is telling this story?" Because the students know this story already, they are able to point out Nia, the little girl in the picture. Label the girl in the picture with *Nia* and *I* and connect this example to the larger discussion before repeating the focus phrase together: *I use pronouns to stand in for nouns*.

After a while, I kind of forgot about Alfie. He didn't do much.
Well, until the morning of my seventh birthday, when . . .

As students discover pronouns in context, they may also notice that some pronouns are used more at the beginnings of sentences: like *he*, *she*, *I*, *we*, and *they*; others are more likely used at the end: *him*, *her*, *me*, *us*, and *them*. But *you* and *it* are tricky! They are used at both the beginning and end of sentences.

I use pronouns to stand in for nouns.

Beginning Pronouns

I
I like to play.

she
She likes to play.

he
He likes to play.

we
We like to play.

they
They like to play.

you
You like to play.

it
It likes to play.

Ending Pronouns

me
The dog played with me.

her
The dog played with her.

him
The dog played with him.

us
The dog played with us.

them
The dog played with them.

you
The dog played with you.

it
The dog played with it.

Choose another page and sentence from *Alfie* that uses pronouns for the compare and contrast lesson. Write the sentence on the chart paper and display it alongside the picture for support. We like the following sentence from Alfie's point of view for this conversation:

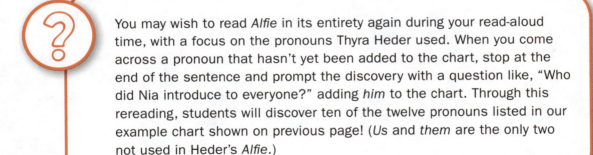

After a while, I kind of forgot about Alfie. He didn't do much.

She told me we were going to be seven, together.

As students compare and contrast this sentence with the ones from Nia's point of view, they may notice there are no names in the second example. When they do, ask them, "Who is in the sentence?" They are likely to say Nia and Alfie. Build on this observation, asking, "What word helps us know Nia is in the sentence?" When they answer *she*, write it on a sticky note and add it to your chart. "Yes, *she* is a pronoun that stands in for the noun *Nia*. Is there another word that stands in for *Alfie*, the one telling this part of the story?" Add *me* to the chart and then see if they figure out that *we* stands in for the two of them together. If they don't, prompt, "I'm thinking there might be one more pronoun here. Who is going to be seven together? Nia and Alfie? Well, Alfie could say 'Nia and I were going to be seven, together,' but instead, he used what word? *We*? Yes! That's another pronoun!" Add *we* to the chart and revisit the focus phrase, repeating it together: "*I use pronouns to stand in for nouns.*" We make a connection to singular (one) and plural (more than one), if appropriate.

You may wish to read *Alfie* in its entirety again during your read-aloud time, with a focus on the pronouns Thyra Heder used. When you come across a pronoun that hasn't yet been added to the chart, stop at the end of the sentence and prompt the discovery with a question like, "Who did Nia introduce to everyone?" adding *him* to the chart. Through this rereading, students will discover ten of the twelve pronouns listed in our example chart shown on previous page! (*Us* and *them* are the only two not used in Heder's *Alfie*.)

Invitation to IMITATE TOGETHER

Interactive Writing

Together, create an imitation of the mentor sentences used in the Invitation to Wonder and Invitation to Compare and Contrast. Begin with a brainstorm of possible people, pets, or things. Then, consider what pronouns you will use to stand in for nouns in each sentence. Use the anchor chart of pronouns to help if needed. An example might be:

> ### After a while, we kind of forgot about the playground balls. They were left outside.

Record the sentence on chart paper, choosing which words you will write and which words your students will write. Because you are writing more than normal during this invitation, you may wish to invite your students to write just the second sentence on their individual dry erase boards.

Invitation to PLAY

Patterns of Wonder Time

Students work with a partner or independently to compose another imitation of the mentor sentences about something they may have forgotten. The point here is to use pronouns, so if they write one sentence that says "I forgot to tie my shoes," celebrate this and then invite them to add another sentence with a stand-in word for *shoes*.

Choice Time

Students read the room, searching for places pronouns are used—in books, on shared writing pieces, in poems, on the word wall, and so on. They can even keep a recording sheet, noting how many times they find each one.

Writing Workshop

Students naturally use pronouns because they hear them in our spoken language all of the time. During writing workshop, have them discover where they have already used pronouns in their own writing and share with a partner.

Invitation to SHARE and CELEBRATE

Students may enjoy the calming and rhyming "Pronoun Song" by Bob the Train (Search for it on YouTube!) as a little review to begin this celebration. Students choose either their imitation created during the *Patterns of Wonder* time or a piece from writing workshop where they used at least one pronoun to share with the class. With the help of your students, make tally marks as you keep track on your whiteboard how many of each pronoun is used throughout the celebration.

After a while, I kind of forgot about Alfie. He didn't do much.
Well, until the morning of my seventh birthday, when . . .

4.10   Verbs for All Seasons: Verbs Show Action

Standards and Connections	Teacher Considerations	Texts
Standard Use frequently occurring verbs. **Companion Lessons** • Lesson 1.4 • Lesson 2.6 • Lesson 3.9 	In this lesson, we move from labeling pictures with verbs to writing sentences that use verbs to show action. This mentor text uses a variety of verbs to show what others do during each season of the year. To extend on this, we invite our students to brainstorm other actions for each season and write a sentence about it, creating a class book about each of the seasons of the year.	*Do I Have to Wear a Coat? A Journey Through the Seasons* Written and illustrated by Rachel Isadora **Alternative Titles** *Some Pets* Written by Angela DiTerlizzi and illustrated by Brendan Wenzel *Move!* Written by Steve Jenkins and Robin Page and illustrated by Steve Jenkins *There Might Be Lobsters* Written by Carolyn Crimi and illustrated by Laurel Molk

Focus Phrase   ❝   I use verbs to show action.   ❞

A note about verbs and time . . .

Verbs also tell time. If students start to notice this, start another collection of verbs that show time. Make three categories or columns: past, present, future. If your writers are curious, keep going. If not, let it slide until they're ready.

Invitation to WONDER

Display the following sentence from the mentor text:

In summer, bees buzz.

As students share their wonderings about the author's choices, have them point out their wonderings in the sentence and discuss why the author made this choice. For example, students may wonder about the comma, calling it a squiggle or even period with a tail. We've heard them all!

"Joan, come up and point to the squiggle you are talking about. Ah, yes, we call that a comma. Why do you think the author, Rachel Isadora, chose to use that comma? Let's read the sentence aloud, paying close attention to the comma." After some discussion about how the comma makes us pause as readers, invite the students to share other wonderings or noticings. "What else do you wonder or even notice?" If students need a little guidance, ask them to think about what the words are telling the readers. When the verb enters the conversation, discuss, act out, and reveal the focus phrase.

Invitation to COMPARE and CONTRAST

Display the following imitation under the mentor sentence to compare and contrast:

In summer, bees buzz.
In winter, some people ski.

Students may notice both sentences use the sight word *in*. They may also notice both sentences use a comma. Honor all noticings and enjoy the exploration of author's purpose and craft. When the students notice the different actions used, revisit the focus phrase, repeating it together.

Invitation to IMITATE TOGETHER

Interactive Writing

Make a four-square chart labeling each square with a season. Together, brainstorm what others do during each season and list on the chart. Choose a season and an action, and then compose a sentence together.

The students in this kindergarten class had fun thinking about each season. Together, they composed a sentence about winter using a verb to show action.

Patterns of Wonder Time

Using the season anchor chart to help them, students choose a season and verb and compose an imitation sentence, either alone or with a partner, and illustrate it. Compile the imitations into a class book about the four seasons in a year.

Writing Workshop

At the end of the minilesson, prior to beginning their independent writing, students go around in a circle, sharing one action they plan to show in their writing today. During independent writing, writers use verbs to show action in their books and share with their partners.

Choice Time

Students notice their own actions during choice time such as dramatic play, building with blocks, or recess, adding some verbs they discovered to a class anchor chart.

Invitation
to
PLAY

Students engage in play and make note of the actions happening. Part of their conversation included "the dinosaur hiding in the forest and a big truck driving through the forest and almost running over the dinosaur." Afterward, the students recorded *hiding* and *driving* on sticky notes for a class-created verb collection chart.

Invitation to SHARE and CELEBRATE

Display a backdrop on your interactive whiteboard or with butcher paper to represent each of the four seasons. Students take turns sharing their class book pages while standing in front of the corresponding backdrop, reading the page aloud twice. After the second reading, the class acts out the verb used.

Even though you've celebrated the work with verbs your writers have done thus far, that doesn't mean the play has to end. Continue the play through choice time, literacy stations, and independent writing, circling back to the focus phrase when appropriate.

4.11   Why? You Know WHY! The End Marks

Standards and Connections	Teacher Considerations	Texts
Standard Use end punctuation for sentences. **Companion Lessons** • Lesson 2.7 • Lesson 2.8 • Lesson 2.9 • Lesson 3.10 • Lesson 3.11 • Lesson 3.12 	Within this phase of writing, students write sentences and use end punctuation to complete their thoughts. In the model text, *Can I Play Too?* Samantha Cotterill uses a variety of end punctuation throughout the book, so it's great for exploring how writers choose specific end punctuation to guide their readers. The book also reminds children how to share and take turns with one another in play settings.	*Can I Play Too?* Written and illustrated by Samantha Cotterill **Alternative Titles** *The Nuts: Keep Rolling* Written by Eric Litwin and illustrated by Scott Magoon *Snail and Worm:* *Three Stories About Two Friends* Written and illustrated by Tina Kügler *Yo! Yes?* Written and illustrated by Chris Raschka

Focus Phrase   ❝   I use end marks to help my reader.   ❞

A note about end punctuation's trifecta . . .

If you're a gambler, a trifecta refers to the first three finishers in a race named in the correct order. With end punctuation, there are technically only three sentence "finishers" and they don't come in any order; they're based on purpose. This lesson brings all the official finishers, or end marks, into one lesson. Writing is a series of choices, and how we end our sentences should be less of a gamble and more of a sure thing.

Invitation to WONDER

Write the following sentences from *Can I Play Too?* or display the page they appear on under the document camera, and ask, "What do you wonder? What do you see? What do you notice?"

This is so much fun!

I LOVE trains.

Did you know some trains can travel 100 miles
per hour through tunnels?

Honor and name all of the group's responses. When students notice the period, ask, "Why do you think Samantha Cotterill decided to use a period there?" Repeat this type of interaction as they notice the other end marks (question and exclamation marks), continuing to steer the reflection toward the author's choices and how those decisions affect the way an audience reads their writing.

At some point, ask your students, "What's your favorite end mark, and why?" Just sit back and listen and you will get an eye-opening miniassessment that no worksheet could compare to.

Invitation
to
COMPARE
and
CONTRAST

Prepare some other sentences that use different end marks, like the following ones, and display them alongside the mentor sentences. Read the sentences aloud with expression and intonation as dictated by the authors' choice of end marks.

This is so much fun!

I LOVE trains.

Did you know some trains can travel 100 miles
per hour through tunnels?

Can we play outside today?

The weather is nice.

Let's go!

As students compare and contrast, celebrate all that they discover, taking time to discuss the author's choices and explore the effect they have on how the text is read. After each end mark is mentioned, mind the punctuation as you reread the sentence aloud together, and continue to repeat the focus phrase: *I use end marks to help my reader.*

Whitney discusses author's purpose and craft with first graders.

It can be very valuable to read a sentence aloud and invite students to read it aloud with you, parroting your intonation. Not only will this reinforce directionality from concepts about print, but you'll also help them develop their dramatic oral reading voice, which impacts the voice they hear when they read independently.

Invitation to IMITATE TOGETHER

Shared Writing

Record statements, exclamations, and questions shared by your students on chart paper. To begin, you might say, "Writers, let's think of some statements we could say that would end with a period. Share with your partner some sentences that could need a period at the end." Listen in on their shares and record a couple you hear. Then, as time permits or in future shared writing sessions, move on to exclamations and end with questions. The completed chart can be used later in the week for a shared reading experience in whole group or small group.

Invitation to PLAY

Patterns of Wonder Time

Students choose a part of the classroom to write about, such as the sink or the teacher table. On sentence strips or a large piece of paper, they write three sentences that relate to it, each one ending with a different punctuation mark. Post their sentences near the part of the classroom they chose.

For example, a child who chose the sink might write:

I wash my hands.
Is there any more soap?
My hands are clean!

Literacy Station

Set up a chart using the Punctuation Collection template included at the end of this lesson and place it alongside several familiar books. Students explore each book, noting the end marks each author chose to use. Remind students to use the end marks to help them as they read each book with expression and intonation.

Writing Center

Students record statements, exclamations, and questions on sentence strips. Create a three-column bulletin board or wall chart (one column for each ending mark) and label it: *I use end marks to help my reader.* Post student-created sentences on the wall, leaving enough space for the class to add more sentences over the next few weeks as they play around with end punctuation.

Students choose a piece of writing they composed during the Invitation to Play and share it aloud with appropriate intonation. Audience members guess their end mark with motions like:

- **Period:** Push the hand forward like you're saying "stop."
- **Question mark:** Tilt the head to the side in a questioning way.
- **Exclamation mark:** Jazz hands and smile big.

Punctuation Collection Template

Make a tally mark for each punctuation mark you find in the books you read. Which mark did each author use most often?

Book Title	Period .	Exclamation Mark !	Question Mark ?	Other Marks You Find
Can I Play, Too?	卌 卌 卌 l	卌 卌 卌 卌 卌 lll	卌 卌	卌 卌

4.12 Is It a *Toy* Turtle, *Pet* Turtle, or *Sea* Turtle? Adjectives Show What Kind

Standards and Connections	Teacher Considerations	Texts
Standard Use frequently occuring adjectives. **Companion Lessons** • Lesson 1.5 • Lesson 2.10 • Lesson 3.13 	Now that students are writing with more conventions, with ample approximations, of course, we continue our work helping them expand their sentences by adding more detail. In this case, we use adjectives to tell what kind. Students use their illustrations to springboard into words they can use in their written sentences to tell readers *what kind*.	*National Geographic Readers: Sea Turtles* Written by Laura Marsh **Alternative Titles** *Truman* Written by Jean Reidy and illustrated by Lucy Ruth Cummins *Brave* Written by Stacy McAnulty and illustrated by Joanne Lew-Vriethoff *Bird Builds a Nest* Written by Martin Jenkins and illustrated by Richard Jones

Focus Phrase I use adjectives to show what kind.

Invitation to WONDER

Share Laura Marsh's sentence with students by either writing it on chart paper, putting it into a PowerPoint presentation, or displaying the page from the book under the document camera.

Sea turtles are graceful swimmers in the water.

Ask, "What do you wonder about this sentence?" They may wonder why *sea* is spelled that way: "That's not how it's spelled on our word wall," a student says pointing to *see* on the word wall. As usual, their curiosity and observations drive your instruction. Sometimes it's worth taking a few detours. This detour leads to how this *sea* is the ocean, leading to a conversation about its purpose in this sentence: "And here it's telling us what kind of turtle. Can you think of other kinds of things?" Continue the conversation until you arrive at the focus phrase: *I use adjectives to show what kind.*

A note about adjectives that show what kind . . .

Adjectives do more than tell *what kind*. They can also tell *how many* (Lessons 1.6, 2.11, 3.14, and 4.13) or *which one* (Lesson 4.14). If a student writes or names something that tells *how many* or *which one*, honor it as a bonus, and don't feel the need to distinguish between kinds of adjectives. We don't want to push in too many concepts, but when they naturally arise from student inquiry, we acknowledge what the adjective is doing and move on. This lesson is designed to build adjective concepts a bit at a time.

Possible Adjectives That Show What Kind		
Colors	**Size**	**Traits**
yellow	long (longer, longest)	cute (cuter, cutest)
red	short (shorter, shortest)	friendly (friendlier, friendliest)
orange	small (smaller, smallest)	pretty (prettier, prettiest)
blue	giant	ugly (uglier, ugliest)
purple	tiny (tinier, tiniest)	happy (happier, happiest)
magenta		weak (weaker, weakest)
blonde		cuddly (cuddlier, cuddliest)
brunette		toy
		real
		fake

Invitation to COMPARE and CONTRAST

Create a sentence about another animal, or use the following example about elephants. Display the two sentences on chart paper.

Sea turtles are graceful swimmers in the water.

Elephants use their long trunks to take a bath.

Students consider what the authors did in each sentence; they may notice that both sentences are about animals. Use this noticing to continue the inquiry: "What did the authors do differently when telling about those animals?"

If students wonder about the word *graceful* telling what kind, explain that this word tells what kind of swimmer the turtles are. Adjectives can describe movements, like *clumsy* or *quick*.

Interactive Writing

As a class, brainstorm a list of animals. Compose a sentence with your writers about one of the animals using adjectives to tell what kind.

Invitation to IMITATE TOGETHER

Sea turtles are graceful swimmers in the water.

Elephants use their long trunks to take a bath.

Kangaroos use their
~~Jog~~ ~~fer~~ and ~~their~~
       feet
~~bwosee~~ ~~Las~~ to ~~iyg~~
bouncy   legs   jump

Invitation to PLAY

Patterns of Wonder Time

Students use blank paper to draw pictures of animals and write about them using adjectives that tell what kind.

Small-Group Interactive Writing

Share a variety of pictures with students of animals. Students choose one animal to write sentences about, using adjectives that tell what kind.

Invitation to SHARE and CELEBRATE

Writers share their imitations in small groups or partners. Choose a few students to share with the whole group. Provide feedback by naming what you notice they did as writers. "Look what you did there! You showed us what kind of tongue the giraffe has: a black tongue. And what kind of neck? A long neck! Wow! You used adjectives to tell what kind." Create a class book about animals with their imitations.

This student chose to use words that tell what kind to write about a giraffe: "A giraffe has a black tongue and a long neck."

4.13 Between *Two* Windows: Adjectives Show How Many

Standards and Connections	Teacher Considerations	Texts
Standard Use frequently occurring adjectives. *Companion Lessons* • Lesson 1.6 • Lesson 2.11 • Lesson 3.14 • Lesson 4.14 	Now that students are writing in sentences, they continue their work to add more detail with adjectives. In this lesson, we focus on using adjectives to show *how many*. Students use their illustrations to springboard into words they can use in their written sentences to show readers *how many*. See Lessons 4.12 for using adjectives to show *what kind* and Lesson 4.14 for using adjectives to show *which one*.	*Windows* Written by Julia Denos and illustrated by E. B. Goodale **Alternative Titles** *Truman* Written by Jean Reidy and illustrated by Lucy Ruth Cummins *Billions of Bricks* Written and illustrated by Kurt Cyrus *Pete the Cat and His Four Groovy Buttons* Written by Eric Litwin and illustrated by James Dean

Focus Phrase 〝 I use adjectives to show how many. 〞

A note about adjectives that show how many . . .

Adjectives that show how many can also be represented with words beyond exact numbers. In this chart, we share some examples. For more learning around articles, see Lesson 4.14.

Possible Adjectives That Show How Many		
Exact	Approximated	Article
one four twenty	several many some	a an

Invitation to WONDER

Display Julia Denos's sentence from *Windows* and ask students to look for what she did as a writer.

> **Between two windows, there could**
> **be a phone, used for good ideas.**

If they don't wonder or notice about the adjective that shows how many, guide them to look at just the phrase, *Between two windows,* asking, "What are the words telling us here?" Emphasize the focus by asking, "How many windows?" and move into the next phrase, *there could be a phone,* leading students to discover that the little word *a* also tells how many. Reveal the focus phrase and read it together.

When students wonder about the commas, honor their thinking and read the sentence aloud, pausing as guided by the commas. Students at this age don't need to master the placement of commas in their writing, but getting a feel for how commas guide reading fluency will plant seeds children will build on in future learning.

Invitation to COMPARE and CONTRAST

Create another sentence following the same pattern, or use the following example. Display the two sentences on chart paper.

> **Between two windows, there could**
> **be a phone, used for good ideas.**

> **Between some chairs, there could**
> **be a table, used for writing stories.**

Students consider what the authors did in each sentence, comparing and contrasting their choices. They may notice both sentences begin with the word *between.* Celebrate this noticing and ask them to read aloud the three-word phrase that begins with *between* and ends with the comma in each sentence. Why did the authors choose to use this phrase? What is it telling us? As the conversation inches to the discovery of how many, point to the focus phrase and read it together.

Invitation to IMITATE TOGETHER

Interactive Writing

As a class, compose an imitation sentence following the pattern of the mentor sentence. If the sentence pattern is too complex with the commas, simplify it as needed, using an illustration to help.

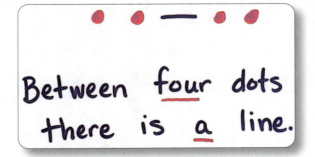

Invitation

to

PLAY

Patterns of Wonder Time

On sentence strips, students create their own imitation of the pattern, using adjectives to show how many. For an added scaffold or STEM connection, students use tubs of blocks to create something and write about it, telling how many blocks they used and how they used them.

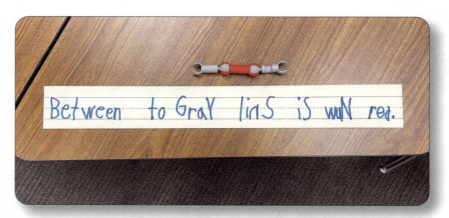

A kindergartner created a pattern from his STEM tub and wrote a sentence about it, imitating the mentor sentence: "Between two gray lines is one red."

Writing Workshop

Students reread their sentences to see if they have used any words to tell how many. They then revise their writing by adding at least one sentence or detail somewhere in their piece to show how many. During the share session of writing workshop, students share out how they revised their writing.

Brain Break

Children choose something in the room to count and orally compose a sentence about it, using an adjective that shows how many.

Invitation

to

SHARE

and

CELEBRATE

Writers share sentences they created during the Invitation to Play/*Patterns of Wonder* time, pointing to the adjectives they used to show how many. Display the writing with the focus phrase in the hallway for anyone walking by as a way to continue the celebration.

4.14 We're Adjectives, Too: *A, An, The*

Standards and Connections	Teacher Considerations	Texts
Standard Use adjectives, including articles (determiners). ***Companion Lesson*** • Lesson 4.13 	This lesson builds on our exploration of adjectives in Lesson 4.13 because articles (*a, an, the*) tell how many or which one. These small high-frequency words have a lot of power in our sentences. *A* and *an* tell us there is one noun, and we choose which one to use based on the initial sound of the word that follows it. *The* tells us which noun we want the reader to know about. We chose Stacy McAnulty's *Brave* to begin our conversation about the article *a* and *the*, and then we bring in *an* during the Invitation to Compare and Contrast.	*Brave* Written by Stacy McAnulty and illustrated by Joanne Lew-Vriethoff **Alternative Titles** *We Are Water Protectors* Written by Carole Lindstrom and illustrated by Michaela Goade *Macca the Alpaca* Written and illustrated by Matt Cosgrove *Giraffe Problems* Written by Jory John and illustrated by Lane Smith

Focus Phrase ❝ I write *a* or *an* to show how many or *the* to show which one. ❞

A note about articles and emergent writers . . .

As you work with emergent writers in this lesson, you may notice that many of them still aren't using the articles *a* and *an* appropriately when they speak. "I had a egg for breakfast!" Since oral language lays the foundation for writing, this will be an issue requiring some instructional flexibility. In this instance, it makes sense to dial things back and proceed with lots of oral rehearsal so students can build some background experience with the correct usage before moving forward with incorporating this standard into their writing expectations.

Invitation to WONDER

Display the following sentence from *Brave* on chart paper, in presentation software, or with the picture under the document camera.

A brave kid leads the team.

At some point during the conversation of wondering and noticing, students are likely to notice the high-frequency words *a* and *the*. When they do, discuss each one separately, discovering their purpose in the sentence, or what they do. How many brave kids are here? How do you know it's only one? Which team? The team. Reveal the focus phrase and repeat it together.

Invitation to COMPARE and CONTRAST

Create another sentence like the model, but one that uses *an* instead of *a*, or use the following one. Display it under McAnulty's sentence.

A brave kid leads the team.
An eagle flies in the sky.

When comparing and contrasting, students are likely to notice that both sentences use the article *the*, but one sentence uses *a* and the other uses *an*. Take a moment for a preliminary exploration of *a* versus *an* by charting out some examples of other words and asking your students to help you determine if you should use *a* or *an* before it. If students are ready for the sophistication of using initial vowels to lead this discovery, follow their lead. If not, help them listen for the differences, calling back to their oral language to help them differentiate. Either way, don't feel that you have to take a deep dive here. Approaching this study from a mindset of curiosity and wonder will help keep things light and playful.

a beetle	an ant
a book	an action figure
a teacher	an animal
a pig	an elephant

Refer to the focus phrase and reread it together: *I write* a *or* an *to show how many or the to show which one.*

Since it's so ubiquitous, emergent writers usually take to using *the* to be specific quite naturally. *The* team. *The* tree in your backyard. *The* book. However, if they confuse the articles *a* and *an*, don't be too concerned. This is an introductory discussion, and emergent writers will refine this understanding as they steep over time in the particulars of the English language. For now, it's enough to work on distinguishing *a* from *an* and simply noticing how they're used differently.

Interactive Writing

Together, develop a list of people, places, and things. If you have a noun chart already up, revisit it, and read each noun together. Choose a noun or two to use in a sentence, and determine which articles you will use. Record the sentence on chart paper interactively, sharing the pen with students who write parts of it while everyone else writes with you on their dry erase boards.

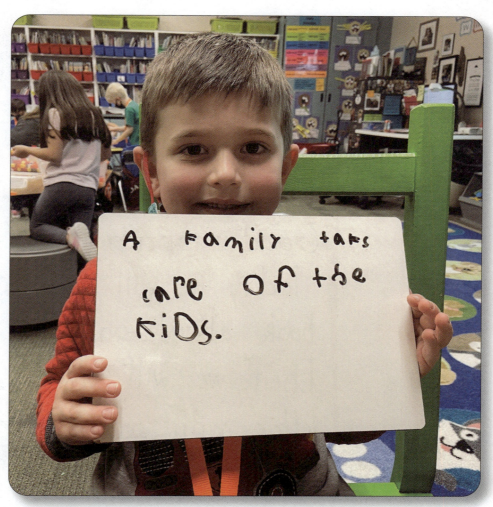

This student's class composed their imitation sentence together and recorded on individual dry erase boards.

Patterns of Wonder Time

On sentence strips, students create their own sentences using articles before nouns. They can use the nouns chart for ideas if they need them. When finished, they place a sticky note under each article they used with an arrow pointing to it.

Literacy Station

Stock a station with a tub of plastic animals. Students take an animal from the tub, saying what it is out loud using an article: *the* pig or *a* pig. If they want to write about that animal, they record a sentence on a dry erase board about it. If they don't want to write about that one, they take another one from the tub, saying what it is aloud using an article. They continue taking from the tub until they find one they do want to write about. Either way, they are getting practice in using articles in a hands-on authentic way.

Morning Message

Display a message for your morning meeting with lines to hold the places of the articles. As you read the message together, invite students to help you add in the article that makes sense: *a*, *an*, or *the*.

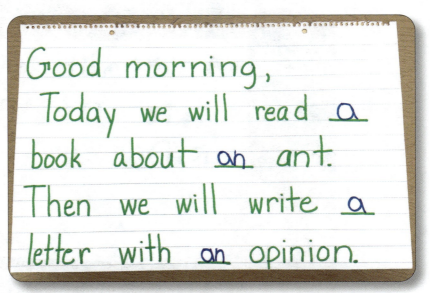

Good morning,
Today we will read a
book about an ant.
Then we will write a
letter with an opinion.

Students helped their teacher determine the articles needed to complete the morning message.

Invitation to PLAY

Invitation to SHARE and CELEBRATE

On your board, write:

It's **a** great day for **an** author celebration in **the** classroom!

Read the sentence together, emphasizing the articles, and use the board as your backdrop for the celebration. Each student sits in the author's chair in front of the board to share their imitation from the *Patterns of Wonder* time, emphasizing the articles they chose to use.

4.15 When and Where? Prepositions

Standards and Connections	Teacher Considerations	Texts
Standard Use frequently occurring prepositions. **Companion Lessons** • Lesson 1.7 • Lesson 2.12 • Lesson 3.15 	Writers in this phase continue to grow as conventional writers, making intentional decisions about the words they choose to create images for their readers. With this lesson, we build on our focus phrase from the companion lessons that prepositions tell where and add to the focus phrase that they also tell when. Students play with elaboration by using prepositions that tell where and when.	*How to Cheer Up Dad* Written and illustrated by Fred Koehler **Alternative Titles** *Hey, Wall* Written by Susan Verde and illustrated by John Parra *Over and Under the Pond* Written by Kate Messner and illustrated by Christopher Silas Neal *One Day in the Eucalyptus, Eucalyptus Tree* Written by Daniel Bernstrom and illustrated by Brendan Wenzel

Focus Phrase I use prepositions to show where and when.

A note about the craft of prepositions . . .

Prepositions ground a reader in time and space. That's the author's craft and purpose of prepositions in our writing, speaking, and reading. To the point, prepositions describe relationships between nouns. When exploring prepositions, connect them to the questions that drive them: *Where* is your backpack? *When* will you have school?

Invitation to WONDER

Display Fred Koehler's sentence on chart paper, in a PowerPoint presentation, or under a document camera and read it aloud.

At breakfast, Dad put raisins in Little Jumbo's oatmeal.

After asking, "What do you wonder?" allow ample time for the conversation to flow in whatever direction it goes. Feed into students' wonderings with your own thoughts and discoveries, or ask other questions like, "What makes you wonder about that?" After some time, if writers need more guidance, prompt them to think about what the words tell us.

> **?** Sometimes students don't just arrive at or even approach the focus phrase. In this case, you can either name it as something you've noticed or hold off introducing it until the comparing and contrasting discussion.

Invitation to COMPARE and CONTRAST

Prepare an imitation of Koehler's sentence like the following one, and post the imitation underneath Koehler's sentence. Read both sentences together and talk about how they are the same and different.

At breakfast, Dad put raisins in Little Jumbo's oatmeal.

During recess, we run on the playground.

When the similarity that both sentences show *where* and *when* is discovered, repeat the focus phrase: *I use prepositions to show where and when.*

> **?** Don't forget the power of the secondary question: "What else?" This powerful question can be asked again and again, which will encourage students to keep scouring the model for ideas, looking closer and closer.

Invitation to IMITATE TOGETHER

Shared Writing

Together, brainstorm a list of words that help tell *where* and another list that tells *when*. Post your lists on an anchor chart and choose a word from each to compose an imitation sentence together. If you want to make this more interactive, students can write the sentence on their notebooks or individual dry erase boards while you write it on the easel or interactive whiteboard. A possible imitation might be:

> In the morning, my sister and I walk across the street.

With teacher guidance, this class brainstormed some prepositions that show when and where and recorded them on this chart.

Invitation to PLAY

Patterns of Wonder Time

Students choose a preposition or two from the anchor chart and compose their own imitation on a sentence strip or index card. It is OK if they only tell when or only tell where. Writers make the choice. After everyone has composed a sentence, students walk around looking for someone who used the same preposition they did and share with one another.

Transition Times

When transitioning from one part of the day to the next, orally rehearse the use of prepositions.

"Time to move to the rug. Where will you sit?"

"In my spot!"

"On the rug."

"Next to my partner!"

"Time to line up for lunch. Where will you stand? When will we go?"

"By the door."

"In a line!"

"Behind Jackie."

"In front of Chase."

"In five minutes."

"At 11:30!"

Invitation to SHARE and CELEBRATE

Students read aloud their imitations created during the *Patterns of Wonder* time. After each student reads, stop to ask "Where?" or "When?" for the students to answer as a way of highlighting the prepositional phrase the author chose to use.

Grayson shares his sentence. "On Friday, I kicked a soccer ball in my backyard."

"When?"

"On Friday!" the class responds.

"Where?"

The class calls back, "In my backyard!"

4.16   BOAS Connect! Conjunctions

Standards and Connections	Teacher Considerations	Texts
Standard Use frequently occurring conjunctions. **Companion Lessons** • Lesson 1.8 • Lesson 2.13 • Lesson 3.16 	Now that students are experimenting with conventional writing, we encourage them to write more by using words like *but*, *or*, *and*, and *so* (BOAS) to expand their sentences. Students use their illustrations to help them discover what else they could write. This may also include adding details to their illustrations before writing more in their sentences. Building on Lesson 3.16 where we introduce *but*, *or*, *and* (BOA), we suggest using the Invitation to Imitate Together to explore *so*, along with examples of how students might use it.	*Last Stop on Market Street* Written by Matt de la Peña and illustrated by Christian Robinson **Alternative Titles** *How to Write a Story* Written by Kate Messner and illustrated by Mark Siegel *The Rabbit Listened* Written and illustrated by Cori Doerrfeld *A New Day* Written by Brad Meltzer and illustrated by Dan Santat

Focus Phrase   I write more with BOAS: *but, or, and, so.*

Invitation to WONDER

Display this sentence from Matt de la Peña's *Last Stop on Market Street* on chart paper, in a PowerPoint presentation, or under the document camera.

She smiled and pointed to the sky.

Read the sentence aloud and ask your writers to consider the choices Matt made as a writer. For further discussion, you might ask, "What are the words showing us? Let's act this sentence out." Upon this dramatization, students discover there are actually two actions joined by the word *and*. Reveal the focus phrase and check to see if any other words from the focus phrase are used in this sentence. Nope, Matt chose to only use *and* this time.

Mnemonics or memory devices can be helpful to young writers, if they're simple like this one. Create a poster to display the focus phrase with the mnemonic and a boa constrictor or a colorful feather boa—whichever matches your personality. Like writers, teachers make choices.

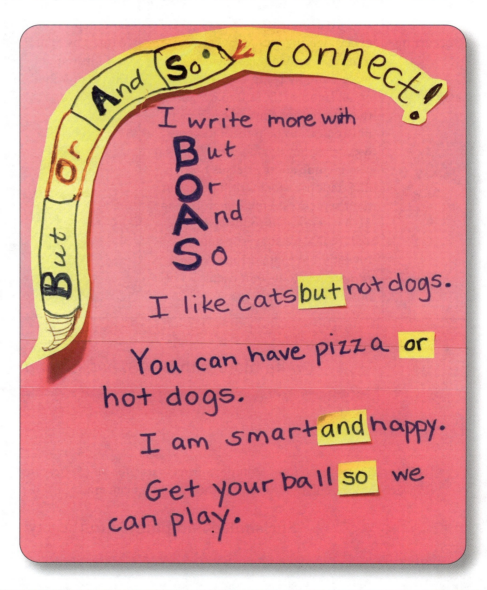

Invitation to COMPARE and CONTRAST

Share the following compare and contrast sentence alongside or below the mentor sentence.

She smiled and pointed to the sky.

I can wash my hands or get a drink at the sink.

When students consider what the authors did in each sentence, they may notice that *drink* and *sink* rhyme in the second sentence but no words rhyme in the first. They might also notice that both sentences use the sight word *the.* Honor all of their noticings, and when they begin to discuss some of the actions that happen in the sentence, act them out and revisit the focus phrase to help guide the conversation around using words like *but, or, and, so* (BOAS) to tell more.

> **?** To help make the connection back to the focus phrase in this invitation, you may find it helpful to ask individuals to come up and point out the conjunctions as they notice them (and, or) in the sentences.

Invitation to IMITATE TOGETHER

Interactive Writing

Students compose a sentence with you using the word *so.*

"Writers, the past couple of days, we have been looking at how writers write more by using words like *but, or,* and *and.* Our focus phrase is *I write more with BOAS:* but, or, and, so. I'm thinking we should try to write a sentence together today that uses the word *so.* Let's think about when it is time for recess. What do we do? Turn and tell your partner what we do to get ready for recess."

As students share with one another, listen in on their conversations and choose one idea to use in the imitation sentence. "Writers, I hear so many ideas for what we do to get ready for recess. Shondra mentioned that we line up on a dot. How about we use that in a sentence with the word *so?*"

Revisit the focus phrase after reading the sentence you compose together, and circle the word *so.*

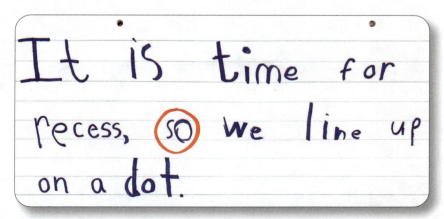

Writers used the joining word *so* during interactive writing.

Once students start to discover the meaning of each of the BOAS, as appropriate, discuss how BOAS are alike (they join or connect) and how they're different (*but* notes a difference, *or* offers a choice, *and* adds on, and *so* links to cause and effect).

Patterns of Wonder Time

Students add more to some of their sentences in their independent writing by revisiting the focus phrase: *I write more with BOAS:* but, or, and, so. When they use these joiners, invite them to circle those words.

Writing Workshop

Some teachers find it helpful for students to have their BOAS words written on craft sticks and kept nearby as a reminder for students to use them during writing workshop.

Invitation to PLAY

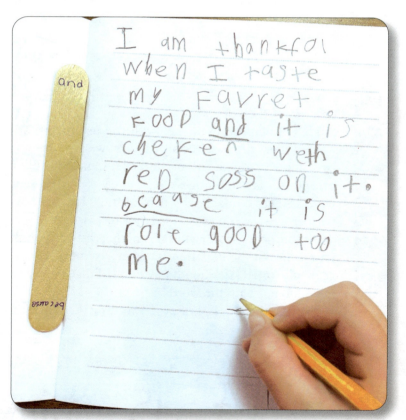

Because students were using *because* so often, Ms. Bleakley added it to the sticks in her classroom.

Literacy Station

Students choose BOAS to join ideas on a pocket chart from the cards included at the end of this lesson. The ideas are not written with conventional capitalization and punctuation because when they're combined, the capitalization and punctuation will change. As students join ideas together into one sentence, remind them to begin with a capital letter and choose an appropriate end mark.

A note about other conjunctions . . .

BOAS are only a few of the more frequently used conjunctions. As students begin to tell more in their writing, pay attention to the other joining words they use and celebrate how they tell more. For example, they may include the words *because* or *when*:

I went to sleep *because* I was tired.

My puppy jumped on me *when* I got home.

Many children will use words they hear often in their writing, and the use of other conjunctions shows a wider range of vocabulary in language composition. The focus here is not about knowing which words are conjunctions. It's about using them to expand sentences to tell more.

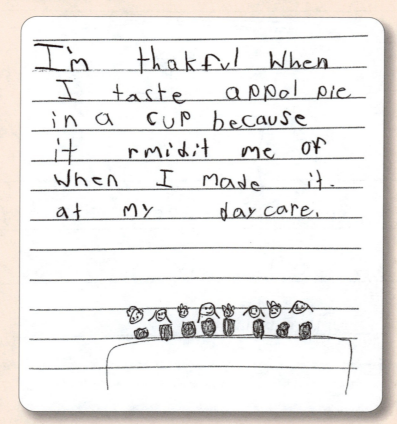

Mackenzie wrote in her thankful journal, using both *when* and *because* to tell more.

Invitation
to
SHARE
and
CELEBRATE

Students choose a piece of writing from their independent writing time and read it aloud, pointing out the BOAS they used. The writer who shares gets to choose the clap they receive when finished.

- **The sizzle:** Rub your hands together making a sizzling noise with your tongue.

- **The silent cheer:** Wave your hands in the air like you're cheering, but with no sound.

- **The snap:** Snap your fingers.

. kensie

Xersis is good for you
Xerise eve day (so) you can
get flxabol.

Kensie used the joining word *so* in her nonfiction book about living a healthy life.

Conjunction Combinations

but	and
or	so

it is cold outside

I grin

I am happy

I have a coat

it is warm inside

I can write

I can read

my friend likes trucks

the dog runs

the cat sleeps

4.17   Planting Seeds: Use Transition Words to Write Order

Standards and Connections	Teacher Considerations	Texts
Standard Use frequently occurring transition words. **Companion Lessons** • Lesson 1.9 • Lesson 2.14 • Lesson 3.17 	Students continue to make books across pages and create pictures that show order, but in this lesson we focus more on the words they write to indicate order. Transitions are used in all forms of writing, but we chose Melissa Stewart's nonfiction book *A Seed Is the Start* for this lesson because it has a page that demonstrates steps in a process with frequently occurring transition words.	*A Seed Is the Start* Written by Melissa Stewart **Alternative Titles** *How to Babysit a Grandma* Written by Jean Reagan and illustrated by Lee Wildish *My Monster and Me* Written by Nadiya Hussain and illustrated by Ella Bailey *Dream Big* Written by Kat Kronenberg and illustrated by Stephanie Dehennin

Focus Phrase   I use order words like *first*, *next*, *then*, and *finally*.

A note about other frequently occurring transition words . . .

The focus phrase in this lesson gives a suggestion for some transition words to help focus your writers' attention. However, these are not the only transition words students could use. Creating an ongoing anchor chart collecting words used to tell something in order over time will expand your students' use of transition words.

Invitation to WONDER

Display page 5 of Stewarts's *A Seed Is the Start*, which shows what happens when you plant a corn seed. Read it aloud, pointing to each circle step as you read. Ask, "What do you wonder? What do you notice?" Students may notice that there are words inside the circles. Invite them to look closely at the words, and reread the first circle again. What do they notice about the words in that circle? What does it tell us? What about the next circle? As the conversation evolves and the transition words are discovered and discussed, reveal the focus phrase.

You have probably noticed that Melissa Stewart doesn't use the word *finally* for her last step, yet, *finally* is in the focus phrase. That's OK, because the transition words we highlight in the focus phrase are suggestions, not requirements.

Invitation to COMPARE and CONTRAST

On chart paper, create an example showing steps in a process similar to the one shown here. Display the page from *A Seed Is the Start* used in the Invitation to Wonder and ask "How is this the same and different from what we see on the chart paper?" When students share that both texts use transitions, revisit the focus phrase, repeating it several times. If they mention other transition words they've heard, celebrate those and add them to a new or ongoing list of other transitions writers use.

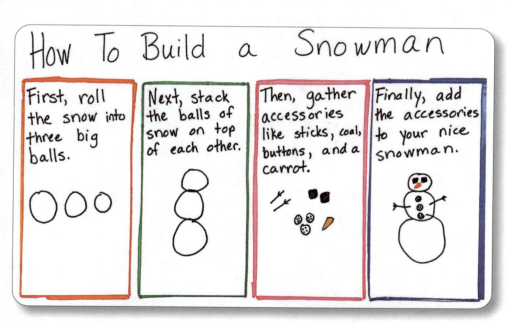

Invitation to IMITATE TOGETHER

Interactive Writing

The students brainstorm ideas for something simple they know how to do. Orally rehearse the steps several times and then sketch each step. Together, orally compose a sentence for each step, beginning with transition words. Then, share the pen as you write out the steps beneath your sketches. If your students suggest using transitions other than *first*, *next*, *then*, and *finally*, celebrate this and incorporate their ideas to show that writers make choices to make meaning.

Invitation to PLAY

Patterns of Wonder Time

Fold a large piece of construction paper into fourths, creating four panels for steps in a process. With a partner, students use transitions to write steps for how to line up for recess or some other routine of their choosing, including a step in each of the four boxes. Stock the writing center with more of these four-fold pages for students to use in writing workshop and beyond.

Lining Up

When preparing to line up to leave the classroom, give groups a card that says a step in a process. Call the steps out in order using transitions. The group with that order word gets to get in line.

Science Discovery Station

Students use magnifying glasses to look for transition words in a stack of procedural books. When they find one, they write it down on a dry erase board or recording sheet. How many different transitions can they find?

Invitation to SHARE and CELEBRATE

Before this celebration, choose a favorite song to play. While the music is playing, the students slowly move about the room. When the music stops, say, "*First,* share your writing with the person next to you." They pair up and share their writing with each other, pointing out the transitions they chose to use. Continue using transition words to keep the celebration going: "*Now* I'm going to play the music again. *Before* you move again, shake your partner's hand. *Then,* you will move around the room some more until the music stops." When the music starts back up, students move again until the music stops. At that point, they find another partner nearby to share with. Continue this method of celebration until the song ends.

This kindergartner uses transition words to teach her readers how to line up at her school.

Conclusion
An Adventure of Curiosity

The *Patterns of Wonder* process invites emergent writers on a path of adventure, punctuated with exploration, play, and curiosity. In early childhood education, it's easy to find ourselves inundated with expectations filtered down from the upper-grade curriculum, causing us to question the times we've set aside for four-year-olds, five-year-olds, and six-year-olds to playfully explore their wonderings. We know the value of play and the time needed for it. However, it is often cut from our day, eliminating the joy we know is so important to learning. The *Patterns of Wonder* process provides a space for this valuable play with the real work of meaning-making—speaking, listening, writing, and reading.

Emergent writers wonder about and notice what writers do. They discover new learning through authentic talk, books, illustrations, scribbles, symbols, letters, words, and eventually sentences. Together, as we explore the books in our classrooms, the beauty of the reading-writing connections unfolds before them. In this way, our earliest writers see why and how authors make the choices they do, they see how the conventions convey meaning, and they see that they can do these things, too. Then, as they try it out together, as a class full of writers, they come to identify themselves as writers who also make intentional choices for meaning and effect.

Invite your young writers to linger in a world where curiosity reigns and stories grow from marks, scribbles, and pictures—and where playful meaning making leaves plenty of room for orange snowmen, expression, and connection. In the land of wonder, anything is possible.

Play is often talked about as if it were a relief from serious learning. But for children, play is serious learning.
—Mr. Rogers

This is, after all, the work before them. And, our work? Our work is to create environments that give time and space for play, approximation, and celebration, which creates more space for writers as they continue on their path of exploring new wonders, making choices, and making meaning.

353

Appendix A
Patterns of Wonder Across Literacy Settings

Although we have found carving out ten minutes a day to devote to the *Patterns of Wonder* process particularly powerful, it might work better for your schedule to integrate the process into other parts of your day instead. When deciding the best course of action, consider how the following literacy settings correspond best to the steps in the invitational process, and set a schedule that supports your learning community best.

Patterns of Wonder Invitation	Literacy Component or Daily Schedule Opportunities
Invitation to Wonder	Shared reading Read-aloud
Invitation to Compare and Contrast	Writing workshop Morning meeting
Invitation to Imitate Together	Shared writing Interactive writing
Invitation to Play	Writing workshop Reading workshop Shared reading Read-aloud Literacy centers
Invitation to Celebrate	Writing workshop Morning meeting

Appendix B
Patterns of Wonder to Patterns of Power

We refer to grammar and conventions as the meaning-making activators that connect reading and writing in both *Patterns of Wonder* and *Patterns of Power*. When working with emergent writers, our development of grammar and conventions most authentically builds through conversations as we help students read their writing and tell their stories. This will lead well into the work writers and readers will do in future grade levels using *Patterns of Power*. Here, we explain how the *Patterns of Wonder* process is compared to the *Patterns of Power* process.

Patterns of Wonder Process		Patterns of Power Process	
Invitation to Wonder	*What do you wonder? What do you notice?* Invite students to explore the text *and* pictures in a picture book, engaging in conversation about their curiosity. When the conversation leads to the focus phrase, reveal it, say it together, and display it throughout the remainder of the process.	**Invitation to Notice**	*What do you notice?* Invite students to explore a small piece of text, engaging in conversation about the choices the author made, focusing on purpose and craft. When the conversation leads to the focus phrase, reveal it, say it together, and display it throughout the remainder of the process.

(continues)

356

Patterns of Wonder Process		**Patterns of Power Process**	
Invitation to Compare and Contrast	*How are they alike? How are they different?* Invite students to compare and contrast the model with another example, such as another page with pictures and words, or another sentence that demonstrates the focus phrase. This example may also be text with pictures and words created by the teacher.	**Invitation to Compare and Contrast**	*How are they alike? How are they different?* Invite students to compare and contrast the model sentence with another one that follows the same structure and demonstrates the same focus phrase.
Invitation to Imitate Together	Through interactive or shared writing, compose an imitation of the model while applying the focus phrase.	**Invitation to Imitate Together**	Compose an imitation of the model, demonstrating the focus phrase, together through shared, interactive, or paired writing.
Invitation to Play	Invite students to try out the focus phrase in other areas such as centers, writing workshop, small-group writing, or any other alternate settings.	**Invitation to Imitate Independently**	Invite students to compose an imitation of the model sentence independently, demonstrating the focus phrase.

(continues)

Patterns of Wonder Process		Patterns of Power Process	
Invitation to Celebrate	Invite students to share what they have tried through their play time with the focus phrase, valuing their approximation and risk-taking.	**Invitation to Celebrate**	Invite students to share their imitations, celebrate their risk-taking, and showcase their imitations.
Continue to explore, wonder, and play with the new skill in multiple settings for as long as necessary. This continued immersion can occur simultaneously with additional work on another focus phrase or an added level of complexity.		**Invitation to Apply**	Invite students to try out the focus phrase in various settings such as writing workshop, reading response, or content areas.
		Invitation to Edit (Editing Conversation)	Invite students to take a look at the different versions of the model sentence with changes applied, and engage in conversation about how those changes affect meaning.

Appendix C
Patterns of Wonder
Planning Template

Patterns of Wonder Planning Process	
Standard/Concept	Review your students' writing samples or refer to your curriculum standards. Choose a standard or concept and break it down. Uncover what it asks writers to do. Decide if you need to have a grammar focus or focus on concepts about print.
Author's Purpose and Craft	Connect the convention to the author's purpose (*why* writers do that they do) and craft (*how* they do it).
Pathways of Writing Support	Determine where your heavy support will be for your writers: oral language, illustrations, written language.
Focus Phrase	Create a focus phrase grounded in the *Patterns of Wonder* Phases of Emergent Writing: kid-friendly language that states a clearly defined learning goal.
Invitation to Wonder	Choose a text that demonstrates the focus phrase, and decide if you will explore a picture, a picture with words, or a sentence from the text.
Invitation to Compare and Contrast	Select or create an imitation of the model that the students can use for a compare and contrast conversation.
Invitation to Imitate Together	Decide if you and your students will imitate the model through shared writing or interactive writing.
Invitation to Play	Incorporate opportunities throughout the day or week for your writers to play (explore, try, talk, act) with the standard in their reading, writing, and speaking.
Invitation to Share and Celebrate	Determine how you will celebrate writers' application of the standard and how you might display and honor their efforts.

Refer to these steps when using the template on the next page to plan for the *Patterns of Wonder* process.

Patterns of Wonder Planning Template

Standard/ Concept	
Author's Purpose and Craft	
Phases of Writing Support	
Focus Phrase	
Invitation to Wonder	
Invitation to Compare and Contrast	
Invitation to Imitate Together	
Invitation to Play	
Invitation to Share and Celebrate	

Children's Literature Bibliography

Agee, Jon. 2018. *The Wall in the Middle of the Book*. New York: Dial.

Alber, Diane. 2019. *Never Let a Unicorn Scribble*. Gilbert, AZ: Diane Alber Art LLC.

———. 2019. *Scribble Stones*. Gilbert, AZ: Diane Alber Art LLC.

Alexie, Sherman. 2016. *Thunder Boy Jr.* New York: Little, Brown.

Allen, Jonathan. 2014. *I'm Not Scared!* New York: Hyperion Books for Children.

Allman, John Robert. 2019. *A Is for Audra: Broadway's Leading Ladies from A to Z*. New York: Doubleday.

Amato, Max. 2019. *Perfect*. New York: Scholastic.

Arnold, Marsha Diane. 2015. *Lost. Found.* New York: Roaring Brook Press.

Atinuke. 2020. *Catch That Chicken!* Somerville, MA: Candlewick.

Ayres, Katherine. 2008. *Up, Down, and Around Big Book*. Somerville, MA: Candlewick.

Baker, Keith. 2014. *LMNO Peas*. New York: Little Simon.

Bang, Molly. 2016. *Yellow Ball*. Cynthiana, KY: Purple House Press.

Barnes, Derrick. 2019. *The King of Kindergarten*. New York: Nancy Paulsen Books.

Barnett, Mac. 2019. *Jack Blasts Off!* New York: Viking.

Bennett, Kelly. 2005. *Not Norman: A Goldfish Story*. Somerville, MA: Candlewick.

———. 2020. *Norman: One Amazing Goldfish!* Somerville, MA: Candlewick.

Berger, Samantha. 2018. *What If . . .* New York: Little, Brown.

Bernstrom, Daniel. 2016. *One Day in the Eucalyptus, Eucalyptus Tree*. New York: Katherine Tegen Books.

Berry, Cate. 2019. *Chicken Break! A Counting Book*. New York: Feiwel and Friends.

Bingham, Kelly. 2012. *Z Is for Moose*. New York: HarperCollins.

Bishop, Nic. 2020. *Joey: A Baby Koala and His Mother*. New York: Scholastic.

Brewer, Heather Dean. 2020. *Love Is Powerful*. Somerville, MA: Candlewick.

Broach, Elise. 2018. *My Pet Wants a Pet*. New York: Henry Holt.

Brodner, Terry. 2020. *Vinny Gets a Job*. New York: Aladdin.

Brown, Lisa. 2016. *The Airport Book*. New York: Roaring Brook Press.

Burleigh, Robert. 2018. *Sylvia's Bookshop*. New York: Simon and Schuster.

Campoy, F. Isabel, and Theresa Howell. 2016. *Maybe Something Beautiful: How Art Transformed a Neighborhood*. New York: Houghton Mifflin Harcourt.

Capucilli, Alyssa Satin. 2016. *My First Soccer Game*. New York: Simon Spotlight.

Carle, Eric. 1969. *The Very Hungry Caterpillar*. New York: Scholastic.

Cherry, Matthew A. 2019. *Hair Love*. New York: Kokila.

Clanton, Ben. 2017. *Rex Wrecks It*. Somerville, MA: Candlewick.

Cleary, Brian P. 1999. *A Mink, a Fink, a Skating Rink: What Is a Noun?* Minneapolis, MN: Millbrook.

———. 2003. *Under, Over, By the Clover: What Is a Preposition?* Minneapolis, MN: Millbrook.

———. 2006. *I and You and Don't Forget Who: What Is a Pronoun?* Minneapolis, MN: Millbrook.

———. 2008. *A Lime, a Mime, a Pool of Slime: More About Nouns*. Minneapolis, MN: Millbrook.

Cook, Julia. 2008. *It's Hard to Be a Verb!* Chattanooga, TN: National Center for Youth Issues.
Cordell, Matthew. 2017. *Wolf in the Snow*. New York: Feiwel and Friends.

Cornwall, Gaia. 2017. *Jabari Jumps*. Somerville, MA: Candlewick.

———. 2020. *Jabari Tries*. Somerville, MA: Candlewick.

Cosgrove, Matt. 2020. *Macca the Alpaca*. New York: Scholastic.

Cotler, Joanna. 2020. *Sorry (Really Sorry)*. New York: Philomel.

Cotterill, Samantha. 2020. *Can I Play Too?* New York: Dial.

Crews, Donald. 1996. *Freight Train*. New York: HarperCollins.

Crimi, Carolyn. 2017. *There Might Be Lobsters*. Somerville, MA: Candlewick.

Cummings, Troy. 2018. *Can I Be Your Dog?* New York: Random House.

Curtis, Jamie Lee. 2016. *This Is Me: A Story of Who We Are and Where We Came From*. New York: Workman.

Cyrus, Kurt. 2016. *Billions of Bricks*. New York: Henry Holt.

de la Peña, Matt. 2015. *Last Stop on Market Street*. New York: G.P. Putnam's Sons.

———. 2021. *Milo Imagines the World*. New York: G.P. Putnam's Sons.

de Regil, Tania. 2019. *A New Home*. Somerville, MA: Candlewick.

Dean, James. 2013. *Pete the Cat: Pete's Big Lunch*. New York: HarperCollins.

Dean, Kimberly, and James Dean. 2014. *Pete the Cat and the New Guy*. New York: HarperCollins.

Deenihan, Jamie L. B. 2019. *When Grandma Gives You a Lemon Tree*. New York: Sterling.

———. 2020. *When Grandpa Gives You a Toolbox*. New York: Sterling.

Denos, Julia. 2017. *Windows*. Somerville, MA: Candlewick.

DiCamillo, Kate. 2019. *A Piglet Named Mercy*. Somerville, MA: Candlewick.

DiTerlizzi, Angela. 2016. *Some Pets*. New York: Beach Lane.

———. 2020. *The Magical Yet*. New York: Disney Hyperion.

Doerrfeld, Cori. 2018. *The Rabbit Listened*. New York: Dial.

Dotlitch, Rebecca Kai. 2015. *One Day, the End: Short, Very Short, Shorter-Than-Ever Stories*. Honesdale, PA: Boyds Mill.

———. 2016. *The Knowing Book*. Honesdale, PA: Boyds Mill.

Downing, Julie. 2008. *No Hugs Till Saturday*. New York: Clarion.

Dunklee, Annika. 2011. *My Name Is Elizabeth!* Tonawanda, NY: Kids Can Press.

Eggers, Dave. 2018. *What Can a Citizen Do?* San Francisco, CA: Chronicle.

Fanelli, Sara. 1995. *My Map Book*. New York: HarperCollins.

Ferry, Beth. 2015. *Stick and Stone*. New York: Houghton Mifflin Harcourt.

———. 2020. *Swashby and the Sea*. New York: Houghton Mifflin Harcourt.

Fleming, Candace. 2012. *Oh, No!* New York: Schwartz & Wade.

Fosberry, Jennifer. 2010. *My Name Is Not Isabella: Just How Big Can a Little Girl Dream?* Nashville, IL: Jabberwocky.

———. 2011. *My Name Is Not Alexander: Just How Big Can a Little Kid Dream?* Nashville, IL: Jabberwocky.

Garza, Cynthia Leonor. 2017. *Lucía the Luchadora*. New York: POW!

Golubeva, Evgenia. 2020. *I'm Not a Mouse!* Auburn, ME: Child's Play.

Gutierrez, Lorna. 2020. *Dare to Dream Big*. Naperville, IL: Jabberwocky.

Hall, Michael. 2017. *Little i*. New York: Greenwillow Books.

Hanlon, Abby. 2012. *Ralph Tells a Story*. New York: Two Lions.

Heder, Thyra. 2017. *Alfie*. New York: Abrams.

Heller, Ruth. 1998. *Merry-Go-Round: A Book About Nouns*. New York: Puffin.

Hurley, Jorey. 2019. *Skyscraper*. New York: Simon and Schuster.

Hussain, Nadiya. 2021. *My Monster and Me*. New York: Viking.

Isadora, Rachel. 2020. *Do I Have to Wear a Coat? A Journey Through the Seasons*. New York: Penguin.

Jackson, Ellen. 2016. *Octopuses One to Ten*. New York: Beach Lane.

Jenkins, Martin. 2018. *Bird Builds a Nest*. Somerville, MA: Candlewick.

Jenkins, Steve, and Robin Page. 2006. *Move!* New York: New York: Houghton Mifflin Harcourt.

John, Jory. 2016. *Quit Calling Me a Monster!* New York: Random House.

———. 2018. *Giraffe Problems*. New York: Random House.

Kim, Jaime. 2019. *Where Are You From?* New York: HarperCollins.

Kitamura, Satoshi. 2019. *Hat Tricks*. Atlanta, GA: Peachtree.

Koehler, Fred. 2014. *How to Cheer Up Dad*. New York: Dial.

Kronenberg, Kat. 2017. *Dream Big*. Austin, TX: Greenleaf Book Group.

Kügler, Tina. 2016. *Snail and Worm: Three Stories About Two Friends*. New York: Houghton Mifflin Harcourt.

LaRochelle, David. 2012. *It's a Tiger!* San Francisco, CA: Chronicle.

———. 2020. *See the Cat: Three Stories About a Dog*. Somerville, MA: Candlewick.

Larsen, Andrew. 2016. *A Squiggly Story*. Tonawanda, NY: Kids Can Press.

Levine, Sara. 2014. *Bone by Bone: Comparing Animal Skeletons*. Minneapolis, MN: Millbrook.

Lindstrom, Carole. 2020. *We Are Water Protectors*. New York: Roaring Brook Press.

Litwin, Eric. 2012. *Pete the Cat and His Four Groovy Buttons*. New York: HarperCollins.

———. 2017. *The Nuts: Keep Rolling*. New York: Little, Brown.

Loewen, Nancy. 2006. *If You Were a Pronoun*. Mankato, MN: Picture Window Books.

Maier, Brenda. 2018. *The Little Red Fort*. New York: Scholastic.

Mamada, Mineko. 2013. *Which Is Round? Which Is Bigger?* Tonawanda, NY: Kids Can Press.

Marcero, Deborah. 2020. *In a Jar*. New York: G.P. Putnam's Sons.

Marino, Gianna. 2020. *Night Animals Need Sleep Too*. New York: Viking.

Marsh, Laura. 2011. *National Geographic Readers: Sea Turtles*. Washington, D.C.: National Geographic Kids.

Martin, Billy Jr. 1996. *Brown Bear, Brown Bear, What Do You See?* New York: Henry Holt.

Martin, David. 2017. *Shh! Bears Sleeping*. New York: Viking.

Martinez-Neal, Juana. 2018. *Alma and How She Got Her Name*. Somerville, MA: Candlewick.

Matheson, Christie. 2019. *Bird Watch*. New York: Greenwillow.

McAnulty, Stacy. 2017. *Brave*. Philadelphia, PA: Running Press.

McDonnell, Patrick. 2014. *A Perfectly Messed-Up Story*. New York: Little, Brown.

———. 2017. *The Little Red Cat Who Ran Away and Learned His ABC's (the Hard Way)*. New York: Little, Brown.

McKay, Jodi. 2016. *Where Are the Words?* Park Ridge, IL: Albert Whitman.

Meddour, Wendy. 2019. *Lubna and Pebble*. New York: Dial.

Meltzer, Brad. 2021. *A New Day*. New York: Dial.

Méndez, Yamile Saied. 2019. *Where Are You From?* New York: HarperCollins.

Messner, Kate. 2015. *How to Read a Story*. San Francisco, CA: Chronicle.

———. 2017. *Over and Under the Pond*. San Francisco, CA: Chronicle.

———. 2020. *How to Write a Story*. San Francisco, CA: Chronicle.

Mora, Oge. 2019. *Saturday*. New York: Little, Brown.

Neal, Kate Jane. 2015. *Words and Your Heart*. New York: Feiwel and Friends.

Neuman, Susan B. 2014. *Swing, Sloth! Explore the Rainforest*. Washington, D.C.: National Geographic Kids.

Newman, Lesléa. 2015. *My Name Is Aviva*. Minneapolis, MN: Kar-Ben.

Norman, Kim. 2014. *Ten on the Sled*. New York: Sterling.

North, Ryan. 2018. *How to Be a T. Rex*. New York: Dial.

Novak, B. J. 2014. *The Book with No Pictures*. New York: Dial.

Pak, Kenard. 2016. *Goodbye Summer, Hello Autumn*. New York: Henry Holt.

Pearlman, Robb. 2018. *Pink Is for Boys*. New York: Running Press.

Pett, Mark. 2016. *This Is My Book!* New York: Alfred A. Knopf.

Petty, Dev. 2016. *I Don't Want to Be Big*. New York: Doubleday.

Pham, Leuyen. 2018. *The Itchy Book*. New York: Hyperion Books for Children.

Polansky, Marisa. 2018. *Hello, My Name Is . . . How Adorabilis Got His Name*. New York: Scholastic.

Portis, Antoinette. 2019. *Hey, Water!* New York: Neal Porter Books.

Raschka, Chris. 2007. *Yo! Yes?* New York: Scholastic.

Read, Kate. 2019. *One Fox: A Counting Book Thriller.* Atlanta, GA: Peachtree.

Reagan, Jean. 2014. *How to Babysit a Grandma.* New York: Alfred A. Knopf.

———. 2020. *How to Read to Grandma or Grandpa.* New York: Alfred A. Knopf.

———. 2021a. *How to Raise a Mom.* New York: Dragonfly.

———. 2021b. *How to Surprise a Dad.* New York: Dragonfly Books.

Reidy, Jean. 2019. *Truman.* New York: Atheneum Books for Young Readers.

Reynolds, Peter H. 2018. *The Word Collector.* New York: Scholastic.

Roeder, Vanessa. 2020. *The Box Turtle.* New York: Dial.

Rosenthal, Amy Krouse. 2013. *Exclamation Mark.* New York: Scholastic.

Rubin, Adam. 2019. *High Five.* New York: Dial.

Saltzberg, Barney. 2015. *Inside This Book (are three books).* New York: Abrams Appleseed.

Santat, Dan. 2016. *The Cookie Fiasco.* New York: Hyperion Books for Children.

Schaefer, Lola M. 2006. *An Island Grows.* New York: Greenwillow.

———. 2004. *Loose Tooth.* New York: HarperCollins.

Scillian, Devin. 2010. *Memoirs of a Goldfish.* Ann Arbor, MI: Sleeping Bear Press.

Shannon, David. 2020. *Roy Digs Dirt.* New York: Blue Sky Press.

Shaskan, Trisha Sue Speed. 2009. *If You Were a Plural Word.* Mankato, MN: Picture Window Books.

Sheneman, Drew. 2017. *Nope!* New York: Viking.

Slyke, Rebecca Van. 2017. *Lexie the Word Wrangler.* New York: Penguin.

Stead, Philip C. 2013. *Hello, My Name Is Ruby.* New York: Roaring Brook Press.

Stevens, Janet. 1995. *Tops and Bottoms.* New York: Houghton Mifflin Harcourt.

Stewart, Melissa. 2018. *A Seed Is the Start.* Washington, D.C.: National Geographic Kids.

Stone, Tiffany. 2020. *Knot Cannot.* New York: Dial.

Stott, Ann. 2018. *Want to Play Trucks?* Somerville, MA: Candlewick.

Sweeney, Joan. 2018. *Me on the Map.* New York: Dragonfly.

Tanaka, Yoko. 2020. *Dandelion's Dream.* Somerville, MA: Candlewick.

Tatsukawa, Maya. 2020. *The Bear in My Family.* New York: Dial.

Thompkins-Bigelow, Jamilah. 2018. *Mommy's Khimar.* New York: Simon & Schuster.

Tsurumi, Andrea. 2017. *Accident!* New York: Houghton Mifflin Harcourt.

Twohy, Mike. 2016. *Oops, Pounce, Quick, Run! An Alphabet Caper.* New York: Balzer and Bray.

Verde, Susan. 2018. *Hey, Wall: A Story of Art and Community.* New York: Simon and Schuster.

Vignocchi, Chiara, Paolo Chiarinotti, and Silvia Borando. 2018. *Shake the Tree!* Somerville, MA: Candlewick.

Willems, Mo. 2007. *Today I Will Fly!* New York: Hyperion Books for Children.

———. 2009. *Watch Me Throw the Ball!* New York: Hyperion Books for Children.

———. 2010a. *Can I Play Too?* New York: Hyperion Books for Children.

———. 2010b. *Cat the Cat, Who Is That?* New York: Balzer and Bray.

———. 2010c. *We Are in a Book.* New York: Hyperion Books for Children.

————. 2011. *Should I Share My Ice Cream?* New York: Hyperion Books for Children.

————. 2013. *That Is Not a Good Idea!* New York: Balzer and Bray.

————. 2016. *The Thank You Book.* New York: Hyperion Books for Children.

————. 2019a. *Busy Creature's Day Eating!* New York: Hyperion Books for Children.

————. 2019b. *The Pigeon HAS to Go to School!* New York: Hyperion Books for Children.

————. 2019c. *Who Is the Mystery Reader?* New York: Hyperion Books for Children.

Wood, Audrey. 2009. *The Napping House.* New York: Houghton Mifflin Harcourt.

Yolen, Jane. 2020. *How Do Dinosaurs Show Good Manners?* New York: Blue Sky Press.

Yoon, Salina. 2016. *Duck, Duck, Porcupine!* New York: Bloomsbury.

Professional Bibliography

Ackerman, Diane. 2000. *Deep Play*. New York: Vintage Publishing.

Anderson, Jeff. 2007. *Everyday Editing: Inviting Students to Develop Skill and Craft in Writer's Workshop*. Portland, ME: Stenhouse.

Anderson, Jeff, with Whitney La Rocca. 2017. *Patterns of Power: Inviting Young Writers into the Conventions of Language, Grades 1–5*. Portland, ME: Stenhouse.

Applebee, Arthur. 2010. "An Overview of the National Study of Writing Instruction." Paper presented at the 2010 Annual Conference from National Council of Teachers of English, Orlando, FL, November 18–20.

Byington, Terea A., and Yaebin Kim. 2017. "Promoting Preschoolers' Emergent Writing." *Young Children* (naeyc.org) 72, no. 5.

Cherry-Paul, Sonja. 2020. "Planning and Leading Culturally Responsive Read Alouds and Book Talks: Virtually and Face to Face." Prerecorded course from Columbia University Teachers College Reading and Writing Project, New York, NY, August 24.

Clay, Marie M. 2017. *Concepts About Print*. 2nd ed. Portsmouth, NH: Heinemann.

Dehaene, Stanislas. 2020. *How We Learn: Why Brains Learn Better Than Any Machine . . . For Now*. New York: Viking.

Eagleman, David. 2011. *Incognito: The Secret Lives of the Brain*. New York: Vintage Books.

Garner, Betty K. 2007. *Getting to Got It! Helping Struggling Students Learn How to Learn*. Alexandria, VA: Association for Supervision and Curriculum Development.

Graham, Steve, and Delores Perin. 2007. *Writing Next: Effective Strategies to Improve Writing of Adolescents in Middle and High School—A Report to Carnegie Corporation of New York*. Washington, DC: Alliance for Education.

Heard, Georgia, and Jennifer McDonough. 2009. *A Place for Wonder: Reading and Writing Nonfiction in the Primary Grades*. Portland, ME: Stenhouse.

Jensen, Eric. 2005. *Teaching with the Brain in Mind*. Alexandria, VA: ASCD.

Mraz, Kristine, Alison Porcelli, and Cheryl Tyler. 2016. *Purposeful Play: A Teacher's Guide to Igniting Deep and Joyful Learning Across the Day*. Portsmouth, NH: Heinemann.

Oxford English Dictionary, 2nd ed. (CD-ROM, version 4.0). 2009. Oxford, UK: Oxford University Press.

Ray, Katie Wood, and Matt Glover. 2008. *Already Ready: Nurturing Writers in Preschool and Kindergarten*. Portsmouth, NH: Heinemann.

Siegel, Daniel J., and Tina Payne Bryson. 2019. *The Yes Brain: How to Cultivate Courage, Curiosity, and Resilience in Your Child*. New York: Bantam.

Sims Bishop, Rudine. 1990. "Mirrors, Windows, and Sliding Glass Doors." *Perspectives: Choosing and Using Book for the Classroom* 6 (3).

Thompson, Terry. 2015. *The Construction Zone: Building Scaffolds for Readers and Writers*. Portland, ME: Stenhouse.

Winter, Caroline. 2008. "Me, Myself and I." *New York Times Magazine*, August 3.

Credits

Chapter 1

Illustrations from *Can I Be Your Dog?* by Troy Cummings, © 2018 by Troy Cummings. Used by permission of Random House Children's Books, a division of Penguin Random House LLC. All rights reserved.

Lessons

A Squiggly Story cover image used with permission by Penguin Random House.

From *Inside This Book* by Barney Saltzberg. Text and illustrations © 2015 Barney Saltzberg. Used by permission of Abrams Appleseed, an imprint of Abrams, New York. All rights reserved.

Shake the Tree. Copyright © 2015 by Minibombo/TIWI s.r.l. English language translation © 2018 Walker Books Ltd. Reproduced by permission of the publisher, Candlewick Press, Somerville, MA.

Lucía the Luchadora cover and interior illustrations used with permission by POW Kids Books.

Snail and Worm cover image and interior illustrations used with permission by Houghton Mifflin Harcourt.

From *The Little Red Cat Who Ran Away and Learned His ABC's (the Hard Way)* by Patrick McDonnell, copyright © 2017. Reprinted by permission of Little, Brown, an imprint of Hachette Book Group, Inc.

Oh, No! cover image used with permission by Penguin Random House.

Tops and Bottoms cover image and interior illustrations used with permission by Houghton Mifflin Harcourt.

No Hugs Till Saturday cover image used with permission by Houghton Mifflin Harcourt.

Knot Cannot cover image used with permission by Penguin Random House.

Swashby and the Sea cover image and interior illustrations used with permission by Houghton Mifflin Harcourt.

Jabari Jumps. Copyright © 2017 by Gaia Cornwall. Reproduced by permission of the publisher, Candlewick Perss, Somerville, MA.

A Is for Audra cover image used with permission by Penguin Random House.

Index

Patterns of Power Family of Resources

An authentic, inquiry-based approach to grammar instruction for grades Pre-K–8

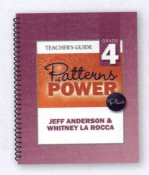

Patterns of Power Plus: 60 Grade-Specific Lessons for Grades 1–5
*(includes grade-specific Teacher's Guide, Lesson Display Flip Chart, Focus Phrase Cards,
25 Student Notebooks, access to Companion Website)*

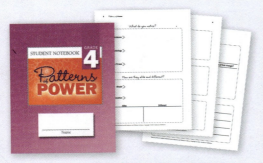

Patterns of Power Student Notebooks
*(included in the Patterns of Power Plus but also available
separately in packages of 5 and 25)*

Patterns of Power Plus Anchor Text Collections

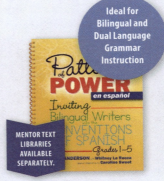
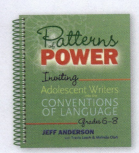

Ideal for Bilingual and Dual Language Grammar Instruction

**Patterns of Wonder
Resource Book, Grades PreK–1
(Available Fall 2021)**
*(includes over 50 sample
lessons addressing the most
common needs of emergent
writers, Pre-K–1)*

**Patterns of Power
Resource Book, Grades 1–5**
*(includes 70 lesson sets
spanning Grades 1–5)*

**Patterns of Power
en español, Grades 1–5**
*(includes 53 Spanish
grammar lesson sets for
Grades 1–5 aligned with
the Patterns of Power
resource book)*

**Patterns of Power
Resource Book, Grades 6–8**
*(includes 55 lesson sets
for middle school writers)*

WWW.STENHOUSE.COM | 800.988.9812